CAMP 21 COMRIE

CAMP 21 COMRIE

VALERIE CAMPBELL

Whittles Publishing

Published by
Whittles Publishing,
Dunbeath,
Caithness KW6 6EG,
Scotland, UK

www.whittlespublishing.com

© 2017 Valerie Campbell
ISBN 978-184995-227-9

Printed by Short Run Press Ltd.

DEDICATION

for Lorna with love

CONTENTS

ACKNOWLEDGEMENTS

Writing a book like this takes many more people than just its author. First and foremost I would like to acknowledge Rolf Weitzel and the late Günther Schran, who brought the book alive with their memories. I am grateful to you both. In addition I thank the following for all their help with research: Hans-Jürgen Kickertz, Theo Hunkirchen, Dave Winter at the Clifton Park Museum, Captain Jerry Mason, Julie Somay at the Commonwealth War Graves Commission, Fiona Davidson, former chairperson of Comrie Development Trust (CDT), Allan Kenny, Grace MacLennan, Heather Lumsden at Dollar Academy, Ian Prentice, Gordon Burns, Bill Oram, and Carol McDivitt at the Crown Office. I also thank the International Committee of the Red Cross (ICRC) in Geneva and the National Archives in London as well as the editors of the *Stirling Observer* and the *Strathearn Herald*, especially Johnathon Menzies. My deepest thanks also go to Ann Petrie at CDT without whom the book would be incomplete and to Anne O'Sullivan for providing several photographs..

Finally I have my nearest and dearest to thank for their continued support – Colette Robertson, Pauline Hurst, Fiona Cramb, Carol Gray, Isabel Binnie, Sophie-Jo Campbell, my children Sam, Lauren and Kirsty, and my partner John Allan. I love you all.

INTRODUCTION

Prisoner of war camps in Scotland have been largely ignored, except by a few dedicated local historians who undertake research and take photographs of what is left of the camps in their district. The Royal Commission on the Ancient and Historical Monuments of Scotland (RCAHMS), now part of Historic Environment Scotland, keeps records of all Scotland's historically important buildings, as well as those at risk. Among these are Nissen huts at Camp 21 Comrie, also known as Cultybraggan Camp. Here thousands of prisoners of war passed through the gates and into these huts to continue their lives as captives. Many camps have disappeared but Cultybraggan is one of the few in the UK which has survived and so can give the visitor an insight into what life was like inside them.

Prisoners of war sometimes find it difficult to discuss their time as captives because of what happened to them, while others involved in the camps were sworn to secrecy – a secrecy that has lasted much longer than the governments of the day could have predicted. In archives all over the UK, the written submissions of prisoners have been carefully stored for more than half a century, with more added in the recent past, but it seems our interest in them is forever growing. We want to hear their stories. We want to know what happened to them.

Following the D-Day landings, a large influx of German prisoners of war began arriving on UK shores. The government had not expected the numbers to be quite so vast. Prisoner of war camps quickly sprang up all over the country. Disused amenity ground, football pitches, estates and agricultural ground all saw the arrival of Nissen huts and tents as well as thousands of men from the Kriegsmarine, Luftwaffe and Wehrmacht. Some were boys, others older men, and others still belonged to Hitler's elite forces. Without some of these prisoners, and guards for that matter, coming forward and giving us the chance to delve into their lives, we would not have a clear picture of what camp life was like.

This book focuses on Camp 21 Comrie in Perthshire, one of the earliest prisoner of war camps in Britain (it is said that its first prisoner was not actually foreign but a sergeant from the Argyll and Sutherland Highlanders). Comrie had another camp, known as Cowden, by the southwest corner of the village, which was for unknown reasons variably numbered Camp 21A, Camp 64 and Camp 242.

For the purposes of this book a prisoner of war camp is defined as a place where segregated German military personnel were sent following capture. The prisoners were deemed 'white', 'grey' or 'black': to all intents and purposes Camp 21 was a 'black' camp, holding those who were deemed to be hard-line Nazi supporters. This will be explained more fully later.

This book is not a full history of camps, nor indeed is it a military history of World War II. It is the story of young Germans caught by the Allies following the North Africa and Normandy campaigns and how they survived during their incarceration, with special consideration given to their time in Scotland. It is perhaps selfish of me to write only about Scotland. However, I have walked in the footsteps of these men. I have walked along the roads and peered into the Nissen huts where they may have stayed at Cultybraggan. I want to tell their stories and give you, the reader, a chance to know more about what it actually meant to be a prisoner of war. That said I also want to give an account of Cultybraggan post-war, for its history did not stop when it closed as a prisoner of war camp. It went on to become a training ground for the armed forces and later housed a nuclear bunker. Today the site has been revitalised and is utilised in many different ways, and its legacy will continue for many years to come.

1 | COMRIE AND CAMP 21

The historic, affluent and multi-award winning village of Comrie lies in the heart of Perthshire in stunning Strathearn. The name of the village is derived from the original Gaelic name *comh-ruith*: *comh* means 'together' and *ruith* means 'running' or in this case 'flowing', as it refers to the confluence of the rivers which meet there, the Ruchill, the Lednock, and the Earn, the former two being tributaries of the Earn. Today its Gaelic name is '*Comraidh*'. Before this, the Romans had named it Victoria and the Picts called it Aberlednock.

Because of its situation on the Highland Boundary Fault line, Comrie has suffered numerous earth tremors (some 7000 were recorded in the 1830s). The first of these tremors was recorded in the diary of John Melville in July 1597 – this affected the whole of Perthshire – while 1788 is widely regarded as the first recording of a quake in Comrie itself. This seismic activity has given rise to the nickname 'Shaky Toon'. Comrie became one of the first sites in the world to have a seismometer installed, thanks to postmaster Peter Macfarlane and shoemaker James Drummond. A replica Mallet seismometer from the Victorian era sits today alongside modern equipment supplied by the British Geological Survey in the so-called Earthquake House in The Ros in Comrie, erected in 1874.

One of the most striking features around the village is the giant granite obelisk, the Melville Monument, at the top of Dun Mor (the Big Hill), to its north. This commemorates Henry Dundas, the 1st Viscount Melville, who became a peer in 1802 taking the title Viscount Melville and Baron Dunira of Dunira, originally a 20,000-acre estate three miles northwest of Comrie. The estate was sold a number of times and during World War II the house was utilised as a military convalescent hospital. It was destroyed by fire in 1948.

In the 1940s Comrie became home to both soldiers billeted in the village and prisoners of war. Tents were erected to house an influx of Commonwealth soldiers such as the French Canadians and Indians, as well as home-grown soldiers from, for example, the Cameronians and the Sherwood Foresters. Units from the Polish army also arrived as well as an influx of nurses and nursing auxiliaries to work at the hospital at Dunira. Thanks to a government initiative some of the troops were also billeted in the local houses and of course locals wishing to do their bit in the war effort were happy enough to take these strangers in. The church was also turned into billets.

Many of the locals themselves volunteered for the Home Guard, the ARP (Air Raid Precautions), or the fire service. Many of the women in the village joined the WRVS (Women's Royal Voluntary Service), while others volunteered for the Red Cross or became Land Girls, working on farms and in forestry as well as other jobs which had been left open as the men were called up to fight.

The camp, two miles south of the village, held thousands of men over the years and was designated as prisoner of war Camp 21 along with the smaller Cowden Camp nearby following a change in its status in the early years of the war. Originally it was selected as Scotland's 'black' camp, holding the most ardent and potentially dangerous Nazis, until in 1945 the camp at Watten in Caithness had its status changed to the most secure camp. Many of the prisoners at Comrie were shipped north to this camp. However, Comrie is famous for the murder, in 1944, of Feldwebel Wolfgang Rosterg who was lynched by fellow prisoners. After the war it became a Polish resettlement camp then a military training camp until the army decided to close it in 2004. Within its grounds is a Royal Observer Corps post and a Cold War bunker which would have housed the Scottish Office in the event of a nuclear attack from the Soviet Union. Today the camp is community owned, and the bunker was bought by Bogons Ltd, a technology firm, in May 2014.

Comrie was not immune to 'hot war' however. On 13 March 1941, during the raids on Clydebank, a German bomber flew over Comrie and dropped bombs in the area, generally up the glens. It is thought the pilot was dispensing his payload. Also in the spring of 1941 a trainee pilot in a Blackburn fighter aircraft lost his way and landed in a field near Dalginross. He was escorted back to base a few days later. By this stage, each person in the village had been allocated a gas mask and an identity card, both of which had to be carried at all times, and ration cards had been distributed when rationing began in January 1940. Throughout the war Comrie never suffered any damaged to its buildings including its iconic white church, known as The White Kirk, Comrie's most famous landmark.

In 2005 the Comrie Development Group (CDG) was formed, following the example of the Westray community in the Orkney Islands which had set up the Westray Development Trust in 1998 to promote the island's economic, social and cultural heritage by involving the general public and help the island develop in an ever-changing world. The CDG took these core values and in October 2005 put them forward at a community meeting to gauge public opinion on the establishment of a similar trust. It was an overwhelming success and in June 2006 the Comrie Development Trust (CDT) was launched, shortly afterwards gaining charitable status. By this time Cultybraggan Camp was up for sale, and the CDT registered its interest in purchasing the base using the Land Reform (Scotland) Act of 2003. However, the Trust needed the villagers to back them so carried out a poll – 72% of the villagers responded, with an overwhelming 97% voting in favour of buying the facility. By September the camp was theirs.

The Trust wanted not only to preserve the camp for future generations but to actually utilise it in a way which would benefit local businesses. The Comrie Allotment Association has taken over some of the land and year after year harvests a range of produce. There is also a community orchard, established in March 2010, and several business have taken up residence in the former camp. Today the Trust has over 800 members and a small shop. A main objective of the Trust is to work closely with local people and businesses, making sure that money is spent on local goods and services. There are numerous CDT Working Groups including the Heritage Group, the Local History Group and the Cultybraggan Working Group. Hut 1 at the gate, formerly the guard hut, is an informative visitors' centre with information on both the camp and the CDT and its work.

Cultybraggan Camp is also the starting point of many long distance races such as the Strathearn Marathon, established by the Strathearn Harriers, and the Original Mountain Marathon. It has also been used during the Scottish Orienteering Championships.

Comrie is full of history, character and charm but it is to its more infamous camp and its impact on the village to which this book now turns.

———

By the summer of 1941 Cultybraggan Camp had emerged on land south of the village. It was built between May and October 1941, by the 249 (Alien) Company Pioneer Corps, made up mainly of German and Austrian Jewish refugees. They laid the foundations and erected the barbed wire fencing which surrounded it. Its first actual prisoner is said to have been a soldier from the Argyll and Sutherland Highlanders who had gone absent without leave to see his pregnant partner. It was originally built not as a prisoner of war camp but rather a training camp for British soldiers, but its role changed following the arrival of the large swathe of prisoners of war captured during the North Africa campaign in 1943.

When the first batch of Italian prisoners arrived, playing guitars, singing and skipping, many of the locals went down to see what was happening. When the Germans arrived in 1943 the atmosphere was entirely different however. These were professional soldiers, arrogant and headstrong, although like the Italians, sang their hearts out as they marched from Comrie railway station to the camp some two miles distant.

On 13 May 1944, the International Committee of the Red Cross (ICRC) visited Camp 21. The camp leader at the time was Oberfeldwebel Martens and his adjutant was Stabsfeldwebel Hummel. Although the camp had capacity for 4500 prisoners, only around 785 were held there at the time. These consisted of 670 army combatants from the Luftwaffe and the U-boats, 115 protected personnel, such as doctors, teachers and ministers, and a handful of officers. Of these 50% were non-commissioned officers (NCOs) and about 25% of protected personnel were from the medical profession. Doctors Baumstrak, Weisser, Schneider and Thange had thought they were going to be repatriated when they had been captured in North Africa but they caused no fuss when they realised they were to spend more time as prisoners of war. Around 300 men had been sent up to Camp 21 from Camp 24, No. 4 General Military Hospital at Knutsford in Cheshire. The Comrie camp was a transit camp at this time, although it became a base camp shortly afterwards, with most of the prisoners being German. They were spending between 4 and 12 weeks at the camp, having passed through a number of transit camps in North Africa and England. There was no canteen, no radio, no gramophone and no library but work was underway to rectify the situation.

The camp was split into four large compounds made up mainly of Nissen huts surrounded by barbed wire, and at the time of the ICRC visit one of the compounds held 54 prisoners. No one in Compounds A, which held protected personnel only, or C complained about their living conditions even though they were rather primitive.

Nissen huts were the brainchild of Canadian colonel Peter Nissen during World War I. There was a need for accommodation to be constructed at speed. In May 1916 the British inspected the first new type of hut at the Pas de Calais and immediately put in an order. Nissen claimed he had been inspired by something he had seen back home in Canada and his huts became an instant success. The British ordered them in vast quantities to provide accommodation for the soldiers in the theatre of war and although there were teething problems, a few tweaks here and there saw the standard Nissen hut evolve. A major advantage was that they were flexible and could create larger living spaces. A downside was that the huge sheets of curved corrugated iron were awkward to transport, but the fact that it took just six men four hours to erect them far outweighed the transportation issue. In the main these huts measured 36 feet long by 18 feet wide and roughly 8 feet high. The corrugated curved roof was held in place with iron strapping. In the summer they were stiflingly hot and in winter freezing cold. The roofs of the huts shook violently in strong winds and heavy rain would be so loud on them that the men would not get much sleep on those nights.

Condensation was another issue as it would form and run down the walls causing blankets to become damp. A few windows were placed along either side, with a brick wall at each end. The hut was lit by electric lighting, although sometimes faults would occur and the men would be plunged into darkness. There was no space for lockers or a table and chairs so the men were forced to sit on the edge of their beds, which were described by the ICRC as 'English army' type. A stove heated the huts but of course fuel was rationed. The prisoners kept a small amount of coal back from their hut's allocation to use in the communal areas if it was raining or cold. As mentioned many of these men had arrived in Scotland from North Africa and were acutely aware of the temperature difference.

———

By June 1944, more prisoners of war had arrived following the Normandy landings, taking the total number to just under 3000. The four original compounds, holding Germans and Italians, were still in place and Compound E had been introduced. This new compound held what were termed 'foreigners'. The camp leaders were Oberfeldwebel Martens for Compound A which held 630 NCOs and soldiers, Oberfeldwebel Gunther for Compound B which held 74 officers and 29 NCOs and soldiers, Stabsfeldwebel Hummel for Compound C which held 1000 NCOs and soldiers (700 of which had been sent up from Camp 24), and Stabsfeldwebel Gorholt for Compound D which held 853 NCOs and soldiers.

By December, the camp was almost at capacity, with 3980 men incarcerated. On the 20th of that month the 7th Polish Guard Company took up their posts, replacing some of the British guards. The camp leaders had changed once more. Stabsfeldwebel Kurt Wilhelm was now the camp leader of Compound A, with Stabsubootsman Gustav Pierau in charge of Compound B, Oberfeldwebel Fritz Hoffman in charge of Compound C, and Stabsfeldwebel Bruno Rikall leading Compound D. Compound A held 999 NCOs and soldiers, Compound B held 954, Compound C held 1000, and Compound D held 996. Nine men were being held in the detention block for the murder of fellow prisoner of war Feldwebel Wolfgang Rosterg, and the camp infirmary held the rest. All of the prisoners were now German and all were housed in Nissen huts. The tents which had been erected to take up the slack while huts were erected had gone. Electricity was still to be installed in some of the huts and those that had it still had recurring faults.

The food rations for the prisoners were exactly the same as those given to the British troops, but the prisoners had complaints. For one thing they did not receive vegetables which they liked, and for another they found the meat to be fatty. The sausages were bulked out with bread and they thought there was too little sugar available. They also complained that they did not receive onions. On the up side they did have salt and pepper, mustard and curry powder. The prisoner of war Wirth spoke to the chefs and between them calculated they could make a cheap, healthy hotpot and soups. Each prisoner had his own set of cutlery and crockery with which to eat.

By June the men had been allocated 10 oz of bread per man per day but the Germans complained that it was not enough, having been more used to the heavier rye bread or black bread back home. They requested at least 16 oz per day. The camp's limitations were still apparent at this time as some of the men had to eat their meals in their hut because there were not enough tables and chairs in the dining room, meaning the chefs had to prepare the food three times in quick succession. The problem still existed at Christmas when some of the men ate in the refectory while others had to eat in their huts. In Compound D they all had to eat in their huts as there was no refectory there.

Christmas was a special time of year for the men. They thought of home and many found incarceration particularly difficult at this time. Grey clouds covered the mountains, which were pitted with patches of snow, and this summed up the mood of the camp. The men lifted their spirits by decorating the hospital and their huts, making decorations out of paper and wood. The altar in the Roman Catholic chapel in Compound C was decorated with different colours of covers on a wooden frame, five chandeliers made from sculpted wood, a crucifix carved in the camp, and a small carved crib. The choir sang for an hour and fiddlers played for the first time at Christmas for the prisoners. Other celebrations took place in the refectories or in the barracks and even the British organised a small celebration, inviting the trusted men and one man from each compound as its representative to join them. The prisoners were each given bonbons and chocolate, the British sacrificing their rations of sugar for them. Each prisoner was also given 'the Führer's Gift', which was a transfer from Germany of the equivalent of £1 – 15 Marks. This money enabled the prisoners to buy small necessities such as toothpaste, razor blades, and cigarettes, which the smokers bought as a two- or three-week supply.

There was no chaplain at the camp but the theology students took the Catholic mass, which was celebrated almost every day with a special service every Sunday. Around 100 men from Compounds A, B and C – and some 150–170 from Compound D – attended these regularly. Only one Protestant service took place every week, attended by around 200 men. The prisoners managed to arrange books to be used in the services.

———

In May 1944 a hospital had been allocated space just outside the camp. A German doctor was responsible for the 30-bed infirmary, along with an assistant who was in charge of its smooth running. A senior British medical officer was responsible for the medical service along with the commandant, and had a good rapport with the German medical officers. In all four Germans were permanently at the hospital and the 28 other members of staff were made up of protected personnel. There was a call for more medicines but at least the camp had eradicated any cases of malaria and dysentery. By December the principal medical officer was a man named Hans Rahne and the infirmary had expanded to hold 40 beds. There were now three distinct rooms – two isolation rooms and one containing a man suffering from angina. There was also now a dispensary, toilets available for those who were ill, and bedrooms for the medical officers. A store, a hospital kitchen with a store, and an office (which was also the sluice room) had also been added. Most of the rooms now had electric lighting and central heating although one room was heated by a stove. A German dental officer had use of a room and equipment to carry out his work.

———

Work at the camp was non-existent, although there was a call for it by the camp leader. This also meant that money was unavailable but ingeniously there was another system in place – a credit system on pieces of card, so if the prisoners went to the canteen they could get items and the purchases would be debited onto their card. However, at this time, there was no canteen at Camp 21 as the local NAAFI (Navy, Army and Air Force Institutes) had not been informed of the arrival of the men. On the instructions of the War Office, with all the NAAFI furniture being uniform, it was hoped the canteen would be up and running before too long after it was requested from Camp 24. Many complaints were made at this lack but they still managed to distribute the cigarettes which arrived in June without one.

Leisure time was spent playing football nearly every day on the large sports ground within the compound. Language courses had also begun, as had maths and other subjects, but there was a problem, namely a lack of paper. As an improvisatory measure toilet paper was used instead. The Accounts Officer too was desperate for paper and tried to expedite the delivery of stationery, but there was a lack of willingness on the part of the British officers within the camp – and because it was a transit camp, with the expectation that the men would stay no longer than three months, there was no provision made for the long term. There was no radio; there were also no games, no musical instruments, no materials for the theatre, and no gardens to tend to. However, the authorities gave carte blanche for the acquisition in London of sporting materials and other items from the Welfare Fund.

By Christmas the men were no longer allowed to play football but they amused themselves in other ways. They made games and model aeroplanes and tanks from wood and metal using old cans. The library was now much better stocked so reading became a favourite pastime. The educational classes had also expanded greatly. For example, in Compound A the classes offered included English, navigation and stenography. In Compound B French was offered as well as accountancy and maths. Compound C offered maths, arithmetic, French, German and English. And Compound D offered botany, agriculture and literature, among others, but they did not have the luxury of books, or paper for that matter. The radio was now being installed in the camp but the prisoners were only allowed to listen to the BBC and musical programmes. The amateur theatre group had also been set up.

Mail was slow in getting through to the camp. The majority of prisoners had not received anything since their capture in North Africa more than a year earlier. What was received in the camp were 108,000 cigarettes, 5 lb of tobacco, over 450 razor blades as well as shaving cream, just under 700 boxes of matches and 144 tubes of toothpaste. In June the ICRC offered to give the men cards so they could write home and let their loved ones know they had been captured but they were not given permission to do so, even though the cards were found to be in stock. More supplies of meat and fruit, biscuits, soap and tobacco did arrive though.

December, however, saw a large number of letters arriving at Cultybraggan. On the 14th, ten sack loads of mail arrived although many letters were addressed to prisoners who had been moved to other camps. Of the 4000 letters, 500 found their way into the hands of prisoners at Comrie. Along with the letters were 123 German Red Cross parcels, mainly containing books. And although over 400 parcels came, many had to be forwarded to other camps, with just 87 reaching their intended recipient in the camp.

———————

The early summer of 1945 saw the last ICRC report, while the camp was under the direction of Lt.-Col. Archibald Kennedy Wilson. Wilson, born in 1890 at Galston in Ayrshire, had been a police officer with Cardiff Police and in 1928 became Chief Constable of Carlisle then of Plymouth the following year. In 1932 he was moved to Liverpool and was awarded the King's Police Medal, and in 1937 was made a Commander of the British Empire. In 1938 he was given command of the Air Raid Precautions Organisation and created the Air Raid Wardens Service. In March 1940, due to failing eyesight, he was forced to retire. He was called up and given command of the Comrie camp on 27 March 1945.

Many improvements had been made in the look of the camp. Flower beds had been laid out, and paths had been constructed. The huts were so close together that there was no space for exercise, but each compound was allowed to use the football pitch twice a week, although the prisoners were not allowed to speak to those from another compound. Protected personnel were now allowed on walks and on the whole discipline was good (there was the exception at Christmas 1944 when a home-made swastika was flown). The prisoners were more content and were healthier, although there were six cases of bronchitis, two with heart trouble, two with cystitis, two with tonsillitis, and a man with a 'distortion of the right ankle', at the time of the June visit by Mr Bieri of the ICRC. Only 10% of the prisoners had been captured before D-Day and there had been a large influx in March. The camp's total number of prisoners of war stood at 3661 with the vast majority (2192) being from the Heer, the army, with 850 from the Luftwaffe and 531 from the Marine, the navy. There were 60 from Hitler's SS. The camp leader in Compound A was now Stabsoberfeldwebel Walter Lindner and Kurt Wilhelm assisted him. In Compound B it was Stabsfeldwebel Helmut Herrman with the assistance of Feldwebel Fritz Brand. Compound C had Oberfeldwebel Fritz Hoffman as leader and Unteroffizier Karl Wenniger as his assistant, and Compound D's leader was still Rikall and he was assisted by Feldwebel Edwin Leydecker.

Some of the huts had now been subdivided to cater for barbers' rooms and first aid posts, and the sanitary conditions had improved. There was only cold water in the washrooms and a hot shower was only available once a week but it was better than it had been. Clothes washing was all done in cold water.

Another improvement was the theatre group and the orchestras. Each compound had its own theatre group with all kinds of improvised materials for the costumes and the scenery. There were 20 members in the Compound A group, 18 in Compound B, about 20 in Compound C, and 40 in Compound D. The orchestra of Compound A was known as DTC – the *Deutsches Theater Comrie* – and had eight members, three of whom played the violin, one the accordion, one the trumpet, one the saxophone, one the clarinet and one jazz guitar. They held a concert on the afternoon of Sunday 10 June at the camp infirmary and Bieri stated 'they played exceedingly well'. The members intended to stay together after their release but it is not known if this happened. Compounds B and D also had small orchestras. All the compounds also had a camp choir ranging from 30 to 36 men.

There was still no canteen and still no real opportunity for work by this stage, although some of the prisoners managed to keep themselves busy doing various jobs for payment. Food rations decreased but the prisoners did not complain. There were only two radios in the whole camp and no films were shown, although British newspapers were made available. There was now a Catholic chaplain by the name of Gefreiter Hans Jamar, who was allowed to hold services in each compound. There was no Protestant chaplain but Dr H. Golzen of the Church of Scotland, a former German soldier who had lost him arm during World War I whilst fighting, held services in all compounds.

––––––––

The next commandant of Camp 21 was 45-year-old Lt.-Col. Darcy Evelyn Mills Fielding OBE of the York and Lancaster Regiment. Born in Islington, London on 12 March 1900, Fielding had seen action in East Africa and Madagascar and on 30 December 1940 had been awarded the Order of the British Empire. When he was in charge, in November 1945, there were fewer than 850 men in the camp, with only Compounds C and D holding them, although Compounds A and B were expecting an influx in the near future. Compound C held 401 including 125 NCOs and Compound D held 433, including four officers. Just over 500 of the men came from the army, 175 from the Luftwaffe and 152 from the navy. Many of the prisoners had been transferred to other camps. Of those left, only 25 were captured before D-Day and all the rest were caught afterwards.

Again things had changed. There was no longer a British medical officer but the German one was Assistenzarzt Fritz Grosche, a trainee doctor, who was assisted by Gunther Lengeling. The dentist was now Stabsarzt Friedrich Urbach. Medicals were now carried out once a month. Some of the prisoners were now allowed to work in agriculture locally and in the construction of buildings, earning 1½d. per hour. And at long last there was now a canteen in each compound, with a fund of £250 available. There was also a change regarding religious services, and both compounds were allowed to come together to worship.

Over 2500 books were available in the library including more than 100 classic German works, 280 language books which were used to teach English and French in both compounds, 50 theatre pieces and over 40 music books for the two camp theatre groups and orchestras. The theatre group in Compound C was divided into two groups of ten. One group concentrated on classic works while the other did variety. There were also almost 50 religious books.

Letters too were beginning to get through from Germany, which raised the mood of the camp. The mood had changed generally with the transfer of so many of the prisoners and morale was at an all-time high, with the exception of those who had relatives now living in the Russian zone in Germany. Reports had also got back to Fielding that the prisoners working outside the camp were doing a very satisfactory job. Overall he was happy with progress.

On 16 May 1946 the ICRC's Inspector Bondeli wrote that Camp 21 was 'a very good, well run camp'. Compounds A and B now each housed 1000 prisoners who were in transit from the United States to other camps or who were about to be repatriated. Their stay was scheduled to last only two or three weeks. Just under 3500 men were held, the vast majority of whom were German, although there were also 25 Austrians, one Polish national, one Italian, and one Slovakian. The camp leader of Compound A was Hauptfeldwebel Herbert Gersching, with Hermann Hansen leader of Compound B. Oberfeldwebel Fritz Hoffman was still camp leader of Compound C, having been in charge of it since at least November 1945, and Feldwebel Walter Pusch was still leader of Compound D. It was only Compound D which had permission for prisoners to work outside the camp. At that time, there were no complaints from the prisoners although the Germans shipped across the Atlantic had been told they were being repatriated, not going to another prisoner of war camp. Their morale was low and they were very bitter about the misinformation.

Mail to the prisoners on the whole was not bad, although letters from the Polish Zone were very few and far between. The prisoners always looked forward to hearing from their loved ones and news from home.

Newsreels were now shown every three weeks as well as a few YMCA films. Books in the library were now old and were 'very dilapidated', according to Bondeli, but there was no point in refreshing them as the camp was beginning to wind down.

———

There were a number of deaths at Comrie, including the murder of Feldwebel Wolfgang Rosterg and the mysterious case of Oberleutnant Willy Thormann, a junior officer. Rosterg was hanged by fellow prisoners who accused him of being unfaithful to the Nazi regime, while Thormann was found hanging just a few weeks before Rosterg. One other death of note is that of 30-year-old Feldwebel Heinrich Schwarz, who died of a bullet wound to the head on 21 April 1945. He was shot by Polish guards without provocation, according to a witness. Anyone outside after the night-time curfew was fair game and it appears he was five minutes late getting back to his barracks following a visit to a friend.

The Polish guards were detested further following another incident during which some liver eaten by the Germans had caused numerous cases of severe diarrhoea. The barracks were locked after 10 p.m. and the buckets the men had been using were simply not big enough to cope. As the men dashed to the latrines, the Polish guards became aware of the activity and began taking potshots at them while they sat in the toilets.

In January 1945 a report had been filed to the Polish military authorities stating that the Polish guards had to refrain from calling the Germans names – on being called names the Germans would retaliate by throwing stones, and the Poles would shoot back at them. It was a wholly unsatisfactory situation which was only resolved when the British guards were re-instated.

Unteroffizier Christian Munz, aged 32, was killed in a truck incident in September that year – again the circumstances are rather sketchy. The others who died were Obergefreiter Gustav Reiss from a stomach tumour two months before his 31st birthday, 26-year-old Unteroffizier Johannes Wöhrle who suffered from tuberculosis, and 21-year-old Gefreiter Kurt Zimmermann who died of appendicitis.

———

Like so many other prisoner of war camps, Camp 21 had its share of escape attempts. A Compound C sergeant who was decorated with the Knight's Cross, a high military honour in Germany, decided to make a bid for freedom. He managed to breach the security but within 24 hours he was found hidden in a haystack and promptly brought back. On 10 March 1945, three prisoners managed to escape and went on the run. Two days later they were recaptured and returned to the camp.

The camp guards also discovered three tunnels. The first two of these tunnels were found on 9 April 1945 in Compound B, one in the compound and the other in a compound store-house. One of these was behind a bookcase in the library and the commandant ordered a search of every man's bunk until the perpetrators were found. On 27 April that year, a third tunnel was found, but in its very early stages. Wilson, the then commandant, had become suspicious as he had noticed a pile of earth, consisting of various colours of soil, get larger over a period of weeks. Following its discovery, the perpetrators were exposed – they all had yellowish-brown soil underneath their fingernails – and were duly sent to the detention block. However, most prisoners had no real interest in escaping into the wild Scottish countryside.

But the camp did have a dark side. In the officers' sections of Compounds B and C the SS and the paratroopers organised a spying ring to find out if other officers were pro- or anti-Nazi. Compound B was the worst for this and organised a section of what amounted to secret police. If they recognised someone who had made an anti-Nazi comment he was targeted and under the darkness of night was beaten or punched. Those who did not do the Nazi salute were also singled out for punishment. This group had spies in every hut and compiled a list of men who appeared to be anti-Nazi, smuggling the list back to Germany by means of an exchange of prisoners of war. There was a general acceptance that if a prisoner of war did anything against the government or opposed it, the government was able to take steps against his private property and his immediate family.

It was rumoured in Camp 21 that a list of anti-Nazis were selected to travel to Camp 13 Shap Fells Hotel at Shap near Penrith in Westmoreland (the camp where German ace fighter pilot Franz von Werra dug a 50-yard tunnel and escaped only to be recaptured when he was trying to fly home). This list, it was said, had been compiled by an Unteroffizier who worked in the interpreter's office at Camp B and had come into the possession of one of these spies or one of the hard-line Nazis who threatened those who were on that list. The ringleader at Comrie was Obersturmbahnführer Jaeckel, a former teacher at the Junker school at Bad Tölz, who was held in Compound C. The camp commandant had to remove six or seven officers from Compound B in which most of the spying happened, and put them into protective custody. One prisoner in that compound ended up with a dislocated jaw and another two were throttled during the night.

It was Major Zapp, who had been captured in Brussels on 4 September 1944, who told the authorities about these underground officers. Zapp had arrived at Camp 21 in October 1944. At that time there were two sections for officers and two or three for other ranks. Camps B and C were the officers' camps, with around a thousand officers in each camp, a mix of navy, SS, paratroopers, railway operating troops and workers from the Todt Organisation. Zapp was in C. The camps were separated only by some barbed wire. During an interrogation he explained that there was a 'whole Kompanie' of parachutists and SS men who would hold a 'vehmic court'. They had their spies in every hut compiling lists and they discovered around 200 men were to be taken to Camp 13. The list was discovered by Jaeckel. All sorts of people were there, including a Sonderführer from the Todt Organisation who had a wooden leg. Many of the officers were petrified, and they were justified in feeling that way, for if the information reached Germany they knew their families would be in danger from the authorities. The spies termed Camp 13 'Free Germany Camp' and threatened to find out who were in these camps and warn the German authorities who would then use the SD (Sicherheitdienst, the intelligence section of the SS) to mete out the appropriate retribution on their families. It got to the point where the prisoners decided not to write home for a short period of time as the camp number appeared on the letters. An order had been issued that any prisoner of war 'occupying a special position or coming under special arrangements or collaborating with the enemy' would pay for it with the lives of all his family and his entire fortune.

The camp leader Prince Urach collected signatures of officers leaving with him and had intended to hand the letter to the camp commandant and for it to be forwarded to the War

Office. In it he had requested he and the 100 or so officers wanted to be moved to a different camp as at Comrie they were 'forced to be in the company of officers' who had acted 'contrary to the international officers' code'. The anti-Nazis were scared as if discovered they would be seen as collaborating with the enemy. Urach himself was frightened, as many of his relations were arrested following the July 1944 plot when an attempt had been made on Hitler's life, and he described Jaeckel as 'a frightful fellow' and the 'terror of the whole hut'. The whole situation caused 'great unpleasantness' among the officers, who wanted to be left in peace. Zapp believed the lists drawn up had been done partly from interrogations, partly from what the interrogators felt and partly according to reputation. Zapp himself was instructed by Oberst von Aulock 'to procure clothing for officers who had none' and he came into contact with the interpreter and camp officer and they would ask questions and make enquiries. From such interactions and a great deal of guesswork the lists were made up.

Zapp was sent to Camp 13, one of 240 officers. Six weeks before the men were to be sent to Camp 13, the officers were called out individually and the authorities stated that they were wanted for interrogation. The Norwegian officers said straight out 'We want to form a new camp. It will be a democratic camp. What are your views? Are you Nazi or anti-Nazi?' But Zapp believed the SS and paratroopers should have had a camp of their own, segregated from the ordinary soldiers. Sixty-two, mainly from Compound B at Comrie, were expelled from that camp by the War Office as they had started to stir up trouble. They had warned the others that they too should be expelled or they would make sure everyone knew they had been in the anti-Nazi camp. Zapp believed Jaeckel had managed to send his spies among the group.

Camp 21 closed its doors to prisoners of war not long after the cessation of World War II, with all 2000 prisoners removed in five batches on the same day in May 1947, and later became a Territorial Army camp. There is evidence that Camp 21A, the Cowden Camp which opened in early 1945 to house the 500 overflow prisoners, was a Polish resettlement camp between 20 August 1946 and 31 August 1948, as hinted at by the written testimony of Major John August's son David. August, from the Welsh Regiment, was posted at Comrie at this time to a Polish camp and given a Polish shield when he was transferred. This camp had around 33 huts, most of which were Nissen huts, to house the prisoners, with 14 huts to the immediate east outwith the perimeter fencing for staff.

As for the commandants, Wilson died in January 1962 after a long and illustrious career, while Fielding, who had been forced to retire on 28 April 1951, died in Surrey in 1988.

2 | THE RE-EDUCATION PROGRAMME

Education and re-education as part of de-Nazification played an important role in all camps. At Comrie a key player in the early days of the re-education programme was Herbert Sulzbach.

Sulzbach was born on 8 February 1894 into a wealthy Jewish banking family in Frankfurt-am-Main. On 8 August 1914 he became a soldier with the 63rd Frankfurt Field Artillery. He saw action briefly on the Eastern Front but was mainly based on the Western Front for the duration of the war. In 1916 he won the Iron Cross Second Class at the Battle of the Somme followed by the Iron Cross First Class after the bloody battle at Villers-Cotterêts in Picardy in northern France. He was also awarded the Frontkampfer-Ehrenkreuz, the Frontline Cross of Merit, which he received personally from Field Marshal Paul von Hindenburg, who later became president of the Weimar Republic between 1919 and 1933. Following the cessation of hostilities Sulzbach, like so many others, was surprised by Germany's capitulation and felt that the treaties at the Paris Peace Settlement were far too harsh.

He began working for the family's bank but found he was not suited to it so his father bought him a partnership in a paper factory. In 1920 he moved from Frankfurt to Neubabelsberg near Berlin where he married and had a baby daughter. The marriage soon began to fail, although his business prospered. Following the breakdown of his marriage he met an actress and remarried, mixing in artistic circles in the city, but soon his world was turned upside down by the rise of Hitler.

In 1936 Sulzbach's factory was sold 'under duress' and in 1937, he came to England and set up another paper factory in Slough, which failed. He returned to Germany a year later to pick up his wife Beate, along with her sister Ruth, in order to bring them back to Britain to escape persecution as he had found out he was on a blacklist. With the little money he had received when the factory was sold they made their plans to escape. He was forced to pay a few thousand Marks in a special tax levied on people wanting to leave the country, although he reclaimed it after the war under the law of restitution. The couple lived in London on money he was sent by his grandfather Rudolf, the founder of the banking business. Following the fall of France in 1940, there was a tribunal and because his papers stated he was German, he was interred as the result of a letter he had written – in 1924 – to his sister-in-law about France invading the Ruhr. Initially he was sent to Liverpool then to Douglas on the Isle of Man, where he was interred on 31 May 1940 along with his wife albeit separately.

During that time Sulzbach experienced what it was like to be basically a prisoner of war and this put him in good stead for his future roles. At Douglas, behind barbed wire and living in empty houses, a little community arose. There were musical evenings and a canteen where they could buy goods if they had money. He became a committee member for 'the university' and a pastry cook taught the internees. Newspapers became available and a camp newspaper was published. The Pioneer Corps were guarding them but they did not understand the difference between Jews and Nazis so thought of them as the enemy. After a while the men were allowed to write to their wives and find out where they were; then they were allowed to meet them but under guard at all times. At one point Sulzbach thought he was going to be deported to Australia but this never happened. During interrogations he was interviewed by Mr Napier, who asked about his past, and Napier soon realised he was no Nazi. He left the camp in October but it was another three months before he and his wife were reunited.

As soon as he was released, he volunteered for the Pioneer Corps, made up of Alien companies following the visit of a recruiting officer to the Isle of Man. He was a private for four years then became a lance corporal. Following the capture of German prisoners of war, a call was made for German speakers so Sulzbach put his name forward and was posted to the interpreter pool. His first posting was to a Russian company near Aldershot where he was unable to understand them, but he was soon posted to Comrie, in January 1945, shortly after the murder of Feldwebel Wolfgang Rosterg. He found Lt.-Col. Wilson, the commandant, 'wonderful' and reports that he gave him 'a free hand to deal with the POWs'. Sulzbach told them about a duplicating machine and went on to produce thousands of copies of leaflets explaining what democracy was and distributed them in the huts. He also had to explain to them why a Labour newspaper could be pro King. It was this kind of work that remained with the prisoners long after they had left the Comrie camp.

On 14 April 1945, before the war in Europe was over, Sulzbach's suggestions for re-education were sent to the Foreign Office at Aldwych in London. In his note he wrote of the '"Dolchstoss-Legend"', the 'stab in the back legend', stating that it would not work this time, and that the British should use rather the '"Übermacht" Legend from the conquered Germans, the legend that they may have only been conquered by superiority of their enemies'. To prevent the perpetration of the lie he believed a very short pamphlet should be produced making it very clear 'once and for all' that Germany alone had prepared for war and had done so for 20 years, that the German victories of 1939 and 1940 were down to inferior and unprepared enemies and that once Germany had met an army on equal terms then it was beaten. He also suggested it should be pointed out to them that for the last four and a half years much of the continent had been working for Germany, whether in factories or in agriculture, and that there had been around 13 million slave labourers, deported against their will, who had worked inside Nazi Germany for the German war machine. In turn, this made 13 million Germans available for the German armed forces. He wanted the Germans to know that until D-Day they had had a 'tremendous superiority of every kind' until the Allies matched them. Germany, he went on, was beaten because the Allied troops were better in every way, 'better spirit, better morale, better leaders, better officers and Right and Justice' was on their side. Eight days later he also suggested that, as the BBC had recorded Hitler's speeches from 1933, his false promises and lies could be shown to the prisoners of war in order to debunk the myths that surrounded him.

Sulzbach later gave more detail regarding his referral to the 'legend'. On 9 May 1945 he wrote to the Political Intelligence Department that the new German Foreign Minister Graf Schwerin-Krosigk had mentioned the word 'succumb' which he believed meant the minister wanted the German people to think that they had only laid down their arms due to Allied superiority. In addition he noted that the German commander in Norway had said in a broadcast that the Allies had not attacked the German forces there, meaning '"our army was never conquered – just like 1918"' – and Sulzbach knew these 'lies' would be believed by the fanatical prisoners. He reiterated the need for the pamphlets but added that a film showing the utter destruction of the German forces was also needed, making clear how they were crushed not only at the Rhine, which some believed was the case, but also at the Elbe, including footage of the Ruhr, Hanover, Kassel, Frankfurt, Munich (München), Hamburg and Bremen. On the eastern side the film had to show 'the Russian victories from the Oder to Berlin'. He said that a well-known captured general should be chosen to tell the fanatics 'how they were defeated – defeated and conquered in the field'. Leaving them as they were was not an option as they would remain a danger for the future, especially on their return to Germany. Footage of Buchenwald or Belsen concentration camps should also be shown to all prisoners, he stated, 'for their eternal shame'. A copy of this letter was sent to Dr Koeppler who responded saying that although what Sulzbach had recommended was excellent, much of it was already being implemented. However, Miss Lankaster, who had forwarded Sulzbach's suggestions, later wrote that she had written to the commandant at Camp 21 'to say that we shall be glad to receive further ideas' from him.

––––––

In early June 1945 both Camp 21 and Camp 21A were visited by James Grant, who inspected many camps to see how education was delivered. At this time, Comrie had a bad reputation – but Grant found it to be the opposite. The atmosphere was good and he believed that this was down to Lt.-Col. Wilson. He was told by the prisoners that letters were not getting through but they believed Wilson would not be withholding them as he was a fair man – although they added that if they stepped out of line, he would punish them without hesitation. Wilson himself was a keen supporter of the education on offer to the men as he knew it was an important part of their re-education regarding the meaning of democracy in their newly defeated homeland.

One of the main issues with the education programme was the lack of paper and pencils but the enthusiasm of the prisoners more than made up for this. English was the most popular class in all four compounds at the main camp and at the Cowden Camp. Of the 700 men held at the satellite camp, 65 men were classed as beginners in English, with nine advanced students. The students here complained that the books in the library were of no use in learning the language and that there were not enough teaching books.

In Compound A of the main camp, 163 pupils were studying under five teachers, four of whom taught English. These were 42-year-old Paul Bennewitz from Erfurt who, although he spoke English, actually taught German history. Grant found him to be a 'fine fellow'. Franz Frey, a 39-year-old former insurance clerk from Brünn, had been taught English at school and privately so taught beginners English. Oskar Link, a 22-year-old from Trier, had just passed his Abitur when war broke out and 19-year-old Fritz Berndt from Kassel had been at middle school at that time. Both could speak English well enough to teach it to the others. Herbert Imunds, a 34-year-old insurance employee, was the last of the English teachers in the compound. There were two advanced sections of students who were taught for four hours a week, while the five beginners sections were taught for an hour a day. There were only 49 copies of the student books but Grant arranged a supply of another 22 copies from London to be delivered. Unfortunately there were no dictionaries or grammar books at that time.

When Grant visited Compound B he found it altogether different. His reception was 'cool' in this difficult compound, notorious for its political hard line. However, there were 150 pupils eager to learn under five teachers. These were Herbert Battermann, a 39-year-old who had previously worked for the Caribbean Oil Company in Venezuela and had married a Venezuelan who was waiting for him in Germany. Battermann was a 'peculiar individual' who declared he taught advanced English, Spanish and constitutional history without the aid of books. Grant discovered it was his intention to move back to Venezuela following his release; he thought him a 'smart Alick' and the 'least satisfactory of the teachers' he met. During a test Battermann allowed fellow teacher cum student 42-year-old Harry Stellmacher, a former ship's engineer, to copy his advanced paper, which Grant only discovered when he was correcting it. Stellmacher claimed he had visited North America, South Africa and some other non-English-speaking countries; as a parting comment Grant wrote that although he never attended his classes 'if they reflect the personality of the teacher, they will be somewhat crude'. The other teachers were Karl Splettstoesser, a 28-year-old from Stettin who had been in commerce before the war, 39-year-old Erich Blitz who had learned English at the Berlitz School in Magdeburg and had taught English at an electric works in Berlin, and 23-year-old Olaf Kussel who had been a chemistry student before the war and had been taught English at school. These latter four all taught beginners courses.

Compound C was the most well-liked compound in the camp, especially in its teaching. Here there were 166 pupils with nine teachers. When Grant mentioned that 110 copies of the teaching books had been received in the camp, the Unterreichsleiter, or deputy, opened up a list for new classes and enrolled 240 pupils; however, only 30 more copies were forthcoming meaning that in total there were just 86 for the group. Luckily there were two Wichmann dictionaries, one of which was held in the Lagerfürher's office. All of the pupils had three lessons a week each lasting an hour.

In Compound D six teachers taught 129 pupils. All the classes were beginners, and in these good progress was being made, although there was also a business English class taught to between 12 and 15 students. All courses here were taught for two hours twice a week as there were only two huts available to them and this made best use of the time.

Following his visit, Grant stated in his report that he considered there was 'ample room for re-education' provided the matter was not rushed. He also called for more pen-nibs, writing paper, study books, dictionaries and German periodicals: Compound A only had *Die Wochenpost*, a German periodical supplied at a rate of three per hut of 75 men; Compound C had the same periodical at a rate of two per 75 men, although it was widely read, and *Ausblick*, which came by chance through a few prisoners of war who worked on building and drainage within the camp (*Ausblick* was also supplied in a very small number to the Cowden Camp). But pencils were highest on the list. In December 1944 the students had received half a pencil each and by this visit they had not been renewed. Due to many of them not working they had no money, although the instructors told Grant that many of the non-students who did work tried to purchase them for their friends. Wilson informed Grant that he had tried for months to get pencils through the NAAFI but to no avail. He also stated that the paper used during the classes was in fact toilet paper – and only after it had been employed in this way was it then used for its normal function in the latrines. Grant spoke to Pastor Denham of the Swedish Red Cross about the situation, as he was working in Glasgow at the YMCA, and showed him samples of the pencils. The pastor agreed to recommend 1000 pencils should be issued from Glasgow and sent to Comrie, but Grant suggested 2000 would be 'a more adequate supply', so Denham said he would do his best. So that the pencils were not given to non-students, lists were to be made up by the Unterreichsleiter in every compound and left with the official who was to distribute them.

During July Wilson wrote to Mr H. King, the Director of Lectures and Broadcasts at the Political Intelligence Department of the Foreign Office in London, regarding the number of prisoners of war who could attend lectures. Only 250 could be accommodated at any one time but he made the suggestion that with '3 lectures per day – one in the morning, one in the afternoon and one in the evening – 750 could be dealt with each day'. He calculated that it would take four and a half days for all the prisoners to attend. In his reply on the 19th, King said he thought most of the lecturers would not be able to spend so much time in one camp but said he would try to arrange 'for as many as possible to do it'. He suggested that some of the lecturers, who he described as 'quite experienced and relatively tough', might be able to give four or five lectures a day, meaning the whole camp would be covered in three days. Wilson wrote back three days later that one of the reasons he wanted the lectures restricted to three days per week was that it was not good for the prisoners mentally or physically to be hanging around the camp all day 'doing nothing, day after day, week after week'. It was not conducive to 'openness of mind which is essential to effective re-education'. Work opportunities were available in the local community and he saw these as important and constructive. In fact employment conditions at the camp were improving anyway. A good number of prisoners were engaged in engineering works at the camp, while 80 went out daily to work in forestry, 20 to a Royal Engineers site, and roughly 100 to different building sites. All of them were from the main camp, which Wilson himself regarded as 'black', and not from the satellite camp which was 'white'. He believed that by giving them some small freedoms and work to do the camp authorities were restoring their self-respect. He went on that with these men away from the camp, some of whom had to travel 'considerable distances', the camp could accommodate one lecture on the morning and one in the afternoon with one, possibly two, in the evening. It was also in this letter that Wilson hinted he would be retiring from the army in September.

Grant returned to Comrie on 18 August 1945 for a two-day visit and was warmly received. On this return visit the changes were very apparent. Compound A had been emptied, with the 'greys' going south and the 'blacks' going to Watten in Caithness. Compound B had only 500 prisoners, with the other two 'rather below' what he had seen on his previous visit. The teachers in Compound B were Oskar Link, who had been in Compound A on Grant's previous visit but with those prisoners gone had been moved. Hugo Strauss, aged 43, was a new teacher. He had learned English at the Oberrealschule at Oberhausen and had attended the universities at Göttingen and Cologne (Köln) passing the Staatsexamen as a Gewerbeoberlehrer, commercial head teacher, and was employed as an Oberlehrer, head teacher, at the Berufs Pedagogisches Institut in Cologne. Another new teacher was 32-year-old Hermann Adam, who had learned English at the Realgymnasium at Bochum. Before the war he had been a wholesale grocery manager. His English was 'distinctly shaky', however. Blitz remained a teacher.

Grant found the compound depressing as the men complained about the lack of letters from home and of course half the men had been removed which had 'upset everyone'. However the compound leader Rücker was trying to 'get the orchestra and theatre group moving' as the leading lights of these had been removed. While there Grant saw their production 'Mann bleibt Mann'.

Because of the change in prisoners some of the teachers from Compound C had been removed. The ones which remained were Kröger – although his time was mostly taken up by acting as interpreter for a builder – and Schriewens, who had been promoted to camp interpreter: both however said they would be available if time permitted should one of the other teachers be unable to attend a lecture for any reason. E. Beyers, who had lost many of his pupils during the change, now had 40 beginners, while Prisoner Weuffen had two groups and Prisoner Paul had 16 of the original advanced pupils. There was also a new teacher called Oskar Hart, aged 20, who had learned English in The Hague. He had been in 4th year at high school when he left to join the army and had intended to train as a Protestant minister. Lastly there was Gunther Jacob, who had learned English at school in Magdeburg and had attended one semester at Halle University as a medical student. He taught 20 beginners. This compound still had the same atmosphere as before. When asked to give a lecture on something other than politics, Grant spoke to them about 'the stages of the development of a novel in England which they appeared to appreciate'.

The change in circumstance also impacted on Compound D. There remained five teachers, these being Mainka, who had 32 pupils, Finger, who had 22 advanced pupils, Zarbock who had 25 pupils, Vogt who had 17, and Frey who had 32. On Grant's previous visit, Frey had been in Compound A.

Many of the prisoners had begun to lose interest in the classes as men were being transferred and they believed they would be next. However, in Compound D there was a thirst for the technical side of English and there was a request for short stories 'in childish English, about things that are not childish'. Not only did they want grammar books but most importantly a dictionary.

Again, Grant paid a visit to the satellite Camp 21A. Sommer and Wehmyer, teachers in this camp, asked for books as the main camp's library books were in a poor state by this time, with almost half missing pages. They believed the books they received were in this condition because, as many of those in Camp 21A were labourers or agricultural workers, it was considered they did not matter. They told him they had been 'greatly and grievously disillusioned' on their arrival and subsequently, and asked if they could have a separate library of their own.

––––––––

On 8 September the prisoners themselves organised a lecture on the question 'Will the House accept the proposal that all POW should be sent home immediately?' Attending this lecture were ten prisoners from each hut, amounting to 120 in total, and Staff Sergeant Sulzbach. It would not seem implausible to expect every man there to agree but it was not the case. The speakers expounded clearly, intelligently and logically and answered their opponents quickly, contradicting them 'cleverly and precisely'. Among the opposition the reasons put forward included the lack of housing following the bombings, lack of food, and staying put until the situation improved back home. What Sulzbach found most impressive was that the prisoners were full of confidence in the Allies and the way they were administering Germany, 'trusting their conquerors as if they were friends'. They had accepted defeat and spoke of the criminality left behind as a result of the Nazi leadership. Sulzbach was also surprised that they believed what they read in newspapers available to them. Here was a chance to re-educate all prisoners of war – for these ones, at least, were willing to learn and abandon Nazi ideologies. He firmly believed that through re-education Germany could be a peace-loving country again.

Shortly before 11 November, Armistice Day, Sulzbach had explained to the prisoners what Poppy Day was and read them the poem *In Flanders Fields* by John McCrae. He then proposed they should meet on the parade ground and salute the dead of all nations who had perished in conflict, whether fighting or in concentration camps. He went further, asking them to vow that never again would such murder take place and that never again would they allow themselves to be deceived or betrayed. He also wanted them to acknowledge that they were not a superior race, that they had no right to believe they were any better than any other, and that they had inflicted much misery on people due to their arrogance. He implored them to return to Germany as 'good Europeans' and involve themselves in reconciliation in the name of peace. Out of all the prisoners in the camp that day only a handful remained in their huts. His message had struck a chord and they stood in silence remembering the victims of war.

By Christmas Eve 1945 little had changed at the camp, except Lt.-Col. Wilson had been replaced by Fielding and Staff Sergeant Sulzbach had been replaced by Captain P. H. Blake. The latter substitution caused some upset to the prisoners but Grant believed the change would be good for the men 'since there is no doubt that the excellent re-education work done by the staff sergeant had probably gone far enough', and it was time the men readjusted. During this visit Grant gave a lecture in each of the compounds. In Compound C, at the request of the compound leader, the subject of the lecture was 'Scottish Christmas and New Year Observances', the leader having explained that the newspapers on that issue were incomprehensible and no dictionary in the world would help the men understand. In Compound D he spoke about dialect and its relationship with English.

On 14 February 1946 Dr Charles Wolff gave two lectures in the main camp on 'Scientific Progress – Both Sides of the Picture', which were so well received that Fielding requested he hold another two the following day. Three hundred and fifty men attended the first set of lectures, with 250 attending the second set. On the 15th, the lectures were held in the afternoon – the first to 300 U-boat personnel who had arrived the day before, and the second to men in the infirmary. On 15th February a talk was given on 'Light and Shade of Technics' which was received well generally, and eight days later Dr Pearse gave a lecture on 'Public Opinion' which received a mixed reception. The discussion following this lecture lasted around an hour and a half with the U-boat personnel clearly showing their fanatical affiliations. The main drawback at that time was that the huts were small therefore only around 130 prisoners could attend any given lecture at a time.

On 28 February 1946, a letter was written to the commandant from L. Hamilton at the Prisoner of War Division informing him that prisoners Walter Dunz, Franz Frey, Herbert Gersching and Josef Höser had passed their exams and that their diplomas would arrive in due course. He asked that the men be informed of their good results and for Fielding to pass on 'that we congratulate them on their success'.

February also saw *Der Wille*, the camp magazine, ready to be published and the camp waiting for materials to do so. Meantime the press review wall, which was all handwritten, contained items of news from the British newspapers, although there were not many and very few read them.

———

Between 22 and 25 March the camp was visited by W. G. W. Aston. Almost 4000 men were held there, with nearly 3000 newly shipped over from the United States. By this time Captain P. H. Blake, the Austrian officer interpreter, had been at the camp since 4 March that year and was responsible for most of the administrative activities regarding the recent intake of prisoners; at that point he did not know very much about prisoners of war or re-education. The other office interpreter was Staff Sergeant Jones, who had been sent to work at Comrie some six months previously. Although he was a good assistant, he did not have the drive or personality to influence prisoners of war with regards to their outlook. According to Aston, Jones was overshadowed by Blake and his somewhat 'aggressive demeanour'.

Of the 1018 permanent prisoners, 987 were in Compound D, and a staff of around 37 in Compound C were scheduled to join them shortly afterwards. The 2898 prisoners from the United States were housed in Compounds A, B and C. Eighteen men classed as C+ had recently been removed to Camp 165 at Watten. The camp leader of Compound C, Oberfeldwebel Fritz Hoffman, was regarded as a 'military type' and was considered senior to Feldwebel Walter Pusch, the camp leader of Compound D. Hoffman, who had been chosen by Wilson before he was replaced, dealt with the prisoners in transit while Pusch, Sulzbach's choice, was camp leader of those who were static or working prisoners of his compound. During the screening process those prisoners from the United States were categorised as 'white', 'grey' or 'black'. In Compound A, there were 4 'white', 805 'grey' and 90 'black' while in Compound B there were 11 'white', 921 'grey' and 67 'black'. However, Compound C held the most 'blacks', with 245 men seen as ardent Nazis; here there were 27 'white' and 726 'grey'. Two men were in hospital at the time and so were unscreened. Fifty-seven billetees were sent to Camp 21A.

Morale was low mainly due to the influence of 270 U-boat prisoners who had arrived from Londonderry, and who were mostly graded C. Their uncertainty regarding repatriation and the poor news coming out of Germany did nothing to boost morale but there was a glimmer of hope when *Die Wochenpost* ran a story about repatriation. The 270 U-boat personnel were segregated in huts together away from the other prisoners and the two did not mix. Pusch considered most of the working compound, apart from them, as anti-Nazi and they seemed to be satisfied with their treatment. Very quickly 80 or so U-boat men fell into line although somewhere between 35% and 40% remained ardent Nazis. Two hundred and twenty U-boat personnel were under 25 years of age, out of a total number of 370 youths at the camp, and presented a real danger to the status quo. The camp had many men who were 'requisite influential prisoners of war'; they found the submariners 'rather recalcitrant and for the time being some sort of segregation had to be imposed'.

As for study, there were 125 students of English at varying levels. Two of the teachers, Frey and Schrader, were said to be 'politically unsound' and the sooner a replacement could be found – at least for Schrader – the better. There were also 20 maths pupils, 20 studying Latin, five studying French and six studying Russian. Twelve men asked to study painting so a request for painting materials was made. Overall the re-education programme was progressing slowly, partly due to the arrival of the U-boat personnel and partly due to the British staff's time being largely taken up with administrative duties. There was also a lack of materials including books on political subjects and pamphlets which could be used in talks, as well as a distinct lack of dictionaries. Other problems were the lack of heating and appropriate rooms. In Compound D, for example, the dining huts were used. There were five huts each seating 80 men but one of these was used for stores, and three sittings were necessary to serve all the prisoners their meals, leaving precious little time for educational purposes. All of this led to apathy and a loss of interest in the courses on offer. Thoughts of repatriation also preyed heavily on the prisoners' minds. Aston recommended that in order to stop this negativity, more books on democracy, modern history, art and economics, as well as biographies, should be sent to the camp, so as to 'awaken interest in all prisoners of war'. He also stated that the younger prisoners should have leaders who were a positive influence on them, and recommended these youths be given special lectures on democratic systems.

On the day Aston left, visiting lecturer W. Beger-Spayne delivered two lectures in the main camp, on 'Democracy in Economic Life' and 'The World Food Position', and the following day gave a lecture on 'The Importance of Curiosity' (on that second day he delivered five lectures in all). Attendance on the 25th was 250 while on the 26th it was 375 in total. After the first lecture there followed a very good discussion on 'Democracy', although the younger prisoners did not really know much about it; that on 'World Food' began slowly as most of his audience was Austrian and they did not feel the subject had much relevance to their country. Yet as the discussion went on, nearly all acknowledged there was an issue with food in Germany which could not be quickly solved. On the 27th, Beger-Spayne gave his original two lectures to around 80 men. The camp report on these lectures was very positive: he had delivered the lectures in a 'clear and interesting way' which was 'very much appreciated'. It was the 'unanimous desire' of all the prisoners that he return and give more lectures in the near future.

————————

Grant's next visit to Comrie took place on 6 and 7 May 1946 at a time when there was continual movement of prisoners in and out. Grant reckoned these amounted to around a thousand or more in a month, all of whom had been shipped back from America. There had been no change in the teaching staff although Captain Blake spoke of his misgivings regarding Franz Frey as he lacked cooperation in lecturing and the camp newspaper activities made him 'suspect politically' or at least would suggest he was 'inert'. Finger had 15 beginner students. The course had started at Christmas and was combined following other courses falling through as a result of transfers and billeting. Erich Berger had 12 intermediate pupils who were the last of various courses and various teachers who had been transferred. Herbert Schrader began with 50 students on 5 April but most were transferred immediately and by May he had only 12. Blake also had reservations about him. Walter Dunz had taken over Frey's class as the latter was in hospital at the time of the visit.

Mid-May saw Max Patrick visit the camp, delivering five lectures in total over three days in Compounds C and D on 'The Future of the Skilled Worker'. The first took place on the 14th in the afternoon in front of 100 prisoners; the Austrians asked for him to lecture them separately which he did. At 8 p.m. he delivered his second lecture in the main compound in front of 150 men. They were interested but quiet as many felt they could not speak up, although one did say it was difficult to judge the situation in Germany from behind barbed wire. One of his lectures was given to newly arrived prisoners from America –this turned out to be very lively as they had been promised repatriation, although of course this did not happen. These prisoners claimed their treatment had been 'barbaric' and against the Geneva Convention. Patrick shot back about the Allied prisoners who had been shot, which they called 'a lie'. Patrick told them that while in the United States they had not been kept up to date on the state of Germany. He implored them to stand up against the 'old-time Nazis' and help build a new, peaceful Germany. Following the lecture a number of prisoners went up to him and admitted they wholly agreed with him. During that month the prisoners themselves discussed 'Modern Upbringing', by Finger, and 'Protection of Workers and Youth Welfare' by Gefreiter Groenwold, which was attended by 160 men. In addition Feldwebel Geese lectured on 'The Structure of Free Trade Unions before '33' – this was attended by 100 men and discussed at great lengths afterwards.

––––––––

A month later the camp received another visit regarding its re-education programme. This time Aston arrived at its gates on 7 June and left three days later. In total there were 3260 prisoners of war; however, only 550 were in the working compound D, as the rest were in transit. Morale in the compound was low as prisoners found the promise of early repatriation to have given them false hope. Letters from home did not help as through them they found out how dire the situation was back in Germany. All of this was on top of their dislike for the way Captain Blake tried to force his ideas on them. They had become dispirited and were becoming increasingly rebellious as well as losing interest in the re-education classes. That said Aston now considered the compound to be 'grey' after 200 U-boat personnel had been moved to different camps. Blake told him he considered there to be 20 'whites', 380 'greys' and 150 'blacks'. The camp leader Feldwebel Walter Pusch informed him he was unsure if any political progress had been made but that he considered 250 prisoners to be truly democratic, 50 to have Nazi leanings but not strong ones, and the rest to be politically indifferent although many remained sceptical of democratic aims. Of these prisoners 80 were under the age of 25 and thanks to Unteroffizier Erich Beyer were able to participate in political discussions. Three other prisoners, Unteroffiziers Strauf, Sandt and Obergefreiter Knechtel, took an active part in youth activities. Fifty youths participated in classes ranging from chemistry and botany to shorthand and commercial arithmetic.

The cultural committee now consisted of Pusch (the chairman), Feldwebel Barth (study leader), Obsoldat Buchholz (camp magazine editor), Unteroffizier Bueschler (head of discussions), Beyer, Unteroffizier Tilgen (head of lectures and discussions), Fahnrich zur See Finger (chief of the press review) and Wilhelm Schirmer (head of theatre and music). Aston called a meeting with the committee to discuss the re-educational activities. During these discussions he saw at first-hand how Blake harangued the prisoners; as they failed to reach agreement, Blake's excitement escalated and Aston called the meeting to a close. Blake's 'dogmatic and overbearing attitude' was already having adverse effects on the re-education system and it had to stop. It should be noted Bueschler was only part of the committee because he had attended courses at Beaconsfield – when he gave a lecture on the Nuremberg process he repeated his notes parrot fashion and could not answer the questions put to him, thus making him a complete failure as far as lectures went.

The committee met once a week and had used up much of the material already submitted. They had been unaware of the Oxford Pamphlets and hoped to receive a set of them for future talks, discussions and debates. However, the prisoners also still had access to newspapers including *The Times*, *The Scotsman*, the *Glasgow Herald* and the *Manchester Guardian Weekly*, *The Times* being the one they saw as official. They also had access to six or eight German newspapers weekly and of course they had *Der Wochenpost* and *Ausblick*. The library also had more books of which 600 were textbooks including almost 400 on the English language. *Der Wille* was still going strong and during his visit Aston asked the two padres why they did not use the camp magazine for religious purposes. The Protestant padre Leutnant Karl Siefkes felt he was not capable of writing a good article while the Catholic padre Gefreiter Ludwig Jamar, a Silesian monk, had believed it was a political magazine but would contribute in future, aiming at those who did not appear at Mass. Lt.-Col. Fielding told Aston he was anxious to replace both these men and Aston agreed with him, believing it would do the camp good.

Although the lectures were successful, the discussion groups were rapidly declining with fewer and fewer people attending them. According to Aston, the prisoners were afraid to say too much as they thought it would count against them when it came to being repatriated. They were under the impression they would be whisked away to a black camp if they did not say the right thing; mention was made of Camp 165 at Watten. Although Aston tried to reassure them, the feeling was deep rooted and Blake's attitude did nothing to help the situation. Aston had noticed how reticent the prisoners were in Blake's presence, and witnessed how the youths spoke more freely in their discussions.

Overall, there were still signs that the re-education programme was working, especially for the younger men, and the cultural committee members were enthusiastic in guiding others towards democracy. However, Blake's attitude held back many of the prisoners from truly believing in the process. He was seen as 'a stumbling block to the peaceful penetration of democratic tenets'.

On 25th, 26th, 27th and 28th July Richard Laufer gave five lectures on 'From British Empire to Commonwealth of Nations'. Total attendance for his lectures was 1200 out of a total of 1700, although only the last lecture was for those permanently held at the camp. Laufer found that the re-education system was making only slow progress but thought this would change when the camp became a working rather than a base camp. Although there was not a discussion as such after the lecture, there were some questions and the prisoners were heard discussing the topic later amongst themselves.

————

Grant visited again on 5 and 6 August 1946 by which time the camp held 1553 in the main camp and 80 billetees. The camp's spokesman for Compound C was Fritz Hoffman and for Compound D Herbert Gersching. There were 134 students of English from Compound C and 115 from Compound D, with each student receiving six lessons per week at their chosen academic level. Two classrooms were in huts, with the theatre hut used as a lecture theatre. The teachers were Helmut Julius, Wolfgang Quandt and Walter Dunz for Compound C, and Hans Georg Müller, Erich Beyer and Werner Finger for Compound D. Julius caused some discomfort for the camp interpreter Blake. Born on 24 April 1916, Julius had been a hardware salesman at Flensburg before his capture and subsequent internment in the United States. He had been graded as C and Blake asked for a ruling about him, to which Grant replied with a suggestion that he could be replaced by Erich Beyer from Compound D; Grant said that if any explanation were needed he could speak of the 'inexperience of the one and the long experience of the other'.

Shortly after Grant's departure another visiting lecturer arrived: G. Guder delivered two lectures on 10 and 11 August in Compounds C and D on 'Ten Years in Great Britain'. On the Saturday he lectured in Compound D and when he had finished talking, the prisoners rose to leave as if they had not expected a discussion. They all appeared attentive enough but, with the exception of the younger ones, seemed to show very little response. The Sunday group in Compound C were much more responsive and asked questions following the lecture. All of them had taken an interest in how in Britain 'anyone can say what he wants and live as he likes'. One of the questions posed to Guder was whether he thought it possible a two-minute inter-rogation was enough to pass a political judgement on a person. He replied no but pointed out that the interrogation was not the only basis for the judgement and other guiding factors were also taken into account by the interrogator.

At the end of August Fielding got a phone call to say K. W. Rothschild would give lectures at the camp, although he never received written confirmation. The lectures went ahead though. The first was on the 31st on the 'U.N.O.', the United Nations Organisation, which had been established on 24 October 1945. Delivered in the main camp to 300 men, there were 'some good contributions from a small minority' but on the whole Rothschild saw it as a 'rather dull camp' where the prisoners only had one thing on their minds, namely when they were going to be repatriated. The following day he delivered the same lecture to around 100 prisoners – afterwards the discussion was 'good' but mainly 'carried out by two or three people'. These discussions lasted around an hour after each lecture.

Five weeks later a controversy landed at Comrie. Dr Rawitzki arrived to lecture on 'Hitler and the Nuremberg Trial' in the main camp on 6 October. Two lectures were given to between 550 and 600 men in what was now a working camp where morale 'was high'. The discussion following the lecture was lively as the debating groups within the camp often dealt with the same subject. Rawitzki was surprised 'to find such a high interest' as he had been told the camp was a transit one and was not expecting such a discussion. He also told the prisoners that he was surprised that lecturers were visiting the camp 'in such long intervals' as the camp was 'entitled to two lecturers per month'. In his report, Rawitzki noted that his remarks had resulted in a growing fear on the part of the prisoners that this was still regarded as a 'black' camp, and feared this would have some effect on repatriation from the camp. 'Right or wrong', Fielding implored the authorities to omit such remarks in the future. He went on to say that the camp was a working camp and that the cultural activities 'regarding political re-education' were of 'a very high standard'. The information given to the lecturer by the Lecture Section at COGA (the Control Office for Germany and Austria) that it was a transit camp with 3000 prisoners who had 'little interest in discussions of this kind is not correct', and the number of men there was less than half their estimate. He also stated the camp should have had an official list from COGA of the lectures given by their lecturers so they could select the ones of interest.

In response COGA informed Fielding that Rawitzki had been inaccurate regarding the number of lecturers which were to visit the camp, explaining that all the lecturers were 'voluntary part-time workers' and that it was impossible 'to guarantee a definitive number of lecturers to any camp'. Fielding was also told that an official list did not exist.

Early November saw the arrival of Paul Emden, who visited on the 4th and 5th of that month. He heard the story from a prisoner about Rawitzki's misinformation and how the camp had been shown in a false light, which Emden wholly agreed with. He found it to be 'full of life and endeavour' and a camp where 'good work has been done'. He went on to explain the camp was split into two, 'Camp C and Camp D'. Compound C still held prisoners shipped over from America – mainly industrial workers – while D held agricultural labourers who had always been held in Britain. Emden gave his first lecture in D on the 4th at 19.30 on 'H.M. Opposition' in front of 240, but as the hut was so small around 50 did not manage to get in. The prisoners took a great interest in it and a 45-minute discussion followed. The following day he gave a lecture on 'Empire and Democracy' to around 190 prisoners but although it went reasonably well it did not engender the same interest and discussion as the previous lecture. At 19.00 that day he delivered his original lecture once more to an audience of 135. The discussion afterwards lasted for one and three-quarter hours. Having spent time there, he classed the camp as 'grey/white' but most definitely not 'black'. Emden made a good impression on the prisoners and they asked him if more lecturers could possibly visit the camp. Fielding endorsed this request.

A few days before Christmas another lecturer arrived, Dr Sinsheimer, who gave two lectures on the 19th and one on the 20th on the subjects of 'What I Learned in My Village' and 'Potsdam or Weimar'. Three hundred prisoners participated – around 35% of the camp – and the discussions afterwards were deemed 'lively'. All the prisoners appeared to be 'very appreciative'.

––––––––

On 28 January 1947, another education survey was undertaken, by P. H. MacDonald. By this time Camp 21 had a total of 855 prisoners, of whom only three were officers. Of these 134 were in billets. The vast majority had been classed as B, B+ or B– with 112 as C and 10 A. Ninety were unscreened. There had been some friction between Fielding and COGA but once everything had been explained clearly to him, things settled down. Captain Blake no longer intervened as actively in re-education and now had a better understanding of the problems relating to it. However, the prisoners of war did not like him and he soon realised that his appearance at camp activities was not welcomed. The prisoners did not take kindly to the way he tried to force his personal ideas on them by ranting and vindictive arguments.

Camp leader Oberfeldwebel Hoffman, a soldier since 1929, still wore his Wehrmacht uniform with badges and polished boots, but his attitude was not unduly militaristic and his discipline was not harsh and the other prisoners of war saw him as a fair man. He gave his full assistance to the re-education leaders, but he only attended the lectures, and did not participate. His deputy was Feldwebel Schmidt who had joined NSDAP (the National Socialist German Workers' Party) in 1931, but he had little influence on the camp and mostly concentrated on his clerical work. The re-educational leader was Gefreiter Pente, aged 49, who had been posted to Comrie the previous November from a training centre where he had been held back to study a second course. He had been a secondary teacher with liberal views and no strong political affiliation, and was interested in sociological issues 'rather than a frontal assault on current politics'.

Morale at the camp was still low as the prisoners knew their camp continued to be seen as 'black'. It also did not help that so few of the men had been repatriated compared with other camps in the area. Grant himself graded some of the unscreened prisoners and this seemed to lift morale a little, although they could not understand why 200 'black' submarine personnel had been repatriated before them. There was also the issue of lack of human contact outwith the camp. Those who worked outside its perimeter did so in isolated parts of the sparsely populated district.

The re-educational activities were overseen by Pente, Feldwebel Euchner (the leader of a newly restarted Youth Group), Feldwebel Winter (a former trade union official) who edited the camp newspaper, prisoner of war Schirmer who ran the theatre group and orchestra, and prisoner of war Martin who ran the sports group. The facilities for all types of activity were excellent and there had been no break in re-education even though numbers within the camp were diminished. The students now had a wide range of newspapers to peruse, from British ones to the *Neue Zuericher Zeitung*, all of which were laid out in the canteen. *The Economist* was also added to the list. The camp library was supplemented in January when Camp 21A was absorbed into the main camp and was adequately furnished with books, although a request was put forward for *A History of German Literature*. Among the lectures to take place were 'Municipal Administration and Politics' and on the 19th of the month Herr Bielik gave a lecture on the 'Reconstitution of Local Government'; although the lecture was considered informative it was felt his theoretical knowledge of the subject far outweighed his practical knowledge. Subjects requested to be covered in the future were the Youth Movement in Germany and/or Britain, the Trade Union Movement, and for Miss Gemmel of St Andrews University to attend and lecture on Education in the British Zone. The discussion group was popular – this would begin with a debate followed by a general discussion and had an attendance of around 50, mainly made up of older prisoners of war. It met once a week under the chairmanship of Pente. Here discussions had included the English Education System, the Conception of the State and Democratic State Reforms. Prisoners also could discuss articles found in the camp magazine *Der Wille* which was published fortnightly by COGA.

New classes were also offered by this stage. A small French course was run by Feldwebel Kroeger. When it was proposed to make Kroeger part of the camp committee, however, Grant vetted him and found him to be 'highly undesirable' and an opportunist who had run a 'Nazi cell in Malaga during the Spanish Civil War'. Prisoner of war Moldenhauer, 'a good honest type with a trade union record', ran a constructional engineering course for five students, while Roman Catholic padre Obergefreiter Grunert ran a Latin class. A combined German language and literature class was run by Pente and prisoner of war Wetzel.

One man picked out for having a negative effect on the camp as a whole was Protestant padre Leutnant Siefkes. Siefkes had joined NSDAP in 1931. He took no part in the re-education programme but somewhere between 50 and 60 men attended his services. This was in complete contrast to the Roman Catholic padre Grunert who took an active interest in cultural activities and who held a number of talks on Human Character and Property. He told Grant that the prisoners sent back from the United States had never got over their disappointment at not being repatriated on their return.

In the main it was thanks to the camp staff that these re-educational activities kept running when some of the teachers were being repatriated. However, the next test was the screening of prisoners which was due to take place in February and how that would affect the programme.

———

On 11 February 1947, Camp 21 received its final visit from James Grant. By now the total number of prisoners was 680; the camp spokesman was Fritz Hoffman. To get to the camp Grant took the train to Crieff then the bus to Comrie, followed by transport to the camp from the bus stop. This time he stayed in the Ancaster Arms in the village, which he rated as 'good'. Now there was only one classroom in the canteen hut, which had electric lighting and heating; the 'dining room's too big to heat now'. A total of 60 students attended the classes with two intermediate English ones having two lessons per week and an advanced English class one lesson a week. Erich Beyer taught 11 students, while Wolfgang Quandt had been at Camp 174 Norton. Thirty of the students were private. There was a shortage of the book *English for All* – only between 29 and 35 copies whereas 50 were needed. Quandt wanted to be transferred elsewhere, as when he returned to Comrie he had found that the long-established teachers were more than capable of doing the necessary teaching. Grant suggested he should be transferred to a camp in need of a teacher, as he could teach not only English but also maths and algebra.

Grant himself had a complaint. When he had called from Stirling to tell the camp about his impending arrival, the commandant who took the call refused for the charges to be reversed and told the operator that he should pay for his own calls. Fielding told him he had never heard of camps accepting surcharges.

Four days after Grant's departure another lecturer arrived. Dr S. Kissin delivered two lectures on the 15th and 16th on 'What is Socialism?' and 'German Labour Movement, Past, Present and Future'. At this stage the camp held around 540 prisoners of war and according to Kissin the camp newspaper was 'more like a scientific review' which would be above the heads of most who read it. He lectured on 'Socialism' on the 15th in front of between 40 and 50 men and during the discussion and questions he found most of them had socialist views, although a few remarks after both lectures 'reflected extremist leanings', and some had communist leanings. Many of the prisoners disapproved of granting compensation to capitalists whose enterprises had been nationalised, at least in Germany. They strongly advocated German industrial reconstruction on the basis of state ownership and expressed a fear of new capitalism under the influence of 'Anglo-American management of the western zone of Germany'. One prisoner however defended Russian Communism, stating that that system 'was apparently approved by the Russian people'. In the discussion following his second lecture on German labour, the prisoners argued for complete unity and attacked German non-socialist parties. The internal issues facing Germany were also discussed by both audiences. They all agreed that there was a need for closer international cooperation and for the creation of a united Europe. Some did voice their concern about Germany's new borders, saying they were unfair, with one man admitting 'Russia and Poland might have justified claims to frontier revision on account of their terrific war losses', but denied a similar claim in the West for France, Holland and Belgium. Topical issues were also covered such as Churchill's campaign for a European Union. Fielding was more than enthusiastic about lectures on such subjects.

The final lecture to take place at Camp 21 happened in March that year. On the 20th and 21st, F. O. Keller arrived and lectured on 'Everyday Democracy' and 'The British Press'. Total attendance was 280 out of the entire camp of 500, with 200 at the 'Democracy' lecture and 80 at the 'Press' one. During discussions the prisoners complained that they no longer got any weekly papers and did not get enough German newspapers.

————

As for the man who instigated the re-education programme, Sulzbach, many years later, received numerous letters from former prisoners at Comrie who still remembered his good work and his 'humane greatness'. Another prisoner wrote to him stating it was his 'heartiest wish' to send him 'a few lines of gratitude' for his 'wonderful help' while he was a prisoner at Comrie between the spring of 1945 and the summer of 1946. In all around 3000 former prisoners wrote and thanked him for his work. Sulzbach left Comrie on 11 December 1945. On that day he received a letter from the German camp leader which stated that he himself had been deprived of his German nationality 'by an evil man but nonetheless you saved our souls for a future Germany' and 'for the rest of our lives we shall never forget Comrie 1945 and your unselfish help'.

Sulzbach was sent to Camp 18 Featherstone Park in Northumberland on the orders of Major Henry Faulk, later Colonel, the Chief Executive Officer at the Foreign Office, German Section, POW Division, where he began work in January 1946. In 1947 he was granted British citizenship and five years later regained his German nationality. He left the army in 1948 then served as the Cultural and Press Officer for the German Embassy in Belgrave Square in London between 1950 until 1981. On the formation of the Featherstone Park Association in Düsseldorf in November 1960, which had been arranged by 20 or so ex-prisoners from that camp, he was elected Life President and over the years many prestigious people accepted his invitations to speak at these yearly meetings in the German city, including Faulk. In 1978 he was awarded the European Peace Cross; he also received the OBE from Her Majesty Queen Elizabeth II as well as the German Order of Merit First Class and the Grand Cross of the Order of Merit. In 1982 the Featherstone Park Association honoured him with a plaque at the entrance of the park. It states that he 'dedicated himself to making this camp a seed bed of British–German reconciliation. Our two nations owe him a heartfelt thanks'. He died on 5 July 1985 aged 93. He worked tirelessly on reconciliation between the two countries he loved and according to Bernard Levin, who attended a memorial service for him, 'he was the soul of humanity'.

3 | A SOLDIER'S STORY

On 4 September 1994, exactly 50 years after he had emerged slowly from the underbrush of a wood with his hands held high in surrender, Rolf Weitzel began writing down his war experiences. It was not straightforward, as with the passage of time, names, dates and places could not be recalled with clarity – nor could the sequence of events for sure – but he chronicled what he remembered, in the main inspired by the 50th anniversary commemorations of D-Day on 6 June.

Weitzel was born in 1924 in the city of Kassel in the northern Hesse region of Germany. In the middle of May 1942 his schooling suddenly came to a halt when he was called up to the Reich's Labour Service (Arbeitsdienst). From the start of the war, secondary school students had been allowed to finish their education and sit their Abitur, their school leaving exam, before being forced into the Arbeitsdienst, from where they were drafted directly into the Wehrmacht. However, by May 1942 this was a luxury the Wehrmacht could no longer afford, and students who would normally have finished school in the summer of 1943 finished a year earlier. Weitzel found the little blue envelope in his letter box one May morning. Inside were the call-up orders for him to serve a three-month period in the Arbeitsdienst, and he was instructed 'to report on 1 June to the Labour Service camp of Steinbach in the Rhön mountains'.

The Arbeitsdienst had been created in 1932 on a voluntary basis to help the millions of people who were at the time unemployed and to get them off the streets. By 1935, however, it had become compulsory, with a six-month service period preceding a two-year stint in the Wehrmacht. Time was spent labouring – the first Autobahn was built using this cheap labour. Weitzel later found out that around a third of his classmates had also received the call-up, all of whom were born in 1924. For those born in 1925 call-up was deferred until the end of 1942 or beginning of 1943. Because there was nothing he could do, Weitzel simply took it all in his stride. All of them had known this was inevitable – their lives were already surrounded by war and their schooling had been interrupted on numerous occasions. During the winter of

1941/42, following a period of severe frost and heavy snowfall, the school had been forced to close due to a lack of coal. Weitzel had spent time shovelling snow and was also mobilised by the Hitler Youth to aid in the supply and delivery of coal to old and sick people living in their area. The coal was 'hauled on sledges since the streets were not cleared from snow'. Another time the students were sent out to the countryside to help with the harvest while the men were away fighting on the front lines. During this time they lived on the farms. The work was very physical for the boys, with a lack of agricultural machinery.

School was also interrupted by Allied bombing raids. As the war continued to rumble on, there were an increasing number of night-time raids on Kassel – if these lasted past one o'clock in the morning, the first lesson at school was automatically cancelled. No classes were ever repeated, except in extreme cases, as the school authorities had been instructed that the students should be available as soon as possible for call-up to the Wehrmacht. And so when the call-up came, the young men 'viewed the future without apprehension, rather as an adventure'. By the summer of that year, the mood of the German people was confident, although neither Weitzel nor his friends 'joined the forces with enthusiasm'.

So it was to the small village of Steinbach situated on the northern flank of the Rhön mountain range that Weitzel found himself sent. The camps were scattered over the whole mountain range and his was situated on a hillside about a kilometre from the railway station, where the 'forest came right up to the camp perimeter'. His first six weeks were spent doing basic training – most of this posed no problem as the necessaries had been drummed into him when he had been forced to become a member of the Hitler Youth almost ten years earlier. Yet the 'spade drill' was something completely new. It was the equivalent of rifle drill in the army, and the young men were barked at with orders such as 'order spade, shoulder spade' and so on with what seemed to Weitzel to be nothing like a spade. They were decorative pieces of equipment used for parades and march-pasts, and they were heavy. It was tedious, repetitive and boring. After three weeks, they were finally given proper spades as well as pick axes and taught specific work with them.

After the six weeks of training the whole unit was transferred to the town of Giessen, roughly halfway between Kassel and Frankfurt. Preparations for a military headquarters from where Hitler and the Wehrmacht had intended to direct war operations against France had been abandoned at the university town, and the young men's first task was to dig up the special communications cable which had been laid there but was now needed elsewhere. They stayed in barracks close to their work. The sergeant of the Pioneer Corps who supervised them located the cable using a site plan and allotted the work to groups. It did not take them long to find the cable, some two metres down, but on a fairly regular basis the sergeant either miscalculated or misread the plans and only following a few hours of digging and no cable were frantic efforts made to find its correct location.

After the cable had been completely unearthed, the men returned to Steinbach, at the end of the first week of September. On 15 September the men were released from the service. Only two weeks later, Weitzel was called up to serve in the Wehrmacht. This call-up order instructed him to report to the local Kassel police barracks where a transport of recruits were to be assembled. Their destination was the Bavarian town of Aschaffenburg. Here there was an infantry depot which dated from the 1890s – by the 1940s it was run down and ill equipped in terms of modern sanitation. The infantry in the Wehrmacht was composed of three battalions, with each battalion having four companies. Three of these were 'light' or rifle companies armed with rifles and light machine guns, with the fourth being a heavy company. This heavy company was composed of one platoon of mortars and three of heavy machine guns and Weitzel had been assigned to the latter; the only difference was that the machine gun was mounted, it was not actually heavy in weight at all. The crew of a heavy machine gun consisted of six men. A sergeant was in charge and Number 1 gunner, the man who fired the weapon, was the most important of the rest of them. Number 2 gunner fed the ammunition, while gunners 3 to 5 were ammunition bearers.

Around 600 men assembled early one morning ready to be transported to Aschaffenburg, each of them carrying a suitcase in which to return their civilian suits back to their families. The day before he reported at the barracks, Weitzel's grandmother gave him a small pouch containing two coins with the Virgin Mary on them to keep him safe. Throughout the war he kept them in the leather bag he wore around his neck along with his identity tag, where they remained until they were somehow lost after he became a prisoner of war.

Life at the barracks was mundane and repetitive, with basic training being undergone once again. A few weeks in rifle training began, at a firing range on the outskirts of Aschaffenburg, and Weitzel beat the rest of his battalion by getting the highest score during the '100 metres in the lying position'. As a 14-year-old he had been given an airgun and had spent time almost every day practising – hence why he was such a good shot. For the next few months he remained consistently the highest marksman, until illness brought his reign to an end.

Around 20 October Weitzel and his battalion were relocated to France for combat training as well as acting as the occupying force. Over the next nine months he was moved to eight different garrisons, beginning in a small village in Burgundy, then on to Digoin not far from Paray-le-Monial in the Loire. Here they lived in makeshift barracks which allowed the cold winds to seep through gaps, keeping the men awake at night. Red wine, which they were able to purchase cheaply from a nearby German customs office, soon helped them sleep. The office sat on the boundary between German-occupied France and the unoccupied zone where the Vichy government of Philippe Pétain exercised limited authority. The German customs officers controlled the border and the cheap red wine was confiscated contraband.

On 11 November 1942, however, Hitler ordered the Wehrmacht to take control of the unoccupied zone and Weitzel and his unit were mobilised two days later, occupying Montluçon where they took over the run-down barracks. Here Weitzel stayed until mid-January 1943, when he was transferred to the spa town of Riom in the Auvergne. In a chateau nearby were residing members of the last French government, notably the ex-prime ministers Édouard Daladier and Paul Reynaud as well as General Maurice Gamelin, and Weitzel's company was charged with guarding the chateau's outer perimeter. In February he was transferred to St Etienne, some 50 kilometres southwest of Lyon in the Rhône-Alpes region, where he spent the next three months. It was here he had his first and only experience of the French Resistance. One Saturday afternoon the men were urgently summoned together at the barrack square, where they were told by the officers that someone from a passing motorbike had thrown a grenade into the officers' mess, badly wounding an officer and slightly injuring others. To show their might, the Germans spent the rest of the afternoon marching round St Etienne and imposed a curfew on the town which was reinforced by nightly patrols. Nothing else happened so a few days later the curfew was lifted and life went on as before. It was during this time that Weitzel fell ill with jaundice. He spent two weeks in the infirmary and the following week was charged with doing barrack duty, including peeling potatoes and scrubbing washrooms. As a result of this illness his eyesight was affected. As mentioned earlier, his rifle shooting crown had been won over by another and the reason was he was failing to see the targets properly, a fact that never occurred to him or his sergeant. Only when he became a prisoner of war was his eyesight tested, during a routine medical examination, and he was issued with glasses while in British custody.

––––––––

At the end of April 1943, Weitzel was made a corporal and transferred to a different battalion. He was now an instructor to new recruits at Montbrison, 30 kilometres northwest of St Etienne. The weapons they were supposed to train with were not German but captured Czech and Polish weapons, and lack of ammunition made the whole exercise impossible to carry out with any satisfactory results. In June he was moved once more, this time to Bourg-en-Bresse where the summer brought very hot weather. Instead of eating the army food he bought himself peaches by the kilo from the market. In mid-July he was finally allowed some leave. He was told that at the end of the leave he was to report to the depot of the 299th Infantry Division in Frankfurt.

On the special Wehrmacht train home to Kassel, his company commander gave him some parcels to drop off with relatives in Kassel. These included coffee and a child's bike that had been dismantled and placed in a sack, which he had to 'drag along in addition to all my regular gear'. The bike was addressed to a woman who happened to be an employee at the District Army Command, and she told him that the 299th Infantry Division was fighting in the central sector of the Eastern Front in White Russia. News of the action there spread and daily reports were coming in from the Wehrmacht High Command. He said his goodbyes in subdued mood and it was to be the last time he saw his home. Three months later, the house where he had been born and grown up received a direct hit during a British air raid and was completely destroyed.

On 1 August 1943, a Sunday afternoon, he reported for duty at Frankfurt's Bergkaserne – the Hill Barracks. They were pretty much deserted with no more than a dozen soldiers waiting to be told where they were being sent. Weitzel, along with three others, was told he was heading to the 529th Infantry Regiment and was given a third class single ticket from Frankfurt to Orel, a town in Russia. Orel appeared in what seemed to be every German High Command report. Most of the reports were fairly positive on the surface but by this point in the war, the soldiers knew 'to read between the lines of the official dispatches'. When the word 'heroic' was used, most knew that in a few days a defeat would have occurred. The train journey was split into three stages. The first leg took the men to Berlin where they changed and caught the special Wehrmacht personnel train to Brest-Litovsk, where they stayed overnight near the station. The following morning had a surprise in store. Weitzel awoke to find he was itching all over, and as peered into the semi-darkness he could see tiny insects jumping about. It was his first encounter with fleas and they went on to plague him for months afterwards. Worse than that, however, were lice, which were also prevalent and are much harder to get rid of. The final part of their journey took them to Minsk, now the capital of Belarus. The men were allowed to stay in the former Soviet Party headquarters, 'a monumental palace'; in the main assembly hall hundreds of soldiers lay sleeping. The next morning they travelled deeper into the countryside, passing vast forests. Sentries stood armed by the windows ready to shoot any insurgents. Trees had been cleared near the tracks by Soviet prisoners of war or forced labour, but when Weitzel was travelling it was at the height of partisan attacks on the railway line between Orel and Brjansk and he saw first-hand the damage done by these guerrilla fighters. The line was guarded by Hungarian troops who occupied posts every 10 kilometres or so, with approximately 15 men ready to attack anyone who tried to blow up the railway line.

The following morning the travelling soldiers were told that the line to Brjansk had been blown up in the night. There was no indication of how long it would take to repair so they were allowed to use the well-stocked Wehrmacht club until such time as they could be transported to their destination. On the third day the line was fixed and they resumed their journey east. From Brjansk they travelled towards Orel on flat open goods wagons, exposed to the heat of the sun and packed together tightly with no room to move. However, the train never made it to Orel. It stopped at Karachev where they were told this was now their final destination. Weitzel knew at that moment that the Red Army had advanced faster than the German High Command had expected. This meant no one knew where the 529th Infantry Regiment actually was in the theatre of war. Three days later the men were told it could be somewhere near a village some 20 kilometres to the east of Karachev. The soldiers made their way there only to find mayhem. There were vast numbers of troops and the soldiers spent two hours looking for the 529th, asking if anyone knew where the regiment was, but without success. By this time it was dark. Every house in the village was bulging with troops so Weitzel and his comrades spent the night wrapped in canvas sheets beneath the night sky.

The next morning the men made their way back to Karachev where they were split up. Weitzel was assigned to the 3rd Battalion, 12th Company where he 'reported to the sergeant major'. Captain Fuchs acknowledged him with a nod and a sergeant assigned him to a machine gun crew. He was now on the front line.

———

By the summer of 1943, the Soviet army was better equipped and better trained than it had been when the German troops had advanced in December 1941 to Stalingrad. It was led by battle-seasoned Marshal Zhukov, who Joseph Stalin had appointed to head the Kursk sector.

However, it was Hitler's intention to outwit the Red Army and cut off Kursk by encircling Soviet troops and annihilating them. The operation was codenamed 'Citadel' and it was to be the last major offensive of the German army in Russia. Fifty German divisions were ready, including several elite Panzer divisions, and the attack began on 5 July 1943. To begin with gains were made, however it became clear they were no match for the Soviet army and soon they were being beaten. The Battle of Kursk turned out to be the largest tank battle in history.

The battle had begun on 12 July and fearing 600,000 men would become encircled at Orel, Hitler agreed with the von Kluge order to retreat. Orel was evacuated on 5 August, several days before Weitzel reached Karachev. According to Winston Churchill, 'the immense battles of Kursk, Orel and Kharkov, all within the space of two months, marked the ruin of the German army at the Eastern Front'.

On the morning of 15 August, Weitzel put his spade training to good use, and dug a foxhole which he camouflaged with the earth. He stayed there waiting. Suddenly, around midday, tanks appeared about half a kilometre away. Guns were no match for the T34s. The tanks moved in different directions then one emerged from a field and 'came at high speed' towards the young soldier. Quickly he lay down as flat as he could in his hole, 'terrorised by the thought that my position had been discovered', then the 26-ton tank thundered past him and as it left its track crushed part of Weitzel's foxhole. He survived without any physical injury.

In mid-afternoon, the Germans shelled the six tanks as they gathered together. Three were badly damaged while the others retreated hastily. It was only at nightfall that the soldiers felt safe enough to emerge from their foxholes and leave their positions. The withdrawal of the 9th Army was complete on 18 August, when it became clear the Soviet troops were exhausted. Weitzel meanwhile was assigned Number 2 gunner on the machine gun; Lance Corporal Willy Krey worked as Number 1. Krey was the recipient of the Iron Cross Second Class and had been at the Russian front since the beginning of the offensive back in 1941.

The long retreat of the Germans continued until early December when they stabilised at the west bank of the River Dnieper. Fortunately the autumn was fairly dry, which was a help as during rain the roads turned to mud, feet deep, bringing the troops to a virtual standstill. The marches had been long and monotonous and Weitzel became a virtual sleepwalker, hanging onto the wagons and being dragged along to his next destination in a catatonic state.

As the Germans withdrew the scorched earth policy inevitably followed. Hitler ordered the burning of houses, blowing up of bridges, killing of livestock and burning of crops so the advancing Red Army had nowhere to stay and no food to eat. The frontline troops were not involved in this – it was carried out by German soldiers bringing up the rear, and the sky burned brightly night after night as Weitzel and the others marched further west. He came across villages which had suffered this fate. The frontline soldiers were against the policy for they knew if they were captured they would be treated harshly by their captors.

By early October the retreat came to one of its many temporary halts, close to the small village of Marino. Both sides had dug themselves in, with 200 metres of No Man's Land between them. On 5 October the Russians began shelling the German positions. The shelling continued for quarter of an hour, and this was followed by a red flare to Weitzel's left signalling 'enemy attack, request artillery support'. Immediately intense rifle and machine gun fire burst over the area. Although it was not directed at him, it was not far off and all the men with him became nervous and on edge. Suddenly about 20 men of the rifle company appeared in their trench shouting 'The Russians have broken through!' and continued to shout their message as they ran on. They were attacking from the rear. Number 1 gunner grabbed his machine gun from his tripod and made off, with the ammunition bearers in hot pursuit. Weitzel, being Number 2 gunner, folded up the tripod and strapped it to his back but lost time doing this so fell behind the others. He peered over the trench and saw 20 or so Russian soldiers advancing. Then the call came from a German lance corporal to stand and shoot as the Soviet troops were on open ground and the Germans in trenches. But the men were in a state of panic and instead ran along the trench until it came to an end. By this stage it was a case of every man for himself, as instinct kicked in. The men made a run for it towards nearby woods. Weitzel, still carrying the heavy tripod, failed the first time he tried to get clear of the trench. The second time he succeeded, but the weight of it dragged his legs into a swamp and he became momentarily trapped. He lay down and removed the tripod, freed his legs and ran towards the safety of the woods. Ahead other soldiers were still running towards it. The Russians, Weitzel knew, had stopped, for he could see the enemy soldiers no more than 80 metres away to his right. Rifle fire began to pepper bullets at the Germans and the first of his 'party were hit and dropped'. He caught up with the rest of the men. By then six of the men were either dead or wounded. While the men were catching their breath under cover of the woods, a counterattack was made and the Soviets retreated. Soon afterwards Weitzel and his comrades were back in the trench. He found his tripod. The bodies of the six men were found, their heads smashed in by Soviet rifle butts. It may seem surprising but during the war years Weitzel never carried a firearm. As Number 2 gunner, then Number 1, he should have been entitled to carry a pistol but they were in short supply. Occasionally he would have a hand grenade but these were dangerous if the pin loosened. Nor, at any time, did he wear the steel helmets which are so much part of the image of a German soldier.

Shortly after this incident the Germans retreated to the banks of the River Sosh, a few kilometres from the town of Gomel. They began to construct a wooden bunker, and during a break in the heavy manual work Weitzel fell asleep. Suddenly two metres of wall collapsed and he became buried under wet sand. He was pulled free by two other men who had been in the pit. It was also here he became unwell. His aching legs now swelled due to the lice, and he had had to borrow a larger pair of boots. He had been scratching and this had caused an infection. He marched over to see the medical team – the doctor who saw him claimed he had 'on purpose let the infection develop so as to get away from the front', and said he would see him court martialled for it. The doctor plastered his legs in black antiseptic ichthyol ointment and covered them up with a paper dressing. After a week in hospital Weitzel's legs returned to normal and after being deloused, he was discharged.

Meanwhile his company had moved on, and he had to ask for directions. He followed the dirt track and came across the hanged bodies of two men and a woman swinging from the gallows where they had died. Finally that November day he reached the orderly room and was greeted by the news he had just walked through partisan country – and survived. He slept in one of the huts and woke the next day covered in bedbug bites. When he drove out to the front he discovered the doctor had indeed written a report about his legs, but Captain Fuchs, after asking a few questions, shrugged and dismissed him without any rebuke.

————

In mid-November skirmishes broke out and more and more intense fighting followed. Through binoculars the soldiers could see the Russians amassing and it became clear they were about to launch a major offensive. The Germans were pulled out of their positions before the attack was launched, taking off under the cover of darkness, not stopping until almost 24 hours later, when they had a break at a village and were given soup which the field kitchen had made throughout the march. After this they continued on but the wagons began to get stuck in the muddy roads and the horses were tired. Eventually the commanding officer ordered the men to return to the village. In all they marched 90 kilometres.

After a good night's sleep, they set off again. The road was no longer muddy and difficult as a frost had set in, which made life easier. But when they were stopped and Captain Fuchs called for the men to gather for a brief meeting, they knew the situation was dire. The Russians were advancing. They had established the first bridgehead on the west bank of the Dnieper back in September and by the end of October had crossed the river at six other points. On 6 November they had taken Kiev. This happened to the south of Weitzel's current position; to the north Marshal Rokossovski with the 1st White Russian Army had pushed forward, crossed the Dnieper on 6 October at Lojev and taken the Reshitza bridge, leaving the Germans in control of only one other bridge. This was at Shlobin and if the Russians reached it Weitzel and his comrades would be cut off. Orders were given to leave all the heavy equipment on the wagons and to carry on the march with rifles and machine guns. They reached the bridge two hours later and were told by an officer there to run across one at a time, ten paces behind the soldier in front. The bridge had been damaged through bombing, and planks of wood covered up the holes. By the first week of December all troops who had been stationed in the Gomel area were able to reach the west bank and relative safety.

The next morning, having slept in a local commandeered farmhouse, Weitzel became aware of a large open wound on his foot caused by the marching. He was seen by a medical orderly and stayed in the infirmary for about six days. During that time his company had to face repeated attacks from the Red Army as they continued to try to break through at the bridge. On the fourth day of his stay in the infirmary, the Russians began shelling his company and the village. The sergeant major burst in and told the men the enemy was breaking through and they must evacuate the village. Weitzel was ordered to 'mount the wagon and drive it out of the village'. He had never driven a horse-drawn cart before but another driver knew what he was doing and Weitzel's horses followed him. A short time later they stopped to let the horses rest and were aware that the noise from the battle seemed to be 'stuck'. They were not making progress or breaking through. An hour or two later, turret-less tanks, which had helped with the counterattack, passed them so they turned around and drove their horses and wagons back to the village, where they learned of how their company had suffered. No one had been killed but many were wounded including Willy Krey and Willy Kayser. Krey had been shot in the shoulder while Kayser had taken a bullet in the abdomen. Weitzel was therefore promoted to Number 1 gunner. Two days later he was released from hospital and took up his position with the gun crew just outside the village.

In early January 1944, Weitzel was called by Fuchs and told that the regiment was raising a training unit and he was to be their instructor. He was to leave in half an hour. Needless to say his platoon commander was not impressed, losing a Number 1 gunner so close to an attack. He and three sergeants left the village at 10 p.m. with the whole of the Soviet front on fire. Several dozen T34 tanks had lain in wait and proceeded to rain down fire on the Germans. By the time the order came to withdraw the battalion had suffered heavy losses.

A week passed at the village where the training was to take place before the first group of men arrived. It snowed continuously and the temperatures plummeted but at least they were warm in the farmhouse where they were staying. They passed some of the time talking about the training programme but most of the time was spent doing very little. This did not last long, however, for soon they were transferred to a poor village in a marshy region, 'the only Wehrmacht personnel there'. The first contingent of 50 men arrived and although things got off to a sticky start, their experiences on the front lines proved invaluable, as opposed to the training manuals which were simply theoretical. Weitzel stayed there for two months and helped to train three batches of reinforcements.

When he returned to his company, many of the faces were new following the heavy losses. At the beginning of April the regiment was moved further north to near Vitebsk and at the end of May Weitzel was granted leave. When he arrived at Kassel railway station he felt like a stranger in his home city. Devastation surrounded him and he stood for a few moments taking it in. As he walked further out of the city centre, he began to recognise landmarks and the destruction was 'less total, the streets were at least partly free of debris'. He found the house where his parents were staying and the family was reunited. It was to be the last time his family sat together. During his leave, the news broke of the Allied invasion of Normandy in France on 6 June 1944. They spent a long time listening to the news and although the broadcast tried to mask the unfavourable development, everyone realised it was a turning point. On 23 June, just as he was about to leave, news came through that a major Soviet offensive was underway against the German Army Group Centre. His parents waved him off at the platform but it was the last time he saw his father Jakob alive. In January 1945, a few days after his 49th birthday, Jakob was called up to the local Volkssturm unit. The decimated units of the 9th Army were to be shored up by the Volkssturm, a group of older men or young boys with little or no training and inadequate equipment. On the night of 2/3 February the Soviet troops annihilated the 13/17 Battalion which Jakob was part of. Around 90% were killed. A comrade of Jakob's visited his wife and explained that the two of them had escaped a Soviet ambush and for several days had hidden in a forest without food or shelter until they found a barn. By this time Jakob's feet were badly frostbitten and he could no longer walk. The next day a Soviet patrol passed. His comrade fled. What happened to Jakob is unknown but it is likely he was killed.

Twenty-four hours later Weitzel arrived at Volkovysk, but his journey plans changed immediately. All the passengers were grouped together then those who were to head east were told to board the train. These were all officers, all members of the Panzer divisions, the Luftwaffe and the SS, and all sergeant majors and armourers, none of which Weitzel was. For three days he waited instruction and during that time the number of NCOs and privates of the infantry regiments grew on a daily basis. On the morning of the fourth day the men were told to board a train but none knew if it would head east to Minsk or west towards Bialystok away from the dreaded Eastern Front. As he settled in his carriage a huge cheer went up. The train was heading west.

The train arrived in East Prussia at an army training centre where a new unit was to be set up, and Weitzel found himself once more on the heavy guns. Among his crew were Lance Corporal Ehmke from Gladbeck in Westphalia and Corporal Karl Kost from Landau in the Palatinate. All three had seen fighting on the front lines. The other two were Polish. The older of the two, Kaminski, was uncooperative, 'sullen and crafty' while Lewinski, the younger one, was friendly and cheerful, and could get his hands on anything from food to pieces of equipment. They left the training centre a week after the division was formed and headed through Prussia and on to Germany where they stopped at another training camp at Wahner Heide near Cologne in early July. However, the men recruited were not exactly fit for soldiering and this 'became painfully obvious when during a field exercise a brief forced march was programmed. An alarming percentage of the marchers fell by the wayside'. It was at this time Weitzel was finally given a pistol, a P38.

———

On 20 July a monumental piece of news broke. There had been an assassination attempt on Hitler and a failed coup in Berlin. The next day an order was issued that all members of the Wehrmacht had been put under the command of Heinrich Himmler, the chief of the SS, and that the regular army salute was to be replaced by the fascist one. The men continued with their training and for the next four weeks kept their heads down. Around 20 August, the men boarded a train and headed west, with Weitzel and his crew designated as an anti-aircraft unit. While the train trundled along through Belgium and northern France they were told that if they saw a plane they were to shoot it down as it would be an enemy one. It was night-time when they alighted at a deserted village and finding their bearings they suddenly found themselves looking out over the English Channel. They now occupied the Atlantic Line, or Atlantikwall, just off Le Portel near Boulogne-sur-mer. Once daylight came Weitzel was impressed when he saw all the German fortifications and firepower in the area. The German High Command wrongly assumed that this, the narrowest point of the Channel, would be where any offensive would take place. The gun crew 'had its own small concrete underground bunker, with dormitory and even a small kitchen'. There were two sites for the machine gun, one above ground to shoot at enemy aircraft and one a concrete turret on the cliff's edge. In the morning Weitzel also, for the first time, saw the white cliffs of Dover. He installed his gun and fired numerous shots down onto the beach at various points to test their trajectory, something which was done on the Eastern Front. No one had told them it was forbidden and their unauthorised exercise triggered panic in Boulogne, and 'afterwards there was an unholy row over the uncouth manners of the soldierly rabble from the Russian front'.

As the days went by it became apparent there was something amiss with the food. It transpired someone had not coupled up one of the food wagons, so the men ended up fending for themselves for a time. One day, they noticed a big wooden box floating in the water. Lewinski stripped off and swam out to it and brought it ashore. Inside were three days of rations for an entire US army platoon. The tins and waterproof packages, containing everything from meat and vegetables to butter and jam, were all intact. That evening Lewinski, who was a very good cook, prepared a veritable feast. Coincidentally it happened to be Weitzel's 20th birthday.

A few days later, on 1 September, Weitzel's battalion was withdrawn from the Atlantikwall. They set off late in the afternoon and moved in a southeasterly direction, pulling their heavy equipment on the carts by hand until they requisitioned horses from farms near a village. The farmers of course resisted but eventually they were allowed to drive their horses and wagons with the Germans' equipment and later returned, unharmed, to their farms. The battalion had marched between 35 and 40 kilometres that night. They were assigned positions at the village they stopped at and dug in. During the night they could 'trail the enemy advance south of our position by sound, as in each village the Allied troops reached the church bells began to ring'.

Early in the morning of 3 September a clanking could be heard on the road. This turned out to come from the arrival of two British tanks, which stopped about 100 metres from where the Germans were holed up. Their defence line, such as it was, stretched across pasture, with Weitzel and Ehmke manning the machine gun post. To their left were the holes of Karl Kost and Kaminski and further left again was the platoon commander Sergeant Fritz and his runner Max. Slowly the two tanks approached and stopped between the holes. A head appeared from one of the turrets. The soldier spoke and although no one understood the words they knew well enough he wanted them to surrender. There was silence for a few moments then Kaminski climbed out of his hole, his hands held high. He was the one and only soldier who became a prisoner of war during the stand-off. The British, seemingly happy enough, moved back to the hedgerow, waited for a while then disappeared. Weitzel believes the British knew exactly where they were because they had been given information by local farmers.

The men stayed in their holes until dusk when all 15 of them, the last of the company, assembled round Sergeant Fritz. The rest it seemed had abandoned their positions or been captured. While the meeting was taking place women and children appeared. One of the soldiers, from Alsace, spoke to them and they told him there were around 10,000 resistance fighters about. The soldiers decided to abandon all heavy equipment, and hoped to make their way to German-held areas. They marched northeast under the darkness of the night. They trekked over fields, crawled under barbed wire and kept as quiet as they possibly could. Just after midnight they reached a densely wooded hill where they were forced to go by the road, where they came to a lonely inn. The frightened innkeeper and his wife let them in and soon realised they were in no danger as all they had wanted was a drink. After a beer the Germans offered to pay – the innkeeper would not hear of it but the soldiers insisted and paid.

At dawn they reached a small wood with thick undergrowth where they decided to grab some sleep. Guards were posted to make sure they were safe. In the early afternoon a group of French civilians approached wielding guns. The leader of the group came straight towards their hiding place. He had spotted them and called out. A few seconds of silence was followed by a burst of gunfire, giving the Germans no time to respond verbally. Weitzel heard cries so jumped to his feet – he aimed at the leader and fired before turning and running. He did not get far when he saw another line of partisans. It was over. He threw the gun into the ticket of brambles then turned and walked to the edge of the wood. When he reached their former hiding place he saw Karl Kost sprawled on the ground. He had been wounded. Weitzel bent down and Kost told him he was done for. Weitzel felt a rifle in his back and knew he had to move on. When he reached the field, others from the group were already there, hands in the air. They were surrounded by around 30 civilians. Two were dead, Sergeant Fritz and the French leader, and three were wounded. Weitzel became a prisoner of war on 4 September 1944.

––––––––

The prisoners were marched away, their hands clasped behind their necks. They were taken to a barn and lined up against the wall but it was only for the purpose of searching them, much to their relief. They were then loaded onto a truck and taken to Béthune, a 30-minute drive from where they had been captured. When they arrived they were surrounded by a troop of resistance fighters who 'were visibly more familiar with military matters'. They were prisoners of the Gaullist FFI, the Forces Françaises de l'Interieur. They were held for two days then inspected by a British soldier and transported to a camp of wooden huts nearby. The camp had earlier housed Russian prisoners of war but they had been transported eastwards following the approach of the Allies.

In total there were around 80 German prisoners of war at the camp and they were the talk of the area. The commandant of the camp gave guided tours to 'a remarkably great number of heavily made up ladies' who silently watched these newly acquired animals in the local zoo. The lack of food also did not help with morale but this was a general problem and not directed at the German prisoners alone. The day after they arrived they had watched as a long column of about 200 men, women and children entered the camp. These were the collaborators – they were forced to stay at the other end of the camp and it was forbidden to speak to them.

On 9 September two British trucks entered the camp and demanded the German prisoners board them. The French commandant had known nothing about this and protested, but the British insisted. The Frenchman acquiesced but asked for the soldier from Alsace to stay behind and act as interpreter. The captain said 'No', jumped into the driver's cab of one of the trucks and gave the signal to depart. That night was spent sleeping out in the open in a field and the following day the small convoy passed through Caen. The town had fallen into Allied hands on 9 July but throughout June and July it had been mentioned almost daily in the Wehrmacht High Command reports so Weitzel recognised it. It had been decimated by war. They continued on to Bayeux, the first French town to be liberated. For 30 kilometres as the trucks passed the prisoners saw a sight that had a profound effect on them. Once a battlefield it was now a gigantic supply base housing weapons, vehicles, munitions and various equipment. They also passed an airfield where they saw numerous transport planes landing at two-minute intervals. That was the day they knew the war was lost forever.

Finally they reached their destination, a large prisoner of war camp some distance from Bayeux. Around 1000 prisoners were held here waiting to be shipped on to other camps. There was no accommodation but some had managed to keep items of their equipment and erected shelters from canvas sheets. However, Weitzel and the men with him had lost everything and remained open to the elements. He could not lie down as the ground was sodden, so he spent much of the night pacing, 'mostly along the barbed wire fence behind which British soldiers were patrolling'. Out of Weitzel's gun crew only Ehmke remained. On one occasion Weitzel asked a soldier on the other side of the wire in English what the time was. The soldier saw how cold and exhausted he was and disappeared, returning soon after with a huge mug of tea. It was an act of kindness Weitzel never forgot.

Following a second cold and sleepless night the men were escorted to the local beach for embarkation to England. Five abreast they marched over the Mulberry harbours, the artificial harbours specifically built by the British in areas where there were no natural harbours, and onto the cargo vessel that would take them over the Channel. In all up to 1000 prisoners were packed on board, then the gate shut them in for the crossing.

––––––––––

In the late afternoon of 14 September 1944, the ship docked at Southampton. The prisoners filed out into the bright sunshine, covered in reddish powder from the rusty floor they had slept on. They were escorted along a busy street but many of the passers-by ignored them. This was Weitzel's first taste of England.

The men marched to the railway station in the docks area, where the train waited. They boarded one at a time. Each compartment was filled with eight men, and when the train was full it departed. However, Weitzel was not on it, nor was Ehmke. There had been no space left for around 30 prisoners. Left at the station they pitched tents by the side of the platform and formed orderly queues to use the solitary tap to wash some of the rusty powder from their hands and faces. The next morning another train and another batch of men appeared. This time Weitzel and Ehmke did board the train, their final destination Kempton Park. They arrived at noon.

Today Kempton Park, near Sunbury-on-Thames in Surrey, is well known for its race-course, but in 1944 it was the main reception camp for incoming prisoners. There were other centres including Trent Park and the London District Cage at Kensington Palace Gardens in London, but these were specifically for the high ranking officers and other special groups. At these kinds of camps the interrogations lasted days, weeks even, but Kempton Park saw hundreds of prisoners pass through every single day. The prisoners were asked to rid themselves of assorted objects which they had managed to acquire since their capture. Weitzel only had a tin which he had used as a cup so threw it on the pile. They then had to fill in a form, giving the officials their personal data, and they were also asked to provide details of the military units they belonged to. Although the British knew that all the soldiers had to give them was their name and serial number, they hoped that further information would be forthcoming. Weitzel, along with others, was not amused by this and decided 'to indicate fictitious units – I doubt our naïve deception has fooled British military intelligence'. Each soldier was then given a postcard from the International Committee of the Red Cross which they were to fill in indicating whether or not they were wounded. Nothing else was to be written on the card and the recipients were told not to reply as they would receive further information in due course. Six weeks after he filled in his card, Weitzel's parents in Kassel received news of their son. Lastly each man was given their unique prisoner of war number, one which they had to memorise. Weitzel's was 984671.

The next stage of the process was to sort out the nationalities of the prisoners. A British army sergeant called out the names of different nationalities and when men stepped forward and had formed a group, one of their compatriots would lead them away. The thinking behind this was to engage these men within units in the British army, such as Poles, French and Russians, who could still fight against Nazi Germany. Once this was done, slightly more than half the original number remained standing. They then 'followed the selection of our former comrades-in-arms first incredulously, then with increasing hilarity. It appeared that by 1944 the Wehrmacht had degenerated into a kind of Foreign Legion'. Delousing followed and lastly they were taken for interrogation, or rather questioning, for they had no secrets to share.

The rooms overlooking Kempton Park racecourse were used for the questioning and it was to one of these on the upper floor that Weitzel was ushered. There were a number of tables in the room and behind each one sat an NCO wearing his usual khaki battledress. His interpreter was a sergeant with a red face, around 35 years old, and scowling. He barked at Weitzel in German, 'Were you a Party member?' Expecting to be asked about military information, Weitzel was stunned into silence before finally explaining he had joined the Labour Service aged 17 and that only those who were 18 could apply to join the Party. The sergeant cut him off and began a tirade that astonished him. He began yelling at Weitzel about the Third Reich, Nazi crimes and the SS, and Heinrich Himmler in particular. It then dawned on Weitzel that at least some of the interrogators were German or Austrian immigrants, Jews or political opponents to the Nazi regime. His reaction was to 'respond with total withdrawal, I just waited in sullen silence'. Eventually the tirade subsided and he was asked if he volunteered for work. He refused and that was the end of his questioning. Of course the British could have forced him to work but hostile workers could do more harm than good. Non-working prisoners could not earn money therefore were unable to buy little luxuries such as cigarettes, but Weitzel did not smoke so knew it would have little impact on him. However, about 10% of the German prisoners of war did volunteer, perhaps for that very reason, before the end of the war. The questioning took five minutes in all. Yet not all prisoners passing through Kempton Park had to endure the shouting sergeant. Adolf Schulte, who arrived there several weeks later, told Weitzel he had been questioned by a civilian and had not passed through the hall of the shouting sergeant. His interrogation was based purely on politics too, although Schulte's answers were deemed impertinent. The Geneva Convention states in Article 2 that all prisoners of war should be 'humanely treated and protected, particularly against acts of violence, from insults and from public curiosity'. Weitzel was never informed of his rights as a prisoner of war.

The night was spent in tents pitched on the racecourse. Occasionally their sleep was interrupted by an explosion and shockwave as bombs landed nearby. Then the following day they were on the move again. They boarded a train, travelling slowly and stopping frequently, all through the night. By the middle of the next morning they had arrived in Scotland 'under a grey Scottish sky and cold drizzle'. They marched the short distance from the station to Camp 19 Happenden, also known as Douglas, in Lanarkshire, some 40 kilometres south of Glasgow.

————

Camp 19 Happenden was at the time a transit camp, used as a base for shipping prisoners of war to Canada. Many prisoners had to be sent across the Atlantic as due to the vast number of men captured there was not room for all of them in Britain. Between July and September 1944 over 100,000 prisoners arrived in the UK and the authorities were caught on the hop with no place to put them all. In October 1944 Sir Percy James Grigg, the Secretary of State at the War Office, declared, 'We captured far more…prisoners than we ever expected, and while this is a great blessing, it is not an unmixed blessing'.

Weitzel stayed at Camp 19 for three weeks, during which 'The days passed in aimless wanderings through the camp; because of its transit character the camp offered no recreational or educational facilities'. There was an upside to this however – it gave him time to recover from 'the stress, exhaustion and the deprivation of the past weeks', something he felt was necessary for his well-being. He was fed three times a day and had somewhere dry to sleep at night. It also gave him time to adjust to being a prisoner. Like all prisoners, it came as a shock to be in that situation and it took two weeks or more before bad dreams of his initial capture melted away. He also had to come to terms with the humiliation of the situation, as well as the guilt. One day he had been fighting in the theatre of war, the next he was in British hands, feeling disgraced. Overnight the soldiers on the front lines 'had turned from unenthusiastic but obedient actors of the drama into powerless onlookers'. He had been separated from the others, leaving them to their own fate, and this caused a feeling of immeasurable guilt. However, there was nothing he could do and over time, these feelings of humiliation and guilt faded as he got on with life and realised that in fact he was a survivor of war. He also realised he had no idea how long he was going to be held so decided to knuckle down and get on with it.

For the next four years, camps were to be his home. It was a 'phenomenon of our time. While formerly [camps'] existence was limited to the military sphere, our century has hatched a host of new varieties – ugly ones such as the concentration camp, the forced labour camp, or the cynically named "re-education" camp; and less odious but still unpleasant ones such as the POW camp or refugee camp'. Although rules were rigid when he first arrived, with the defeat of the Nazis and the end of the war some prisoners were allowed to leave the camp to work locally. But it was friendship that became most important to Weitzel. At Douglas he met Helmuth Wetzel, who came from Chemnitz and was the same age as him, and the pair were to be held together for the next 11 months. Forming friendships was important for the mental

Above: Inside a prison cell at Camp 21.

Right: The heavy cell door slammed shut on many a prisoner during the lifetime of the camp.

The corridor showing the cells on either side of the narrow passageway.

Above: The white church is a local landmark in the village of Comrie.

Right: The showers at Cultybraggan Camp originally only had cold running water but hot water showers when they came were welcomed.

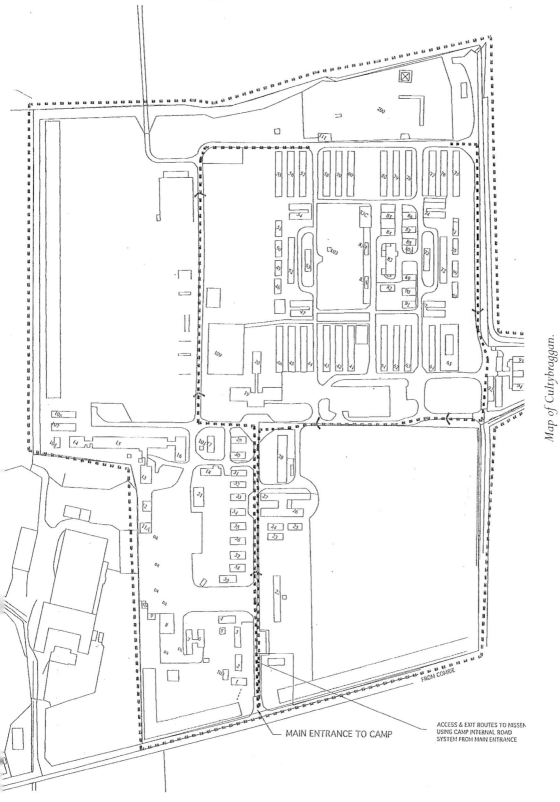

Map of Cultybraggan.

MAIN ENTRANCE TO CAMP

FROM COMRIE

ACCESS & EXIT ROUTES TO NISSEN
USING CAMP INTERNAL ROAD
SYSTEM FROM MAIN ENTRANCE

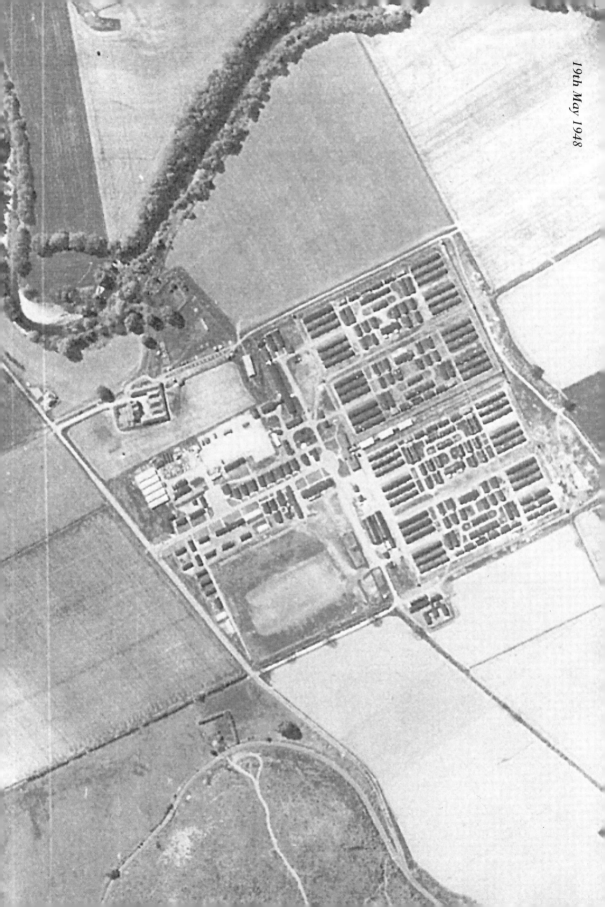

19th May 1948

Left: The camp is well hidden by the trees from the approach from the south.

Below: An extended Nissen hut was used by the Argyll and Sutherland Highlanders after it became a military training camp.

Bottom: Cultybraggan Camp as it looked around 1950.

Günther Schran
Bochum-Hordel
Sechs-Brüder-Str. 6

Bochum-Hordel, den 20. Sept. 1948

V e r z e i c h n i s

der nach England mitzunehmenden Bekleidungsstücke u.Gebruchsgegenstände.

1 blauer zweireihiger Herrenanzug
1   "   einreihiger Sportanzug
1 grauer zweireihiger Herrenanzug
1 Harris Tweed Sportjackett mit grauer Flanellhose
1 brauner zweireihiger Herrenanzug
1 amerik. Militärjacke
1 Herren-Wintermantel
1   "   -Winterüberjacke
1 blauer Herren-Popelinmantel
6 Paar kurze und lange Unterhosen
2 Unterziehhemden
3 Oberhemden mit Kragen
2 Pullover
5 Sporthemden
6 Paar Herren-Socken
3 Paar Herren-Halbschuhe
1 Paar Lderpantoffeln
6 Binder
12 Taschentücher
2 Herren-Hüte
1 Oelgemälde mit Rahmen
1 Damen-Handtasche
2 Damenringe und 1 Anhänger
1 Plectrum-Guitarre mit Kasten

Gunther Schran, former prisoner of war at Camp 21, became a British citizen in 1948.

    Ich erkläre hiermit an Eides Statt, daß die obenaufgeführten Artikel mein persönliches Eigentum sind und ich dieselben dringend für meinen Aufenthalt in England gebrauche.

Die Richtigkeit vorstehender Unterschrift beglaubigt
Bochum, den 21. 9. 1948
Stadtoberinspektor

A complete list of Schran's personal belongings in September 1948 which includes suits, an American military jacket, shirts, handkerchiefs, and his guitar in its box.

*Right: Gunther Schran
as a prisoner of war.*

*Below: Schran's identity card while
he was a prisoner of war at Camp
668 at North Tidworth.*

Bottom left: Gunther Schran.

*Bottom right: A news article
about one of the concerts the
local prisoners of war put on
in Speenhamland, a district of
Newbury in Berkshire*

IDENTIFICATION
My Name *Günther Schran*
City *Bochum* State *Germany*
At present: *German P.O.W.*
Nr. *536246*
668 P.O.W. Camp
IN CASE OF ACCIDENT OR SERIOUS ILLNESS NOTIFY
Mrs. E. Schran (Westfalia)
Street *6 Brüderstr. 6* City *Bochum Hredel*

PRISONERS GIVE CONCERT
13. **At Speenhamland** *1947*

Town residents and local prisoners-of-war together filled St. Mary's Hall, Speenhamland on Saturday evening and enjoyed a spirited performance of light music given by an orchestra from P.O.W. Camp 25, at Lambourn. Strauss waltzes and marches were followed by dance music and were all played with artistry.

One of the prisoners compèred the programme with much good humour. The concert was organised by the local P.O.W. Club.

*Above: Schran was a member
of the HitlerYouth.*

*Left: Schran became a Freemason
and was very proud of his achievement.*

A b s c h r i f t .

Kaufmännische Privatschule R o h l o f f . Köln.

Z E U G N I S

für Th. Hunkirchen

Klasse. Allgem.Handelsklasse   Dauer des Schulbesuches 6 Men.

Lehrfächer	Gesamtzahl der Unterrichtswochen.	Urteil
Schriftverkehr	26	gut
Handelsbetriebslehre	26	gut
Kaufmänniches Rechnen	26	i.g.gut
Reichs-Kurzschrift	26	95 Silben pro Min.
Maschinenschreiben	26	120 Anschl.pro Min.
Handschrift	13	i.g.gut
Einfache Buchführung Doppelte Buchführung und Bilanzwesen Amerikanischeu.Durschreibebu.	26	gut
Deutsche Sprachlehre	26	i.g.gut
Bürgerkunde	26	i.g.gut
Wirtschaftserdkunde	26	i.g.gut

Anzahl der versäumten Unterrichtsstunden   30

Bemerkung: Betragen und Fleiss waren einwandfrei

Köln, den 30 März 1935

der Klassenvorstand: Stempel   Die Schulleitung.

Fräul. Zimmermann   Dr. Rohloff.

*Report on Theo Hunkirchen during his education dated 30th March 1935
where his industriousness was said to be impeccable.*

Above left: A young Hunkirchen as a naval cadet.

Right: Hunkirchen in later life.

Left: Herbert Sulzbach was assigned to Camp 21 Comrie as a translator shortly after the murder of Feldwebel Wolfgang Rosterg.

Weitzel spent time in various camps in various conditions. Here tents were supplied rather than huts which did not go down too well with the prisoners when they arrived at Camp 663, Shipton Bellinger at Tidworth on the Salisbury Plain.

Inside the ColdWar bunker at Cultybraggan.

The men made the most of Camp 663 at Tidworth.

Weitzel and some comrades with two ladies from the kitchens.

welfare of prisoners but subsequent separation could have a profound effect on them. It was worth the risk of separation, however, to have someone to talk to and share experiences with. Both of them enjoyed their endless walks along the perimeter of the camp fence, talking and whiling away the hours.

A few days after his arrival at the camp, when it had finally stopped raining, Weitzel wandered over to the main lane in the camp and watched a stream of prisoners moving in the opposite direction. Suddenly one of their number broke free and ran towards Weitzel, hugging him. He couldn't believe his eyes for it was Karl Kost, the man who had been shot at Béthune woods. Incredibly he had survived. Weitzel stood speechless and in shock as the man pulled back his tunic and showed him the dressing wrapped around his chest. Kost explained what had happened. The bullet from the machine pistol had 'hit him obliquely from above, had entered his chest, slid along the sternum and issued again, leaving a long but shallow wound'. The FFI fighters had taken him to hospital along with Max, Sergeant Fritz's runner, who had been hit in the leg (which due to the damage he later had to have amputated). Kost had been released from the hospital some days later and transferred into British custody. He had been shipped to England and then Camp 19. It was one of the happiest moments ever experienced by Weitzel during the war. However, the reunion was short-lived for a few days later all the men with surnames beginning A–K were shipped off to Canada. Both Ehmke and Kost fell into this group. The L–Z men were to be shipped off a fortnight later. They said their goodbyes and said they would meet in Canada but it was not to be. Government policy changed and the transfer of prisoners overseas ceased as more prisoner of war camps were erected in the UK.

There was now a decrease in the arrival of prisoners, from a vast influx in September to a small trickle by early October, and Weitzel and Wetzel were informed they were to be transferred. Along with around 30 other men, Weitzel packed his kitbag with all his worldly possessions – two shirts, two pairs of long johns, two pairs of socks and two towels – in less than two minutes after the order for departure was given. His next destination was Camp 21 Comrie in the heart of Scotland.

———

At the time Weitzel arrived, Camp 21 was divided into four equal compounds, A, B, C and D. Each compound was now occupied by between 800 and 1000 prisoners and it was to Compound A that Weitzel and his comrades were sent. A vivid record of its layout has been recorded by Adolf Schulte, who arrived four weeks after Weitzel. The compound was rectangular in shape with 12 long Nissen huts arranged in two rows, with huts 1 to 6 in one row and huts 7 to 12 making up the other. Each of these corrugated black huts held 80 men and was lined, although it made no real difference to the temperature. A central passage separated the 20 bunk beds up either side of it, and was furnished with a stove in the centre which was to heat the whole hut. In reality, unless the men were huddled round the fire, they did not get much benefit from it but the coal was used as economically as it could be. Between these two rows of huts were situated the kitchen, the dining hall, the library, the theatre, the washrooms and the latrines. A broad central road was where the daily roll call took place. At each of the four corners of Compound A were watchtowers, which were manned by armed guards 24 hours a day. The living quarters and offices of the camp administration were situated outside the compound.

The camp was mainly made up of naval personnel who had fought and defended the Atlantic Wall between Calais and Boulogne in September 1944 rather than general naval personnel. They later told fellow prisoners that, while waiting for invasion, much of their time was spent rearing chickens and rabbits for food. Much to Weitzel's amusement, these prisoners insisted on using nautical terms. When the jovial and corpulent sergeant major of the group welcomed the new prisoners he explained the layout in such terms as 'the galley is to the port side'. The infantrymen had no idea what he meant but it is certain they would have found the kitchen without the sergeant major's direction. The morning following Weitzel's arrival, after a relatively uneventful night, the petty officer woke the men by blowing his whistle and calling out 'Rise, rise!' which infuriated some of those sleeping but over the next week or so everyone got used to it. The arrival of more army and air force personnel in October saw the demise of the navy's influence on Compound A, and with their arrival the compound was filled to capacity.

Days were spent routinely. Three meals a day were provided and roll call was held at the same time every day. In between the meals and roll call, the men had to amuse themselves. If the weather was good Weitzel and Wetzel went for long walks around the perimeter fence, taking hours to do so, walking in an anti-clockwise direction all the time. The reason for this was just that it was the way they always did it, but Weitzel found out that British prisoners in German POW camps such as Stalag Luft III at Sagan did exactly the same. Walking was a good way of keeping both physically and mentally fit. Weitzel and Wetzel often walked in silence though, lost in their own thoughts. When they wanted to talk they did so, but generally they never walked alone. It gave them a break from being surrounded by other prisoners in the Nissen huts, which caused Weitzel to develop a phobia of crowds and his 'taste for rural calm and solitude'. Often there would be others on these walks but the infantrymen were the ones who kept going the longest. The naval personnel were only occasionally seen out walking the circuit.

When it was wet the men were cooped up inside so passed the time playing chess or card games such as skat, both of which Weitzel only learned at the camp. Cards were plentiful in most prisoner of war camps. At Comrie this was thanks to the gunners of the coast artillery, who had pocketed their decks before their surrender. Chess equipment on the other hand was not so plentiful, although a few ingenious prisoners managed to create boards from wooden crates which they sanded down with stones, painting the black squares using a hot iron from the stove in their hut. Chess pieces were carved from pieces of firewood. The men also whiled away the hours making model aeroplanes, tanks and so on from wood or tin cans. The late autumn of that year provided the men at Comrie with a lot of time for playing these games, as it rained frequently, sometimes for whole weeks. If it was wet in the morning, the men would position themselves on the edges of the lower bunks after breakfast, two on each side, and begin playing skat, only interrupting it 'for meals and the roll call and finish[ing] it, numb and dazed, just before lights out'. Others would visit the well-stocked library but during his whole time at Comrie, Weitzel never read a single book. The noise from the crowded huts made it difficult to concentrate.

There were other duties the men had to carry out in the camp regardless of the weather. These included cleaning, or fetching the hut's supper ration from the compound kitchen and taking it back to the men. And each hut had to take their turn at peeling potatoes. The sacks were emptied onto the hut floor and they spent the entire morning sitting on the lower bunks peeling them to feed the thousand or so prisoners. Rations at the camp were adequate. Prisoners were given exactly the same quantity of rations as the British who incarcerated them in compliance with Article 11 of the Geneva Convention. But the Germans had to adapt to British food. No longer could they have ersatz coffee, a coffee substitute made from grain. They had to have English tea, without milk and sugar. Breakfast was porridge, which was odd to the Germans but they soon got used to it. Weitzel remembers the first time he was served lunch. It was rice served with a green gravy and as he eyed it up he thought it looked terrible. Tentatively he had his first mouthful and liked it. It turned out to be curry, something which had been unknown in Germany pre-war. Bread, of which they were allowed a ration of 10 oz, was something else they enjoyed initially. It was white and fluffy and seemed like a delicacy to them, but their view soon changed when they realised it would not fill them up like the wholemeal black bread they had been used to in the army. The compound spokesman frequently asked for rye flour to make more dense bread but this request was repeatedly refused.

However, bread was not the main issue of concern to the Germans. It was cigarettes. The heavier smokers among the troops suffered severe withdrawal symptoms and the days of having nothing to do exacerbated the problem. The smokers had to find a substitute, which they did, remarkably. They gathered up the soaked tea leaves from the kitchen, which comprised a fair amount having served a thousand men twice a day, dried them out then smoked them in hand-crafted pipes. Although Weitzel never smoked himself, he remembers it smelling 'atrociously. The air of the hut was heavy with the acrid, pungent stench which saturated everything and clung to our clothes'. A year later the practice stopped when cigarettes became available as a form of wages, much to the relief of smokers and non-smokers alike.

One other issue for the men were the sanitary conditions. For the first few months of Weitzel's incarceration there was only cold water available in the washrooms, although the men could have a hot shower once a week. Washing clothes was also done in cold water. There was also a lack of nail scissors, so Weitzel used a rough stone to keep his fingernails and toenails in check until he found a proud owner of a pair of scissors who, once they were better acquainted, offered him use of them.

In October the weather improved, with sunny days and relatively mild temperatures. The hills surrounding the camp bloomed with purple heather and Weitzel enjoyed looking at them as it was the first time he had ever lived in a mountainous region. He promised himself that some-day he would return as a free man and tour the region. In 1957, he and his wife Marie-Luise did return, but to Oban, not Comrie. On 27 October 1944, the first snow fell on the surrounding hills at Camp 21 but during November the rains returned mixed with snow and gales. In a diary entry for 4 December, Helmuth Meyer, a fellow prisoner at Comrie, wrote, 'Blizzard in the mountains, here in the valley it rains continually'. Hence the men were confined to their huts, playing chess and cards once more. The rain stopped for an hour or two every afternoon as the front passed over, and this gave a window of opportunity for daily roll call, although roll call was actually just a head count. The men were lined up in rows of five and a British officer and a sergeant would move along the lines, counting the heads and murmuring numbers as if to remember them accurately. Once complete the numbers were tallied up and as often as not the count had to be re-done, sometimes twice more, as someone had either forgotten their count or miscounted in the first place. In the 11 months Weitzel was held in Compound A no one escaped from it.

It is interesting to note that although many commentators have classed Camp 21 as a Nazi camp, according to Weitzel it was no such thing, or at least not when he was there. Many of the men had been selected randomly to go there and 'if Camp 21 housed indeed a higher proportion of Nazi elements than other camps' it was purely accidental. He has no recollection of a united body of men, nor for that matter any fanatical groups, but rather one of a diverse group of men who had one simple bond – that of being in the military. There had however been a number of small groups who had for some reason managed to stay together, such as the gunners from the Atlantic Line, a submarine crew and members of an anti-aircraft battery which had been stationed near Boulogne which included Meyer and Schulte. This diversity, instead of everyone pulling together in the face of adversity, caused more of a fragmentation and led to many a solitary figure behind the wire.

As 1944 came to a close, the camp was almost at its capacity of 4000, holding 3980 men, and the same routines were still in place. The days were monotonous, knowing that no mail from home would come. When they first arrived the men had been hopeful for letters or packages, but they now resigned themselves that nothing would be appearing. Weitzel had sent home two or three letters in mid-October but had received no news back. Of course, the postal service had been interrupted but after a while all hope had gone. The mood in the camp was sombre. Helmut Meyer wrote in his diary words which sum up the mood – 'We wait, we worry, we hope'. In this atmosphere, being in such constant close proximity to people with nothing to do, small irritabilities were blown out of all proportion and sometimes led to violence.

––––––––

Camp 21 was not without its serious incidents to break the monotony. During October and early November the camp was guarded by a unit of Polish guards. It was an uneasy situation, for the guards despised all things German following the invasion of their country in 1939 – some of them had served with the Wehrmacht, but it was a personal history they wished to forget. They tended to be harsh on their German prisoners. For example, if two prisoners from different compounds tried to speak to each other through the wire, the Polish guards fired two warning shots, as this was forbidden. The spokesman for the four compounds repeatedly raised this with the camp commandant but to no avail. One day a prisoner was speaking to another in a different compound through the fence when a shot rang out – and this time the guard had killed the prisoner of war. This was Feldwebel Heinrich Schwarz. The reaction of the rest of the men was immediate. All the prisoners who worked for the British camp administration, most of whom worked in mess kitchens, walked out in protest. Further to this the spokesman for Compound A informed the commandant that if nothing was done the men would go on hunger strike. The commandant dealt with the guards and replaced them all within a few days with a contingent of elderly Scottish reservists who went about their duties quietly and professionally 'in a placid and unemotional manner'. Another reason for the swift action was that any POW death had to be reported to the Protecting Power working for the International Committee of the Red Cross, who also inspected the camps from time to time to make sure things were running smoothly. In hindsight the British using Polish guards was an extremely unwise decision, which is why they were so swiftly replaced at Camp 21.

Another story of note which broke the monotony came in the form of news from home. On 16 December Feldmarschall von Rundstedt launched the last Wehrmacht offensive at the Ardennes along with two Panzer divisions and members of the 7th Army. News got back to Comrie and the prisoners were kept up to date with developments, something which was rather unusual. Not long after Weitzel's arrival the jovial sergeant major who had caused so much hilarity with his naval speech was ousted as spokesman. There followed a power struggle which the ordinary prisoners of war knew nothing about until a small group of troublesome POWs took command of the compound. Most of these were Nazis or at the very least had strong Nazi leanings, and the first thing they did was have a news blackout. They were given the newspapers every day but did not pass on the information to the other men. When questioned about it they merely said the papers were full of propaganda, while the real reason was that Germany was losing the war. But now, in December, they had something to crow about. The mood in the camp changed. People began to dare to hope and became excited. Men huddled in groups talking excitedly about the news, which was reported twice a day, hoping that this was a turning point. The British administration quickly became aware of this turn of events and beefed up security all around the camp. The guards were doubled and barbed wire obstacles were placed at the compound entrances in case escapes were attempted. However, after less than a week or so the German counterattack began to founder when American troops launched an attack. In the camp, the news bulletins became less frequent and the stories would relate to a number of days previously when Germany had been winning the battle. Soon the bulletins stopped altogether. Now 'the short-lived euphoria was again replaced by sullen dejection'.

––––––––

Soon it was Christmas at Camp 21. According to Helmuth Meyer's diary, heavy dark grey clouds hid the tops of the hills and 'on their black slopes gleam patches of fresh snow'. But Christmas brought a surprise to Compound A – a swastika flag was flying over it, which of course was not acceptable. When they found out about it guards came racing and ripped it down. Weitzel is uncertain whether it was Nazi fanatics or simply the Germans playing a practical joke on the British. After all, 'Teasing the Tommy' was a fairly popular pastime for them. One example of this 'which also contained an element of defiance was the salute we were requested to give to any British officer passing through the compound'. As mentioned, before the attempted assassination of Hitler on 20 July 1944, the Wehrmacht had used the traditional military salute but then were forced to use the fascist salute of the open hand, which had been resented by the Wehrmacht. The British of course insisted the prisoners greeted in the traditional military way – but inevitably they saluted with their right arm outstretched. The British saw it as fanatical; the Germans saw it as being insubordinate and defiant and the only thing they could do which was truly mischievous. But on the whole the prisoners were ambivalent in regard to the guards. The vast majority of them were content with their fate, knowing they had a bed to sleep in and food to eat.

Christmas also meant little extras. On Christmas Eve the men were given Christmas cake and brioche. Compound A also had the privilege of eating in the refectory while all of Compound D and half of Compound C were forced to eat in their huts. They were also given 50 cigarettes extra. However, the one thing the prisoners did not get that Christmas was a walk, as there was a lack of guards.

It was around this time permission was given to the prisoners to listen to the radio. There were to be allowed to listen to the BBC broadcasts and classical music programmes. The necessary work to receive them got underway and they were up and running shortly afterwards. It was a goodwill gesture which was appreciated by the men.

By January 1945 winter had arrived in earnest. There was heavy snow, and severe frosts had set in. The little stoves were inadequate in the uninsulated Nissen huts and coal was in short supply and still rationed. Only one bucket was allowed for each hut per day and this lasted only a few hours. In Weitzel's hut though, a ship's stoker tended to the stove and managed to use the coal much more efficiently, using up every last piece of it. Every morning was the same. He would set himself in front of the stove and nurse it throughout the day. At regular intervals, according to Weitzel, he would 'gently rattle the grate, collect the still glowing but not yet fully burnt out embers which dropped through; [he would then] douse and then dry them and feed them a second or even a third time to the stove'. This kept the fire going all day; although every time the embers were used they gave off less and less heat it kept the temperature at a reasonable level. The stoker 'was a jewel and nobody grudged him the privileged place in front of the stove'.

———

As already mentioned the monotony of camp life could be destructive, yet the men of Camp 21 began to harness a creative energy that flowed through it by starting up educational groups and entertainment. In the autumn of 1944, various talks began to take place. These varied from literature, art and history to 'more down to earth topics such as bee keeping'. There were also lectures available and Weitzel decided to take up book-keeping which he thought might come in useful one day. Popular entertainment came in the form of an orchestra made up of a dozen musicians and a 40-strong choir. The submarine crew set up a sailors' choir, singing shanty songs, some of which Weitzel can still remember the words to this day. There was also a drama group which performed several plays during the winter and early spring of 1945. All were amateurs apart from one, and although they lacked the professional skill, they more than made up for it in enthusiasm. Sometimes the men had to dress up as women – they did not make them like the infamous pantomime dame but rather kept them in the character they were meant to be. As for the historical costumes for the plays, they 'were dazzling…and the stage settings had genuine artistic quality'. Much of the setting and background was the work of Helmuth Meyer who was a professional commercial artist, and he was given much credit for his scenery painting. The orchestra was well supplied with musical instruments and there was 'a special and quite generous fund from which musical instruments, material for costumes as well as canvas and paint for the scenery were bought'.

Politics did not impinge on the men of Compound A particularly but occasionally the ideological tensions would spill over and fights would take place. One morning when Weitzel went to the dining hall for breakfast he saw a pool of blood and some teeth on one of the tables. Standing beside it was 'an army corporal who I knew to be a student of theology'. Apparently he had made a defeatist remark regarding the war situation and a political hard-liner had taken umbrage and landed 'several savage blows' on him. But this was to be utterly insignificant compared with the tragedy that took place in Compound C a few days before Christmas 1944 when Feldwebel Wolfgang Rosterg was murdered by a group of fellow prisoners.

At the time Weitzel and his comrades in Compound A heard only 'confused rumours about a lynched traitor'. He believed this was not an isolated incident, that other murders probably took place in other prisoner of war camps, which of course they did.

Another crime connected with Camp 21 concerned around a dozen U-boat crewmen in Compound A. They were petty officers of the German submarine U-852. On 13 March 1944 U-852 was patrolling the waters in the Gulf of Guinea when it torpedoed and sank the cargo boat *Peleus*. Although a Greek vessel, *Peleus* had been chartered by the British Ministry of Transport. The U-boat captain, Lieutenant Heinz Eck, ordered his men to kill all the crew who had survived by firing at them with machine guns or by throwing hand grenades. Following the massacre the U-boat continued on its way to the East African coast. Off the Somali coast two British planes attacked it and it was severely damaged. With the submarine no longer able to dive, the captain beached it near Aden, where the crew were taken prisoner. Had it not been for two incredible occurrences the crew of the U-boat would most likely have got away with it. First, they had not banked on anyone from *Peleus* surviving, but five weeks later three crew members were picked up alive by a Portuguese vessel. They had managed to stay afloat on a raft which had enough provisions for their miraculous survival. The second extraordinary event was the U-boat's log turning up. It had not been destroyed, 'contrary to explicit orders', and fell into British hands. Although it did not mention the *Peleus* it did log the submarine's exact position on 13 March and the link was made.

At first the U-boat's crew were taken to Alexandria in Egypt where they were interrogated, then they were shipped over to Britain. The commandant and the officers were imprisoned in London while the petty officers were sent to Compound A at Camp 21. At the camp they kept very much to themselves, perhaps because the atrocity they had carried out gave them an unbreakable bond. They all lived in the same hut with the exception of one. He found himself in the same hut as Weitzel but kept himself to himself, and had absolutely no contact with his former comrades. According to Weitzel, he was a 'withdrawn and dejected individual'. There was a rumour that when he had been interrogated in Egypt this petty officer had betrayed his crew by telling the authorities what happened to the *Peleus*. In 1945, the case came to trial in Hamburg before a court martial. Eck and two of his officers were sentenced to death and executed. A petty officer was sentenced to 15 years for his part in the atrocity.

––––––––––

During his time in captivity at Camp 21 Weitzel had no inclination to try to escape the confines of his compound. Indeed, he believes that it was a myth that every prisoner of war wanted to, one propagated for example by both British and American films such as *The Great Escape* and *Colditz*. Eric Newby, another former prisoner of war, agrees, pointing out that very few prisoners actually had the necessary skills to do so. In total less than 2% of prisoners even tried to escape, and most of them were recaptured. Weitzel did not want to engage in fighting again and was content to be sheltered and fed three times a day. It 'would have been difficult enough to overcome the technical obstacles of double barbed wire fence, searchlights and guards and what then?' The likelihood of recapture far outweighed the risks involved in trying. However, during the time Weitzel was held there one man decided to have a go. As already mentioned, a Compound C sergeant who was decorated with the Knight's Cross, a high military honour in Germany, decided to attempt an escape but was recaptured 24 hours later hiding in a haystack.

The camp administration tried to stop such escape attempts by conducting spur-of-the-moment inspections of the prisoners roughly once a month, which they were considerate enough to do on dry days. They searched the whole compound for up to three hours while the men stood surrounded by guards at the sports ground just outside the camp. The sports ground was for the exclusive use of the British guards, and no prisoners were ever allowed on it except during these inspections. When they returned to their huts a scene of chaos met them. Kitbags had been emptied, mattresses upturned with blankets strewn on the floor, and the guards sometimes even emptied basins full of soaking laundry and threw it over the whole mess. This angered the men. It continued like this until April 1945 when on a particular occasion they were held in the sports field for an entire day while their huts were checked. No lunch was provided that day either. Guards raced about and the prisoners knew something serious had happened. That night when they were allowed back to their compound Weitzel and his fellow prisoners heard that a tunnel had been found hidden behind a large bookcase in the library hut, and it had breached the perimeter of the camp. The guards had known where to search so someone must have told them. One prisoner was quickly removed and sent to a different camp – it is thought he might have been the one who informed the authorities and he was removed for his own safety. The escape 'had been thwarted, a pity we felt'. Eight prisoners of war were identified as the tunnel diggers and were sentenced to 28 days arrest each, as was standard procedure.

———————

Early in 1945 the prisoners at Camp 21 were sent for interrogation for political screening from which they would then be categorised as A, B or C, white, grey or black. Those who were graded A were seen as no threat whatsoever to Britain. They had been conscripted and had little interest in Nazism or the Nazi regime, caught up in a war they had neither voted for nor wanted. They wanted democracy in their country, not dictatorship. Those graded B were the ones the interrogators had doubts about. These men seemed to them to have Nazi leanings although they strongly believed that, over time, they could be re-educated. However, the C category of men, or 'blacks', was a different case altogether. These were the hard-liners, the ones who believed Germany could win the war and Hitler would do as he promised and give them a better, stronger Germany, and no one was going to tell them otherwise. They had been members of the Hitler Youth and were members of the Nazi Party.

The segregation officers came from various backgrounds. Some were German emigrants while others were from German-occupied European countries, which did not go down well with the prisoners. Many of the prisoners decided not to take the screening seriously, which had dire consequences for them. They tended to go into the room and give the Hitler salute for one thing and that usually categorised them as C, a hard-line Nazi, immediately. When Weitzel went into the room, he, like so many, gave the salute out of sheer insolence. However, the interrogator, a Norwegian who had moved to Britain following Germany's invasion of his country, ignored it. He was a teacher and his German-language skills were good. He was rather cool towards Weitzel but not openly hostile. He asked him two questions. The first was did Weitzel think it had been a mistake for Hitler to attack the Soviet Union, to which he replied no. The second was did he believe in a German victory to which he replied yes. The Norwegian nodded, made some notes then thanked him. He was dismissed. He had been prepared for a full-blown confrontation and instead was in the room for less than two minutes. He felt 'let down' as he had wanted to 'have some fun' with the interrogator.

However, both the answers he had given were untrue. He had fought on the Russian front for ten months and following the retreat he knew it had been a disastrous miscalculation by the German authorities. He also had lost his belief in a German victory 'several months ago, somewhere between Caen and Bayeux'. These answers he had thought were an act of defiance but his Norwegian interrogator took them at face value and he was given a C+ ranking. This meant he was seen as a dangerous, fanatical hard-line Nazi.

———————

By now spring had arrived and in Europe the Third Reich was in its death throes. Despite the news blackout still being enforced by the German spokesman and his men in the compound, news reached the prisoners that the Allies were mounting a fierce final assault and that they had reached Germany. They were informed that Cologne had fallen on 7 March and Kassel, Weitzel's hometown, had been occupied on 2 April. They then learned of Hitler's death on 30 April. Most of the prisoners were indifferent to the news, having expected Germany to capitulate at any moment. Some of the prisoners decided that the news could just be rumour, which frustrated the British in the camp. But the British came up with an ingenious idea. In early May they set up a loudspeaker in the compound and announced a news bulletin of a German radio station would be transmitted. At 5 p.m. a crowd of men stood and listened silently to the news. It came from Flensburg in northern Germany near the Danish border. This was still an unoccupied area of the country and it was here the short-lived replacement government under Admiral Dönitz had taken refuge. The German 'announcer read the daily bulletin of the Wehrmacht High Command which fully confirmed the disastrous news we heard. It was clear the Third Reich had but a few more days to live'. When the news bulletin was over, they dispersed silently.

A few days later the British again told the prisoners to gather for a news bulletin. This time it was to inform them of Germany's unconditional surrender. This news was met by complete indifference. Weitzel and his friend Helmut Wetzel proceeded to embark on one of their long walks around the perimeter. Hardly a sound came from Camp 21.

The following day, 9 May 1945, the theatre group performed its first play, *William Tell* by Schiller. The prisoners of war 'followed the great German playwright's passionate appeal against tyranny and for liberty... Still fully under the shock of our country's debacle, we followed the action on the stage in a state of excitement and inner turmoil'.

Weitzel was to spend a further three months at Camp 21 and it was during that time of 'discouragement and hopelessness' that the horrors of what the Third Reich had done reached the men behind the wire. They sat 'incredulous and dismayed' as they 'stared at the visions of horror that became visible behind the heroic façade of the Reich when the Allied troops discovered the inferno of the concentration camps'. The men swore after seeing this that never again 'would we engage ourselves for any idea, party belief or aim', and the images had a lasting impact.

With the fall of the Third Reich the men began turning their thoughts to their own lives. Rumours were rife that they would be held as prisoners for 25 years or they would only be released once Germany had rebuilt Europe. Perhaps they would be kept as a labour force to rebuild Britain, something that is not altogether fanciful as this was indeed considered. Life in the camp changed too. No longer were there educational classes, and cultural activities ceased. Motivation for such activities disappeared along with conversation and rank. Until May 1945 men had belonged to the Wehrmacht where rank mattered and 'discipline remained intact'. However, after the 8th, insignias were ripped from uniforms as were the swastikas which had remained on tunics. There was now little to distinguish one prisoner from another and all were dejected. Even their status changed. Germany as a political state no longer existed therefore the prisoners lost all their rights under the Geneva Convention. During the war they had been protected by it but now this fell to the International Committee of the Red Cross which had very limited power by comparison. However, for Weitzel and the prisoners at Comrie this in fact changed little.

In mid-June the prisoners were ushered to the camp theatre, which had been exclusively for the British guards. No one knew why they were there. Then a 20-minute film reel began. It showed the British liberation of Bergen-Belsen. When 'confronted with those unbearable images, we reacted stunned and dismayed but also [with] incredulity… It was the expression of our inability to comprehend, and accept, the inconceivable'.

At roughly the same time the food rations reduced. Although this was likely a result of the shortage of food worldwide, many German prisoners believed it was linked to the guards wanting retribution for what had happened within the confines of the concentration camps. There does seem to be some evidence to support this. What used to be 25 sacks of potatoes to be peeled dropped down to five or six the following day. The prisoners felt they had to accept it without complaint. The rations at Comrie were still adequate compared with overseas camps, although during a medical check-up two months later all of the men held at Camp 21 were underweight.

The summer held something positive for the men too, however. The weather had improved and they now had use of the football field for exercise two days a week for each compound. The general look of the camp had also improved. Flower beds had been laid out and were blooming and paths had been constructed. Some improvements had been made to the latrines, and additional ones were underway, but it was still the case of a hot shower only once a week for each man. The prisoners were also issued with new clothes. Their old uniforms were threadbare so they were given brand new British uniforms, which had been dyed a rust brown colour and had a distinguishing mark to show they were indeed prisoners. The mark was on all their clothing – tunics, trousers and overcoats – and was yellow, green or blue cloth cut into circles or squares which covered the patch cut out of the original garment. But the men at Comrie did not care about the patch or the fact it was bright. Around 50% of the men were now in possession of a complete uniform.

Another thing that lifted the men of Compound A's spirits, Weitzel recalls, was the orchestra, made up of three violinists, one accordionist, one trumpet player, one saxophone player and a clarinet player along with a jazz guitarist. Called the *Deutsches Theater Comrie*, *D.T.C.*, they held a concert in the infirmary on the afternoon of Sunday 10 June at which it was reported they played exceptionally well. The music had all been handwritten. All of musicians said they intended to stay together as a band after their release. It was another highlight in a still fairly dreary existence.

At the end of July Weitzel's time in Perthshire came to an end. Around 150 prisoners of war from Compound A were transferred to other camps and it became clear to him that the category C men were being segregated from the others. Due to his Norwegian interrogator and his own misguided answers he was in this group. It was a sunny morning when he said goodbye to his friend Helmuth Wetzel, who was remaining behind. They were marched to Comrie railway station and boarded a train. At that point Weitzel had no idea where he was going. He felt as though he was probably being deported. In fact he was heading north to Caithness in the far north of Scotland.

————

The train journey north through the beautiful Scottish Highlands was lost on the men being transported. It seemed inhospitable, wild and untamed, broken only by the sheep. The train travelled through the night until finally, around noon, stopped at Watten station. The prisoners disembarked and marched past Loch Watten and along Station Road until they reached Camp 165.

Watten's prisoner of war camp had begun life in 1943 as a military training camp. It was completed in August that year at a cost of £30,000. Before its completion, the men to be stationed there had to live with locals. When complete it had, amongst other facilities, barracks for the soldiers to sleep in, a mess hall and canteen, a first aid post, a repair shed and an armourer's shop. In May 1945 the first prisoners of war arrived, transported on trucks and trains. Most had been captured since June 1944 in northern France. Many of them were young conscripts while others, such as Paul Werner Hoppe (the Stutthof concentration camp commandant), Gunter d'Alquen (the prominent German propagandist under Hitler) and even Max Wünsche (Hitler's one-time personal adjutant), were advocates of the Nazi cause. Weitzel believed the reason for those men being transferred so far north was to separate them from civilisation as much as possible. Only a month after it became a prisoner of war camp Watten already had 500 prisoners of war, housing them in 77 huts, although these also included a dining room, a reading room and a detention hut. By the time Weitzel arrived it had been divided into two compounds and four observation towers had been built so the guards could keep watch over the prisoners day and night.

At the time of Weitzel's arrival the camp was made up of wooden huts – it would be some time before the Nissen huts would be erected to accommodate the larger influx. These were homely compared with Comrie's huts and housed 20 men each, making conditions more spacious. In the centre of the camp was a smaller compound which housed segregated prisoners who believed the news they had been given was misinformation and propaganda. Weitzel went over to this compound a few times but the men remained silent and only 'hostile faces stared back'.

During the train journey north Weitzel had spent time with Adolf Schulte, Helmuth Meyer and Fritz Keller, who had been the camp librarian. These men had been the 'driving forces of the cultural life at Comrie' and Weitzel hoped this would continue at Watten. As luck would have it he was assigned to the same hut as the three men, and although he always felt like an outsider, he was happy in their company. He took a renewed interest in his new surroundings, and 'a faint hope in the future began to stir'. It also helped they were now allowed to do some work, which passed the days more easily. But shortly after their arrival, the main topic of conversation in the camp was an escape attempt. It was to be the first of several in the lifetime of the camp.

On 27 August a prisoner managed to break out, making his way across the fields into the barren wilderness of the county. He headed towards the coast and made it as far as the village of

Latheron where he was spotted by Special Constable James Fraser, who was also the Governor of the County Home for the Poor in the village, as he was still wearing his distinctive German uniform. Fraser notified the local policeman Constable Kennedy and the soldier was soon arrested. Although over six feet tall, and very fit, he was so exhausted and hungry that he didn't put up any resistance. He was returned to the camp after just ten hours of freedom. There were numerous other escape attempts at Watten, including a prisoner stealing a motorbike which had been left with the engine running, in *Great Escape* movie style.

As mentioned, Watten provided the men with things to do, a far cry from the endless days of playing chess or cards. It also meant they were not spending hours on end wondering about their families back in Germany. They were assigned jobs and although these were not physically demanding, they passed the time. The jobs were 'for the most part dull and dreary' but on the whole not unpleasant. They worked weekdays and had the weekends to do what they wished with within the confines of the camp. One of Weitzel's jobs was as part of the dance hall working party. Just outside the camp was an oversized Nissen hut the British used for dancing and every Saturday night, and sometimes Wednesdays, the British staff would dance the night away. It was also here concerts were held every two or three weeks. His team of six prisoners were responsible for cleaning and heating the hall as well as maintaining the road and 'the upkeep of the surroundings'.

The camp orchestra of 20 or so were full-time musicians and were exempt from other work. News soon reached other parts of the county about the best orchestra north of Inverness and personnel from other military sites in Caithness travelled quite some distance to hear them play. Weitzel recalls many were RAF personnel stationed at the meteorological and radar stations along the east coast of the county. The women who came wore their Women's Auxiliary Air Force (WAAF) uniforms, not dance dresses, but they all had a wonderful time.

Two prisoners were always in attendance at the dances and were often there late into the night. They kept the two stoves burning and emptied the buckets which were placed in two small cubicles and acted as toilets. These had to be emptied several times 'in view of the impressive beer consumption at the dances'. The following morning the men were greeted with leftover food, broken bottles 'and a lot of other, much more unpleasant residues to be cleared away'. Then the floor was swept, wiped, waxed and polished until it gleamed. This took them all day to complete. Sometimes when there was not such a mess they could stand round the stoves and chat.

Weitzel stayed in that job for the entire six months he was held at Watten. Not once did he leave the camp, unlike his friend Schulte who at first worked at RAF Wick then later at the radar station at Tannach.

————

Because of their classification the men had expected to be treated harshly by the camp commandant Lt.-Col. Rupert Murray. However, these category C prisoners were nothing more than 'rather subdued and slightly undernourished individuals'. Like so many others who encountered Murray, Weitzel had nothing but respect for the man who 'stood nearly two metres tall, of startling gauntness with a hooked nose and a thick black moustache. He was…austere and unsmiling but what distinguished him particularly was his absolute fairness. He was a soldier and treated us as soldiers'. Murray had been a prisoner of war himself and his experience served him well at Watten.

During World War II, Murray was commander of a pioneer company when he was captured on the island of Crete. He was interred as a prisoner of war until his release in 1945. While in captivity he became gravely ill with dysentery and this, compounded by poor rations, caused him to become very weak. He recovered, however, and his experiences stood him in good stead in his new role in Caithness as he understood the needs of the prisoners as well as the risk of disease and the effects on men of being incarcerated. During his time in captivity he became a temporary lieutenant-colonel as he automatically succeeded his group commander. When he and his fellow prisoners were liberated and returned to Scotland, they were brought up to date at Dunbar in East Lothian then given their commissions. Murray's first posting was a prisoner of war camp in Edinburgh, after which he took up the Watten post.

The prisoners affectionately gave him the name 'Black Watch' after his regiment. Whenever he had to sign an order or announcement he always signed it with his rank and name followed by Black Watch. He took roll call wearing the kilt and Weitzel remembers on the freezing mornings seeing his knees blue with the cold. Murray was held in high regard at Watten, not just by the prisoners like Weitzel but by the guards too. These included Englishman Alan Noble who had arrived in the advance party in February 1945 and had helped to set up the camp to receive the prisoners.

———

Due to work commitments, leisure pursuits were much curtailed. The camp orchestra mainly played for the camp staff and visitors while the theatre group tended to work on operettas, light entertainment and musicals. Instead of throwing himself into these, Weitzel took to learning English, reading newspapers with the aid of a dictionary. Amazingly, Fritz Keller, who had been in Rommel's Afrika Korps, managed to bring in an old wind-up gramophone along with some classical records to supplement the two radios at Watten. He was allowed to keep them and every Sunday night after lights out, when the men were in their beds, he would play records for them, using only a candle to see what he was doing. Although 'the programme would vary', it always ended with the finale of Puccini's *La Bohème*. They all stayed still, 'everyone lost in their own reveries'. Weitzel imagined himself 'at home at the opera in a dark suit and a tie'. To this day when he hears that piece of music he is transported back to his days in Watten, lying in bed, listening.

The resumption of the postal service with Germany also lifted spirits. The prisoners were given a postcard in two parts. One part had the words in German 'A member of the defeated Wehrmacht seeks his next of kin', with the second part to be used to reply in no more than 50 words. No personal messages were allowed to be written on them however. Some prisoners took exception to the phrase 'defeated Wehrmacht' but no one in Weitzel's hut ripped up the card or refused to send it. The cards were posted off and the men could do nothing but wait and hope for a reply. Just before Christmas Weitzel received one. It was from his mother. She was well, as were his grandparents, but his father was missing on the Eastern Front. It was the first news from home he had received since August 1944. She had used all 50 words allocated to her. By Christmas Day everyone in Weitzel's hut had received news from home, although it was not always good. Christmas was hard for the men who had families. Helmuth Meyer for example had a wife and a son who had been born in 1944 but who he had yet to see and hold. He was repatriated in the spring of 1948 and saw his son, now aged four, for the very first time.

On New Year's Eve, or Hogmanay as it is known in Scotland, the lights out at 10 p.m. rule was relaxed. At midnight the men went outside and saw a spectacular sight. The Aurora Borealis, or Northern Lights, lit up the night sky with vast swathes of green. They toasted the New Year with cups of tea.

Early in 1946, the British re-education programme reached Watten for the first time. The high principles it set were simply impossible to adhere to, however, and overall the project failed because these men were held in isolation and not allowed to fraternise. The name did not help either, causing many to oppose it. However, one aspect did have some success and that was the visiting lecturers. Only one of these speakers was truly stimulating for Weitzel while others were acceptable but their talks too general or simplistic. It also did not help that sometimes their German-speaking skills were lacking. By the summer of 1946 the programme was beginning to stall and by the end of the year had ceased altogether.

Weitzel believes his own understanding of politics and intellectual and cultural life came from reading the British newspapers. One article stands out more than any other and that was the defeat of the wartime Prime Minister Winston Churchill in the June 1945 General Election to Clement Attlee, which astonished him. He could not understand how this wartime leader could lose to a man who had 'a personality totally devoid of charisma'. Only later did he understand that although Churchill had been a great leader during the war, the country needed someone to tackle the social changes that were coming. He believes it was the abolition of the non-fraternisation policy in December 1946 that truly made inroads. No longer were prisoners isolated from the outside world, and this proved to be a much better way of 're-education' than lectures in a room.

During his four years in captivity, it was only at Watten that Weitzel became unwell. In January 1946 he was diagnosed with a severe bout of influenza. An epidemic swept the camp that January and February, with 270 reported cases in all. One man, Jacob Lanzarth, succumbed to it and died on 17 February. Shortly after his own battle with it, Weitzel's eye tooth became infected, causing his face to swell up badly within a couple of hours. Even his friends did not recognise him. But it was successfully extracted by the dentist. The medical staff and the dentist were qualified, although prisoners of war, and 'we only regretted that nursing services were provided by German medical orderlies rather than pretty British nurses'.

———

One evening in early February a list of men was issued containing the names of those who would be departing the following morning. Prisoner transfers were always announced this way, only a few hours before departure. On that list was Rolf Weitzel. To be transferred with him was Adolf Schulte, and it soon became evident it was the younger prisoners who were leaving. These younger men had not been indoctrinated with Nazi ideology, according to Weitzel. They had been interested in the usual adolescent concerns such as football, music and girls, not politics. As he succinctly puts it: 'immature we had been, obedient and naive but not fanatical'. And it suggested that the Foreign Office had reassessed the screening programme which, as far as Weitzel was concerned, should not have placed him at the Watten camp.

This time the journey took place mainly during daylight hours and the destination could hardly have been further away. The train headed to the far south of England. When the passengers arrived it was dark, and they were in for a shock. As the first of the group passed through the gates 'a horrified cry went up: "Tents!"' Morale changed in that instant. After a year of being in Nissen and wooden huts, a tented camp came as quite a shock. As Weitzel and Schulte crawled into their pitch black tent and pulled up the covers, they thought of their fellow prisoners up in Watten with a great deal of envy. He had arrived at Working Camp 663, at Shipton Bellinger, Tidworth on the Salisbury Plain, a small camp that held around 250 prisoners of war who were housed in nothing but bell tents.

Prisoners of war had been covered by the Geneva Convention but here it seems the Convention was completely ignored. Article 10 states that any prisoner of war should 'be lodged in buildings or huts which afford all possible safeguards' in relation to hygiene, general health and well-being. It goes on to say that the accommodation should be free of damp and there should be adequate heating and lighting with appropriate 'fittings and bedding materials'. Unfortunately Camp 663 broke all of this, much to the indignation of the Germans.

The day after their arrival, the men were assigned to various working parties and the job Weitzel was given, along with 25 other prisoners of war, was to unload artillery shells from a wagon at the nearby railway station and load them onto a truck. These shells were 'large calibre shells and handling them [was] hard work'. They all agreed this seemed to be a rather unsuitable job for them so on their return they spoke to the camp spokesman who in turn spoke to the camp commandant. They never did this work again. Weitzel was then assigned to work at the Royal Engineer Corps depot where he was to remain for the next five months. At first he helped with painting, including of the new living quarters for the NCOs and their families, and it was during this time he learned a new way to tell the time thanks to the pioneers he worked with. They saw the prisoners as their equals and got on well with them. One day Weitzel asked the simple question of what the time was and received the reply in strong language. The Germans 'adopted it cheerfully'. The pioneers had an 'inexhaustible supply of foul language' and it was used to great effect when one day the unthinkable happened. The lorry which brought round the tea and biscuits did not appear so, shouting profanities, the pioneers went on strike. Weitzel did not know whether he could join in the strike or not so continued painting until one of their number came up to him, removed the paintbrush from his hand and told him 'no tea, no work'. He 'really liked those pioneers'.

In May, Weitzel was reassigned to another team, this time to do some dismantling. A massive ammunitions depot had been erected in preparation for the invasion of France, with the ammunition stocked in what was essentially five very low Nissen huts, 'just high enough… to stand upright in'. The ammunition had been removed some time before and now it was their task to loosen the screws, pile up the corrugated sheets and load them onto the truck when it came in the afternoon. They worked as quickly as they could and managed to finish their stint by three in the afternoon. They could then enjoy some leisure time outside as the summer of 1946 was a pleasant one. Weitzel now always carried a Penguin book in his overall and for a few hours it felt like he was a free man. It was also at Tidworth that he became close friends with Adolf Schulte and their friendship endured long after their time in captivity.

Some of these young men had something else on their minds other than work, however. Many had left school without their Abitur, the school leaving certificate, and knew that if they wanted to go to university they would have to go back and sit it. Without any books, they each decided to give a lecture on the subject they knew well from school. Weitzel, after some persuasion, took the Latin class. The camp administration saw these efforts as admirable and gave them use of half a Nissen hut in which to study. For the first time in two years, their thoughts had turned to the future.

Newspapers were available in the camp to keep the men up to date with current affairs. Some of the prisoners did not have a very good command of the English language, however, so those who did decided to translate the stories of interest, type them out and post them on a wall which was changed as and when new stories were ready. Weitzel and his friend Schulte were in charge of cultural stories on literature, art and music and from mid-1946 until the end of January 1947 the two served as culture editors. This led to a new job too in the accounts office, under the auspices of Captain Stevens. Weitzel would spend his mornings assisting two prisoner of war clerks then return to translating the articles with Schulte in the afternoons. With no calculators, the weekly payrolls became somewhat of a challenge. One month into the job, in August, he was promoted, unwillingly, to chief accounts clerk when the two regular accounts clerks were repatriated. Fortunately he acquired two assistants to help him with the task.

In Watten, Weitzel had not been paid for any work he did but now he was given a shilling for his eight hours of work per day. On a Friday evening he would receive a list of the working hours from each working party, and wages were paid every fortnight on a Saturday morning. He would also go out to Bulford where 80 men worked at various locations as cooks, kitchen helpers and mess waiters to pay them their wages, using a jeep provided by the camp authorities. In return for news, and of course the wages, Weitzel and his assistant were offered a meal in each of the three mess kitchens, none of which he refused, then picked up by the jeep in the afternoon.

The prisoners could pay some or all of their money into a savings account, but the money was only token money and could only be used in the camp canteen where they could buy toothpaste, soap, cakes and of course cigarettes. They were also entitled to three cigarettes a day. The cigarettes were distributed by Weitzel's office 'whereas paying the wages was the privilege of the camp's three British officers, the only sovereign act they still performed'. The accounts office also gave Weitzel a little luxury: part of it was cordoned off and there was a bed, small table and two chairs which was a huge improvement on the tent. The office itself was one half of a Nissen hut. The other half was the living quarters for the camp commandant. He was Lt.-Col. Noel De Pletron MacRoberts, who had served in the Royal Sussex Regiment during World War I and had seen action in West Africa during the inter-war years. He was the professional solider through and through and although he could be gruff, he had a good-natured side and the prisoners liked him. Through the partition everything could be heard, however, and at 11 o'clock every morning they could hear his booming voice as he participated in the German-language course which was being transmitted on the radio. It caused quite a lot of fairly quiet giggling in the accounts office.

The prisoners, although on the whole well-behaved, responsible men, when it came to procuring items from the British army did not hold back. For example, the chemistry class run by Gottfried Haese acquired all its materials from the Royal Army Central Medical Store where Schulte was charged with making an inventory of pharmaceutical and chemical stock. Twenty-four hours before the class Haese would tell Schulte what he needed and this was duly pilfered. No one in the camp administration batted an eyelid when they saw all the chemical equipment and chemicals in the class. Weitzel himself managed to acquire both a German–English dictionary and a Latin dictionary through an intermediary in the camp. He still has those books today. However, as far as the prisoners were concerned the best was still to come.

The United States army had been based at North Tidworth but had departed and in their wake had left a lot of brand new overcoats. The storehouse was more or less unguarded so the prisoners working there had little difficulty getting in and taking some of the coats. The price was camp money and cigarettes. At night a group of 'burglars left the camp which presented no problems, marched to Tidworth, entered the depot, gathered the required number of over-coats, and returned to the camp'. They were then dyed navy blue by the second team using the huge kitchen kettles and procured dyes before being handed over to the third team who filed down the buttons with the American eagles embossed on them until the whole garment was no longer recognisable as American.

———

In October 1946 the news came that the tents were to be replaced by huts and special working teams began pouring the cement foundations. Dismantled Nissen huts at now disused sites were reassembled at the camp. In November bunk beds arrived along with mattresses, just in time before the onset of winter.

Then in December news came that the non-fraternisation decree had been lifted after 19 months. The immediate result of this was invitations from locals to go and spend Christmas with them. Weitzel received an invite as he was part of the camp administration but he declined, wishing instead to spend the time with his friends. As a well-liked commandant, MacRoberts received a cigar box in the shape of a Nissen hut as a gift from the prisoners. The camp spokes-man as he presented him with it said, 'You gave us our huts Sir, now we wish to give you one in return'. It moved him to tears.

Early one morning in February 1947 the men awoke to two surprises: a heavy snowfall and an announcement that the following morning the camp was to close. Weitzel panicked.

The accounts office had 24 hours to get its house in order. With two assistants he left in a truck, together with two camp guards, to go to the various outposts and collect all the token money held by the prisoners there. They made it as far as Bulford but no further, due to snowdrifts. When he got back he worked diligently in the accounts office until 5 a.m. the next morning. By 9 a.m. most of the prisoners had lined up and signed their accounts sheet, and they were now marching towards Tidmouth through the deep snow. Weitzel was not with them, however. He and a number of others stayed behind and for ten days he and his staff battled with camp money, paying bills and closing accounts in the eerily deserted and silent camp. He finally left the camp around the middle of the month, along with the others who had stayed behind to wind up affairs. MacRoberts had come into the accounts office and given them a short speech commending their work. He gave them each a work certificate which was in both English and German. The reference he gave Rolf Weitzel was glowing. The following day when the truck arrived to ship them out, MacRoberts stood at the gate, shook hands with each of them and wished them well for the future.

The train journey was the first where Weitzel and the others intermingled with civilians. Only one soldier, rather than a guard, accompanied them to Camp 702 near King's Cliffe, a small town 15 miles or so from Peterborough. This was only to be a transit station for them however. This camp was for those who were to be worked in the service of the Royal Air Force and from here assignments to an RAF station were made. Camp 702 was blanketed in deep snow when Weitzel arrived. After they had been shown to their Nissen hut on the periphery of the camp they were left to their own devices, which involved much pacing to keep warm as there was no coal for them to use.

Five or six days were spent at King's Cliffe then Weitzel was assigned to a small group of prisoners and sent to the basic training centre at RAF Innsworth near Gloucester. Here he and his 30 or so comrades were housed and rationed in exactly the same way as the 3000 recruits who lived there. His group was divided into three distinct working parties, 'delegated respectively to the Officers', Sergeants' and Privates' Mess'. Weitzel was assigned the Sergeants' Mess.

During his time at Innsworth Weitzel felt contented on the whole, as he had a degree of freedom which had been but a distant hope in the early days of his captivity. His living quarters were good, as were the food rations, but slowly his thoughts turned towards his enduring captivity and he wondered when he would be repatriated. By the summer of 1947 moves were underway to repatriate the men, and Weitzel figured his turn would come in March 1948. He was apprehensive, though, as to what he would find back at home and what he would do for a living as he did not complete his Abitur. Adding to his uncertainty was the fact that since he had been at war, and a prisoner of that war, he had taken orders on a daily basis and it had become routine. He wondered how he would cope making his own decisions for the first time in five years.

In 1945 the YMCA had begun courses for prisoners of war in theology, with English and mathematics following, and at Norton in Northamptonshire an education camp for prisoners was opened. When the chance arose at Innsworth Weitzel applied to study German and

English on a six-month correspondence course, so he could go further and gain his Abitur at last. He managed to carry out some study around his work schedule and in August 1947 he was informed the course he wanted to attend was to begin in October. 'Without hesitation' he applied to the Norton camp. He was excited at the prospect, only to have his hopes dashed when he was sent north again, to Camp 63 Balhary near Alyth in Perthshire. There was little to do here. However, in early October he received news that he had been accepted onto the course at Norton so once again he was on the move.

––––––––

Camp 174 Norton was situated at Cuckney near Mansfield and had been made into an education camp after it had finished being a prisoner of war camp in 1945, at the suggestion of the Swedish pastor Birger Forell. The YMCA had a huge impact on the prisoners for it looked after their cultural and spiritual welfare like no other organisation during their time in captivity. It disregarded any political leanings and concentrated on the wellbeing of the men, mainly by providing education which would be of use to them once they returned home. They were the ones who had provided film screenings and they had published what were known as 'wren books' which 'comprised a selection of texts by both classic and contemporary German authors'. The Norton camp was placed under the Hamburg School Authority, and in the autumn of 1947 a Hamburg inspector even visited the camp to assess the competence of the teaching staff, appraise the courses on offer and inspect the facilities.

Around 200 participants arrived to be split into classes. There were four obligatory courses – German, mathematics, history and geography – with an option of studying two more; Weitzel chose English and chemistry.

Another Christmas came and went but for the first time Weitzel's mood was cheerful, for the prisoners knew that by next Christmas they would be home with their families. The United States had already repatriated some 400,000 prisoners within six months following the capitulation of Japan so the returning troops could get the jobs back from the prisoners who had taken them. In Britain, however, the government needed the prisoners as many soldiers were still required to stay in various former theatres of war within the Empire. There was also a gap due to the military losses and demobilisation could not fill the labour gap left in the war's wake. By April 1946, almost 210,000 prisoners of war worked in agriculture, amounting to around a third of the workforce. However, under increasing pressure the government was forced to set out a timetable, and by the autumn of 1947 repatriation on a large scale was underway. It further snowballed with the threat of Sweden and Switzerland boycotting the Olympic Games to be held in London in 1948, with July of that year being when repatriation of all prisoners was to be complete.

In January around a third of the students were dismissed from the classes as they were not performing well, but Weitzel continued and it was due to his study that his repatriation –which should have taken place in March – actually happened two months later. He passed all his exams and was given a piece of paper signed by the Secretary of the YMCA and two prisoner of war teachers, the course director and the chairman of the examination board. When Weitzel produced it later 'this unusual school leaving certificate has invariably caused a surprised rising of eyebrows but its validity has never been questioned'.

On 3 May, three weeks after his exams, Weitzel left the Norton camp. At Leicester he entered the last camp he would ever set foot in on British soil. It was a transit camp. Prisoners from other camps converged there and waited for transportation to Germany. Weitzel spent three days in the camp then on 7 May boarded a train to Harwich. There he 'embarked on a big transport vessel' and at noon the boat left the harbour bound for Hoek van Holland. Following disembarkation, the prisoners boarded another train which travelled through the night to Munsterlager on Lüneburg Heath, a military training centre which was at the time the central processing and discharge centre for the prisoners held by the British. The prisoners were then divided into four groups with each group corresponding to the four Allied occupation zones. Weitzel was designated to the US zone. After nine days here, Weitzel received his discharge document and rations cards for the first few weeks of his freedom. He was also paid money he had saved in his prisoner of war account. However, his money was virtually worthless following the currency reform of July 1948 when the Reichsmark became the Deutsche Mark. On 17 May 1948 he was released and was finally a free man.

Weitzel took the train to Kassel. The city had not changed much since his last visit. It was still strewn with debris, battered by the heavy Allied bombing, but at least he was home. He turned into the street where his family had taken refuge and 'saw someone leaning over the balustrade of the balcony then I heard my mother's voice, choked with emotion: "Rolf, is that you?" My throat was dry, my "Yes" hardly audible'. Moments later they were in each other's arms, happy to be reunited at last.

Following his return home, Weitzel went on to train as a librarian. He gained his diploma in 1951 and secured a position at the State Library Kassel, known as the Murhardsche Bibliothek der Stadt Kassel, the city's second state library. In January 1958 he joined the World Health Organization, which had been set up in 1948, and worked for 26 years as a member of the WHO library staff in Geneva. In January 2006 he left Geneva with Marie-Luise his wife and returned to Kassel, where he continues to live. His wife died in October 2010. They had a daughter, Ruth.

Weitzel now lives in a two-bedroom apartment in a residential home, with books filling shelves from floor to ceiling. Books remain an important part of his life.

Helmuth Meyer returned to Watten in 1985 and did a sketch of the main crossroads in the village. He wrote on his drawing, 'Nothing has changed in 40 years'. The prisoner of war camp at Watten continued to take prisoners, eventually closing its gates in April 1948. Little of the camp remains today, but a small plaque commemorates it near the former football field.

4 | THE GERMAN BAKER

When the Smith Bakery on London Road, Newbury changed hands in 1974, it brought the business to the end of an era. For over 20 years it had been run by baker's daughter Agnes and her husband, former prisoner of war Günther Schran. The couple had taken over the business at the end of World War II following their marriage. When the reins were handed over to Albert Wild, it meant that for the first time in years the couple would be able to go on holiday and there would no longer be 4 a.m. starts for Mr Schran. What follows is his story.

Günther Caspar Schran was born on 10 June 1921 in Bochum in the heavy industrial part of the Ruhr in the state of North Rhine-Westphalia, Germany. The main industries in the area were iron, steel and coal. Schran's father was a mining engineer so this no doubt influenced his choice of career. He went to the Volksschule at Bochum Hordel, where he studied for eight years, and later went on to mining college. Before college, however, he spent two years at a Hitler Jugend (Hitler Youth) camp which was combined with an educational establishment in East Pomerania near the Polish Corridor, close to the town of Kersleen (now in Poland). The Hitler Youth had evolved from an official Nazi Party youth movement founded in 1922 in Munich; this disbanded in 1923, then re-emerged three years later under the title Hitler Jugend, Bund Deutscher Arbeiterjugend (Hitler Youth, League of German Worker Youth), with strong associations to the Sturmabteilung, the paramilitary wing of the Nazi Party. By the time Hitler came to power in 1933, and in the run-up to World War II, this was the first step for German boys towards joining the forces – it took on some of the roles of the now banned Boy Scouts and included military training. In 1933 there were almost two and a half million members and by 1938 over seven million. In 1939 it became compulsory and all young people were conscripted into it, regardless of any objections from parents.

The motto at the Hitler Youth camp which Schran attended was 'Always be what makes you hard'. And they certainly did make the boys hard. For example, if one boy misbehaved, they all had to suffer for it – in this way they made the bond between the boys stronger. Amongst the physical events which strengthened resolve, if nothing else, were the extensive marches Schran and the other boys had to endure. During the six-week summer holiday they did long marches, between 25 and 30 kilometres a day, with rucksacks on their backs. They were aged between 14 and 15 years old. They walked from Lagge on the Baltic coast all the way along the Polish Corridor to Schneidemuhl (which is now Pila in Poland). They carried canvas tents and when luck was on their side, farmers would put them up in one of their big sheds. This 'holiday' usually took place in July and August when the weather was good. They had their lessons and were indoctrinated with the beliefs of the Nazis. When not being taught they helped out on the farms for four or five hours a day. When Schran became part of the Hitler Youth, boys had to become a member, due to the pressure put on them. Before this Schran had been a member of the Young Men's Christian Association (YMCA), in 1933, as he was a Protestant, but they were more or less taken over by the Hitler Youth when Hitler came to power, and so he became a member of the latter not through choice but by fate. He had already also become a member of the Deutsches Jungvolk, the German Youth Group, before it too was taken under the umbrella of the Hitler Youth when he left school.

When Hitler came to power Schran's father was a nationalist but he never really sympathised with the Nazis, or the socialists or the communists for that matter, which was why he supported Paul von Hindenburg's independent party. When the young Schran wanted to join the SS as a volunteer his father refused to give his consent, and later he was relieved this was the case. At the time, however, he thought it was terrible, being denied the opportunity to join. His interest in the SS later came to light after he had joined the German navy – they approached him following their discovery on his application form that his father had not given his consent when he was 17, the age at which young men could apply to join them. However, the Kriegsmarine refused to let him go and he later stated that he felt doubly lucky that he had not become a member of Hitler's Schutzstaffel.

———

Schran had been brought up believing that Hitler had done a lot of good in Germany. He enjoyed the drum beating, the uniforms and the discipline of the Hitler Youth, and he became a member of a band as a trumpeter, soon becoming a Schaftsführer then a Gruppenführer, and at that point in his life he truly believed in Hitler. When Hitler came to power in 1933 there were around six million unemployed. Reparations from the treaties of the Paris Peace Settlement after Germany capitulated in 1918, followed by the Wall Street Crash of 1929 as well the United States calling in all its loans, had destroyed the German economy. Although measures were taken to stem the impact, such as cutting expenditure and reducing wages, the working population began to lose faith in the Brüning government and many were taking an interest in communist ideology. Businessmen became anxious and the middle classes could see that only a strong government would get them out of the economic doldrums. In 1932 President Paul von Hindenburg dismissed Brüning and appointed a new chancellor, Franz von Papen, but he only lasted six months, to be followed by Kurt von Schleicher who lasted just two. By July 1932 the Nazis had over 200 seats in the Reichstag compared with just 12 four years earlier. Hitler saw his chance. Hindenburg and Papen offered him the post of vice-chancellor but he refused. He became chancellor and one of the first things he did was to declare himself as absolute ruler of Germany. He promised Germans the one thing they were desperate for: employment. He also promised an economic market to farmers, to rebel against the Treaty of Versailles, and to rid Germany of the corrupt politicians and of course the Jews who were seen as a dangerous and money-grabbing people but more importantly as a 'sub-class'. Once these problems were dealt with Germany's economy would be world class. The industrialists supported him unequivocally. The threat of Communism was too great for them not to. By 1936, Germany's unemployment had diminished, the Rhineland was re-occupied as Hitler chipped away at the treaty that had caused so much frustration since 1919, and he had reintroduced conscription. He had already abandoned the League of Nations back in 1933, and had declared himself Führer following the death of Hindenburg in August 1934. The Nazi Party was the only legal party in the country by this time, and those who did not share its ideology were dealt with by any means at hand, whether beatings, shootings or being shipped off to the new labour camps such as Dachau, followed in 1937 by Buchenwald and the subsequent concentration camps.

Schran remembered the unemployed miners and tradesmen hanging about, not knowing what to do with themselves while no work was available. With nothing to do tensions rose. Schran witnessed street fighting in the town once, and there was a point during this he found difficult to watch. The police came to stop the fighting between the communists and the Nazis. They arrived in open trucks with long benches on either side carrying 12 police officers, who jumped off and used their batons immediately. The fighting was brutal: there was a lot of bloodshed and people were killed. Schran was around 13 when he witnessed it. He thought the way it was handled was wrong and at the time blamed the communists, not the Nazis. He and others who saw it unfold felt the communists probably deserved it because it seemed like it was them who had started it – but in all fairness he never actually saw who started it. His father dragged him away as he did not want his son to see such brutality. This incident stayed with Schran all his life.

The Nazis persecuted the communists from the very start, taking them off the streets and transporting them to labour camps. Many were severely beaten, especially ones they knew for sure were communists. There was a deep level of hostility shown towards any communist, in line with Nazi doctrine. One family Schran knew of had one son who was a member of the Nazi Party and another who belonged to the Communist Party, dividing the family along political lines. Schran's mother steered clear of politics although she was awarded the gold Mother's Cross for bearing ten children, of which Günther was the youngest. He had two brothers and seven sisters. He remembered his mother was proud when she received it from the Führer but recalls her wearing the cross only once, when his sister told her to wear it for a photograph.

At school in early 1934 the teachers who had been in the military had joined the Sturmabeitlung (SA) or Brownshirts. The SA's main role had been to protect members of the Nazi Party at rallies but included also disrupting meetings of those opposed to the Party such as communists and trade unionists. They had special celebration dates and came to school in uniform so students and teachers alike could tell who was sympathetic and who was not. Schran's head teacher Hector Balke was a member of the Deutsche Volkspartei, the German People's Party, which was a liberal party during the Weimar Government.

Later that year, with rivalries growing between the SA and the SS, Hitler ordered the capture of the head of the group Ernst Röhm and the other high-ranking members of the SA, on 30 June. Hitler personally placed them under arrest at Bad Weissee. Many were shot but Hitler had wanted to spare Röhm for all the things he had done for the Party. However, persuaded by Heinrich Himmler and Hermann Göring, on 1 July he gave him the option of committing suicide. When Röhm refused he was taken out and shot by two SS officers, Theodor Eicke, who later became commandant of Dachau, and Michael Lippert. Both later stood trial, in 1957, and were found guilty of the murder. According to records it is known that 85 men lost their lives but estimates by historians suggest it more likely to have been between 150 and 200. In the days that followed news was released of Röhm's death, as was the information that Röhm, together with other high-ranking members of the SA, was a homosexual (something Hitler had known for many years). It was Hitler's way of making sure order was restored and it was justification for his actions as far as the public were concerned. The whole incident became known as the Night of the Long Knives. The SA numbers diminished following it, although in November 1938, following the assassination of German diplomat Ernst vom Rath by the Polish Jew Herschel Grynszpan, the SA instigated and participated in what became known as Kristallnacht. On the night of the 9th/10th of that month thousands of Jewish shop windows were smashed by members of the group. By the outbreak of war the SA had been overshadowed by the SS and, as numbers diminished further, became little more than a military training group.

Although he had witnessed the fighting between the rival groups, throughout that time Schran never once came across anyone who circulated leaflets in order to stir up trouble. He believed the ordinary people were probably too scared, and with teachers wearing the SA uniforms, students were unlikely to become involved with rival groups for fear of repercussions in the classroom.

––––––––––

Bochum Hordel itself was a large estate in the mining area built by Krupps for their workforce, many of whom were turning towards Nazi ideals. The houses were well equipped, with inside toilets and baths. After his abdication, Edward VIII visited Bochum Hordel with Mrs Simpson following their enforced exile from Britain. The houses looked like middle-class ones, not miners' houses, as care was taken of their outward appearance and the gardens were carefully tended. The miners were mostly socialist although some had deep sympathy for the communists. Tradespeople, teachers and the intelligentsia were more inclined to join the Nazi Party. After Hitler took power the miners turned away from the socialists as coal mining prospered. They were given all sorts of incentives. Sometime between 1936 and 1937 travel was introduced so they could go and spend a holiday in Madeira or Italy or on liners, which only the middle or upper class could afford. Another incentive was the fact that if they joined the

SA they would be given a free uniform. So if not by conviction they probably got them by the temptation of the extra goodies offered by Krupps.

Later Hitler introduced the Volkswagen, the people's car. Schran's older brother started paying in for one in 1937 but whether he saw it or not he did not remember, and when war broke out they were used by the Wehrmacht. It cost around 600 Marks, the equivalent of £40 or £50, and as they started paying in for them the miners felt they were getting a good deal. They had been successfully won over by the regime.

Hermann Göring, the ace fighter pilot, came to the Ruhr to make propaganda speeches to the miners to get them to produce more coal. He was well received as he was a jovial figure and could relate to them better than many of the other politicians. Only two people who lived in Schran's road that he knew of were ever arrested over their political activity. One was a socialist and the other a communist. They were set free after a year in a concentration camp after they had been 're-educated'. He never spoke to them about what had happened to them as he felt it would be inappropriate for a boy of 14 or 15 to ask a man of 30 how he had been treated.

And yet much of this so-called prosperity was an illusion. Germany had lost its Jewish workforce as law after law was brought in until it strangled them and they had either left Germany or were being forcibly removed to camps, so the Jews had simply been replaced by the German workers. Women were encouraged to stay at home and look after their families rather than work, leaving the jobs open for the men. Wages in real terms were no better than they had been at the time before the Wall Street Crash. Men did have work but the terms were strict and they knew there was no option to refuse no matter what the work entailed. The threat of being shipped off to a concentration camp was all too real. Much of the employment was geared towards war, including the mining and steel industries which were physically demanding and dirty jobs. Life was hard, possibly even harder than it had been under the Weimar Government. They could not afford to go out and spend money on German-produced goods even though Hitler implored them to do so. As unemployment fell Hitler stated there had been an 'economic miracle'. By 1939, some 22% of the workforce were employed in a military industry, as war drew ever closer. One of the benefactors of Hitler's war footing was Krupps. In 1933 Krupps made a profit of 6.65 million Reichsmarks. In a year this had almost doubled and by 1939 the profits stood at 17.8 million Reichsmarks.

At Bochum Hordel some Jews still lived in the area in the mid-thirties, as Schran remembered. One of his married sisters went to see a Jew regularly, and when his younger sister joined the Bund Deutscher Mädel, the League of German Girls (the Hitler Youth for girls), she needed a little jacket but her mother could not get it in an ordinary Aryan shop so she said she was going to Bloom, who managed to get it for her. A Jewish shopkeeper had helped to get his sister a Nazi jacket. The irony is not lost on Schran. There were pickets at Jewish shops but hardly anyone ever broke through because of the unpleasantness which would have resulted. Even if they wanted to shop there, people could not for fear of being made an outcast – they were absolutely terrified, so boycotted the shops instead. Schran had no Jewish friends in his class but this could be partly explained by the fact that there were no Jewish miners. However there were some at the Gymnasium.

When war broke out in September 1939 Schran was more surprised about Britain's move than Germany's. He was not surprised when Hitler marched into Poland on 1 September, as Nazi Germany had already annexed Austria and Czechoslovakia; but when Britain declared war on Germany, he had not been prepared for it. In Germany jokes were made about whether people wanted a piece of Czechoslovakia or Austria but suddenly war was all too real. As the Germans attacked Polish targets the British and French sent an ultimatum for Germany to withdraw immediately, on the 2nd, but this was the same day they annexed the Polish Free City of Danzig, now Gdansk. On 3 September it was not only Britain that declared war but also Australia and New Zealand, as well as India. In the days that followed Canada and South Africa followed suit but by then Britain had suffered its first loss, in what was to become known as the Battle of the Atlantic. Within hours of war being declared the SS *Athenia* had been torpedoed by U-30 northwest of Ireland with the loss of all passengers and crew.

In 1939 young Schran joined the Reichsarbeitsdienst or RAD, the compulsory working service which everyone had to serve in for six months. RAD had been formed in June 1935 and although geared towards the military side of the economy, some sections worked in agriculture and after Schran had served three of his six months, the boys were sent to East Prussia to help the farmers. It was while he was there that Germany marched into Poland. They worked on little farms and smallholdings which were actually in Poland – and now they were fighting the Poles. The husband at the farm where he was working had been called up to fight and the women were not pleased. For the boys, their displeasure was wholly aimed at Britain and her declaration of war on Germany, for as 'members of the Hitler Youth, we had learned it [of the invasion of Poland] from English boy scouts and found them [the English scouts] superb to get on with'. They would sing songs around the campfire including 'It's a Long Way to Tipperary'; every Hitler Youth boy knew the words to this song and while the English sang it in English, they did it in German, translating it almost word for word. That kind of camaraderie had now come to an abrupt end. The atmosphere among them in East Prussia was one of shock, and the ordinary Prussians were surprised too, although they probably had more of an idea what was coming as Hitler had ordered soldiers to the region. To the boys it was all a bit of an adventure. They had been sent by ship to Königsberg as they could not go through the Polish Corridor. After about two weeks the communist Stalin regime had joined the Nazis and had entered into Poland. The Hitler Youth had been told time and again the Soviets were the lowest of the low, the arch enemy, but now Hitler had made a pact with Stalin. Schran and his comrades were confused by this turn of events, especially after all the Nazi proselytisation. They had marched into Poland on 17 September from the east. Joachim von Ribbentrop, the German foreign minister, had met his Soviet counterpart Vyacheslav Molotov and they had signed the Treaty of Non-Aggression on 23 August in which both sides publicly guaranteed non-belligerence and that neither would side with the other's enemy. Secretly however the Ribbentrop–Molotov Pact also divided up conquered territories so each side had its own sphere of influence in a given area. Schran stated that he and his friends could not understand why England had declared war on Germany but not on Russia. Hitler after all had been given an ultimatum, but when the Russians then attacked Poland Schran believed the British should have 'been morally obliged to declare war on Russia but didn't'.

Shortly after the war started the boys came back to Bochum, as war broke out in France. Schran decided to stay with the working service after his six-month compulsory stint and became a member of staff as a troop leader so he signed up again. In 1940 they were ordered into France, following Hitler's invasion of the country, and built aerodromes for the Luftwaffe with the help of French farmers who came and levelled the ground to make it possible for the Luftwaffe to build airstrips. Schran's job and that of his superior, Feldmaster Feldmann, was to pay the French farmers for the work they had done so they went around distributing the funds. These airfields were built in northern France near Peron, not far from the Belgian town of Mons, and consisted simply of a strip for the planes to take off and land on, nothing more. In the summer of 1940 French citizens were frightened of the German soldiers. They had been ordered to leave their homes and were told that when they came back they would be treated 'humanely'. Schran and his comrades stayed in the private villas and chateaux in the region which were found to be well stocked with food and there was plenty of wine. There was an order that when the French came back to reclaim their homes, the Germans had to give the villas back and live in the servants' quarters. Schran was in the villa of the managing director of a big sugar factory, Monsieur Lizard, who had fought in World War I and could speak some German as he had studied at Tübingen. Schran had learned some French so the pair could communicate to a certain degree, and in the end they became quite friendly. The director's son had been taken prisoner in Germany so his daughter-in-law did not like these men who occupied her home and her country. However, she slowly warmed to Schran and the others as they gave the children chocolates and sweets and 'we very often gave her extra rations as food was scarce in those days'. Much of the food produced in France at that time was commandeered, either for the occupying troops or to be sent over the border to Germany, causing a ripple effect in French households. Farm production fell due to lack of fuel, fertiliser and workforce while transport was often disrupted so supplies did not reach the shops. Lizard, who had spent holidays in Germany, thought the whole situation was terrible.

During this time the German soldiers always had to be armed. Schran was dispatched between one camp or aerodrome and another, and he was always ordered to take his Luger pistol. He became friendly with Lizard's maid and she invited him to her house to cook for him because he brought meat and had helped her in the past. Her husband at this point was a prisoner of war, and Schran and this woman ended up in bed together. He still had his Luger pistol to hand however. He remembered her eyes when he laid it aside and she asked him what he needed that for. He explained it was a direct order that the pistol had to be kept by his side as there had been cases of German soldiers being shot by the French when they were ambushed. Where Schran went his Luger went with him. No hostility was shown to his face but Schran was sure there was some behind his back.

Later on, when stationed at Cap Gris Nez in the Pas-de-Calais, he became friendly with the son at a nearby farm, and one of their ladies did all his washing, so he had quite an amicable relationship with them. Years later he returned and could still see parts of the bunkers which belonged to the heavy coastal battery once stationed there, at the edge of Wimeroux golf course. Proudly he pointed out to the French golfers 'This was my bunker', much to their bemusement.

———————

Schran was called up on 1 June 1941. All men had to do National Service in the army, air force or navy. He was called to the Kriegsmarine. He did not really want to go into the navy but thought it was better than the army. He did his training in Schleswig-Holstein, and while there he volunteered for the U-boat service but due to his eardrum bursting he could not withstand the air pressure. At Schleswig-Holstein they underwent the ordinary training which everybody had, with guns, square bashing and so on, for six weeks then they were sent to the different batteries. He was recommended to go to an anti-aircraft school at Port Saint Louis in southern France. There they were told how to use light anti-aircraft guns. A corrugated iron plane used to fly with a huge balloon like a large sausage and it was this that the men had to try to hit. They practised their skills on this sausage and knew they had made a hit when a little flash was seen; every hit was recorded. From there he was sent back to Wimeroux and given an anti-aircraft gun.

After four weeks of training the men were let out of barracks. In the Arbeitsdienst they had to wait up to ten weeks for their leave. He was then posted to the anti-aircraft guns. He never became a member of the crews of the heavy guns, however – his job was to help protect the heavy guns from low-flying planes and this he did until 1944 when the Canadians came and over-ran Calais. They would be bombarded by planes for several days, and in the early days 'we used to get low-flying planes that had been involved in dog-fights during 1940 and the Battle of Britain'. Adolf Galland, the German flying ace, and his men used to engage in dog-fights over the Channel. The planes –Messerschmitts, Spitfires or Hurricanes – would come quite low over the battery and once by mistake the Germans fired on a Messerschmitt, one of their own planes. When the aircraft came in very low and fast they were difficult to distinguish as British or German, although the Spitfire was readily recognisable. Schran and his colleagues did however shoot down two Spitfires.

On 11 February 1942, a new part of the Atlantic campaign got underway. An hour or two before Operation Cerberus (also known as the Channel Dash or Channel Breakout) the men were told 'to expect low-flying planes and of course we could hear the gunfire' – then suddenly out of the mist there came planes. The aircraft were slow and were unfortunately sitting ducks. They had no chance and the air force 'must've had heavy losses'. The Swordfishes were over the sea coming into France when they were shot down by the gunners, with Schran and his crew credited with hitting two of them. He saw someone bail out as one of the planes plummeted down. They also had to contend with heavy flak from the battleships in the Channel. They were told the next day that in spite of the heavy bombardment by the British, the German boats had arrived at Kiel without a single loss of life. It was a propaganda feed – in fact over 30 German sailors and airmen were killed between 11 and 13 February, with 22 aircraft destroyed and six boats damaged.

In September 1944, following the Normandy Landings by the Allied forces as they sought to recapture France, the German battery got one full hit straight into the opening of the camp, which was heavily protected by hefty chains. One of the Ermaat's, or sergeants, had been lying on these heavy guns directing the fire and was killed by this direct hit. Schran's battery was at the Pays de Calais. Boulogne had already fallen – the battle for the town had started on the 17th and raged for four days at the Frederick August battery – but Schran was still with the air guns, not the heavy ones. All the crews of the heavy guns were in concrete bunkers but they were outside and expected to fight off enemy fire, so they were far more exposed than the heavy gunners. On several occasions people were sent out on missions to find where the enemy was, in this case the Canadians. On one of these missions the lieutenant was killed and the Obermaat, a sergeant, was badly wounded. They called for medical orderlies to bring him in but without any orderlies whatsoever Schran opened the door, ran out and dragged the injured man in. He believed that he must have been in the field of the Canadians and they could easily have killed him but they did not shoot so he saw this as an act of compassion. Schran never told anyone about this incident until long after the war had ended. A day later Schran was awarded the Iron Cross because of his actions on that day.

Schran's battery eventually capitulated on 23 September. They were completely surrounded by the Canadians. Such was the mood of the soldiers that they all knew it was useless to continue; the officers were actually threatened by the men to surrender or they would revolt and shoot them – so the white flag was raised and their surrender complete. There were tears in the eyes of the old man who raised the white flag. Schran was told he would be shot by his comrades, because he had been using the last gun, but he felt he did his duty to the end. They all knew the war was lost but they had held out hope following the information they had received about secret weapons: the V1 had been developed at the Peenemünde Research Centre and launched via a mobile frame on the French coast targeting England; the V2 likewise began raining down on England in September 1944, hitting London, Norwich and Ipswich and killing over 1400 people. If the commander had not given the order to surrender when he did, Schran was sure there would have been a mutiny.

When captured Schran and his fellow Germans were treated relatively well, but as mentioned Boulogne had just fallen and the Canadians had taken thousands of prisoners of war and did not have shelter for everyone. For ten or more days the new prisoners of war were forced to lie in a field above Boulogne waiting to be shipped to England. By now it was October and the temperatures were dropping. In an effort to keep the cold out and to stave off pneumonia they dug in, lying underneath the earth, although one or two were accidentally killed when the earth collapsed on top of them. Schran did not blame the Canadians, 'as they didn't have transport as the port wasn't open'. They moved on to just above Calais. They were given food once a day and it was just about enough to sustain them. Schran recalled of this time: 'One idiot actually tried to break out and run through the barbed wire and of course the guards started shooting at him, first over the head, but then in the end in the legs', at which point he fell down but he was not killed. Schran felt this was again an act of compassion on the Canadians' part as they shot warning shots over his head first, then instead of aiming for his body shot him in the thigh. Soon after this incident the Canadians handed the prisoners of war over to the British. This was sometime between leaving the camp and boarding the boat but Schran could not remember the precise moment as during this time one event seemed to just melt into the next one.

————

When they came to England, the prisoners were transported to Kempton Park. Although only there for a very short time, they were deloused and given new British military underwear which was 'quite good we all thought and we kept our uniforms'. (When Schran was captured his navy pass was taken away but in a twist of fate when he became a British citizen in 1954 the War Office sent it back to him, meaning he could now claim a pension in Germany as he, having signed on, was classed as a serving German officer.) They were then put not in cattle transports but in proper trains and sent to Comrie. Schran arrived at the camp in late September 1944.

After alighting from the train at Comrie's small railway station, the soldiers, including Schran, marched the two miles to the camp, many singing songs defiantly. The following day he was interviewed by his commander Korvettenkapitän Dickmann who presented him with the Iron Cross and promoted him to Kriegsmarine Maat, saying he had deserved both due to fighting the Canadians until the last gasp. He was also interviewed by the camp's administration and 'asked if Germany could win the war. Being a cocky so-and-so I said of course we could win the war. It was out of spite rather than conviction. That made me straight away somebody to be sent away under heavy guard'. Subsequently he was stripped of his war medals by the guards.

Two compounds were for officers and a third compound held ordinary navy crew and submariners who were classed as C. The Geneva Convention states that no prisoners of war should be classified in this way and the prisoners protested against the practice – so were all classified C. Once again they protested.

The treatment at Comrie was 'actually quite good. The food was quite good. We could leave the camp on word of honour' in groups of about 30 or 40 to go for walks but of course this was only ever allowed to certain inmates. Every man kept his word and no one absconded. That Christmas in 1944 'was rather moving' he recalled, but nothing was said of the death of Feldwebel Wolfgang Rosterg. It was all kept 'hush hush'. As it was Christmas he received a gift of 20 Reichsmarks in tokens from the Swiss government via the International Committee of the Red Cross and a book inscribed by the commandant 'War, Christmas 1944' and signed by him. On Christmas Eve, carols were sung both inside and outside the barracks and he remembered getting a salami sausage, hot tea and Christmas biscuits.

News of the Battle of the Bulge broke in late December. Many still thought Hitler could win but Schran did not and according to him it was doubtful that many of the prisoners held out any real hope of a victory. It was better to keep any thoughts of defeat quiet, however. While the war was ongoing the prisoners absolutely refused to join work parties due to the Geneva Convention regarding the behaviour and treatment of prisoners of war, but after Germany capitulated in May 1945 Schran and many others did volunteer if for no other reason than to pass the time.

One morning whilst attending roll call the German prisoners noticed a swastika flag flying high up on the top of a tree, which one of the guards had to recover, much to the amusement of the prisoners. On another occasion, in the spring of 1945, Schran witnessed an argument between one of the German prisoners and a Polish guard. They called each other unpleasant names and eventually some shots were fired. After this incident the Germans sought for a suitable punishment for the guard – but the camp administration did nothing. The prisoners took it upon themselves to go on hunger strike in protest. Their rations were brought up to the gate and remained there for several days. A few days later things resolved themselves, thanks to their commandant who always did his best to restore law and order. A few days after this they were all asked to leave their compound, which they did, and a British search party entered and turned it upside down looking for what is now known to be an escape tunnel.

Some of the prisoners, once they were deemed trustworthy, were allowed to head into Comrie to the parish church where they would sing in the choir with the rest of the congregation, and others were allowed to work on local farms.

————

Schran's time at Comrie came to an end when he was sent up to Caithness to Camp 165 at Watten, where he spent the very cold winter of 1945/46. There he decided to join the working parties. He helped in the kitchen for the guards and unloaded items at Watten train station. He became friendly with the stationmaster Mr MacKay, with a hole in his eye (they made fun of him simply because it rhymed) who he thought was a 'lovely little chap, but he had two lovely daughters, Millie and Anna'. He received 'little treats' from the girls and did odd jobs for MacKay and found none of them hostile either towards him or to any other prisoner of war – indeed the exact opposite was true.

Following his reclassification after several more interviews, he volunteered to do more and in 1946 he was sent to the military hospital in Tidworth where there was also a prisoner of war camp. From there he applied for a job in the hospital where they needed someone who could speak English – 'my English was passable back then'. At the Tidworth hospital, there were German orderlies and two German doctors who could speak English, and Schran became the general helper. He helped in the kitchen and took care of two dachshunds which belonged to the commanding officer Major Salmon, a woman who was also a Harley Street doctor. Schran recalled 'I was a blue-eyed boy. I liked it'. He stayed there for 14 months, and at the end received a certificate from the matron stating that he could be recommended as a cook, that his behaviour was excellent and that his work was exemplary. He made friends with nurses and medical personnel and with the quartermaster Captain Clark with whom he became quite good friends. However, the prisoners were still subjected to some indoctrination. They were forced to watch films about 'the dreadful things that happened in the concentration camps… and we were shocked by it'. Many people left the cinema with tears running down their cheeks – 'we just couldn't believe anything like that could have happened'. Of course the hard-line right wingers claimed it was propaganda but most of the men soon realised it was not. Schran went on: 'I was ashamed calling myself German after seeing that. We did not know about the camps. Those guarding the camps were sworn to secrecy and not allowed to talk about it on threat of death so kept their mouths shut and I assure we did not know. We knew the Jews were rounded up and sent away but we did not know about this genocide. This was inexcusable, dreadful'. Knowing the difference between dictatorship and living in a democracy was an important lesson to be learned by these young Germans and it had the desired effect on many of them, including Schran.

Schran attended the student association to join classes which were run by German Jews, some of whom he became quite friendly with. There was a man called Schumacher who came from Berlin, and who ran the course, and he found many of them amiable. At Kempton Park they had been taunted by the German Jews who had sought refuge in Britain, and Schran would hear them say such things as 'Here come the chosen people, the Meisterrasse. How do you feel being members of the Meisterrasse?' but there was none of this at Newbury where the classes were run.

Meisterrasse, or Master Race, was a term used by Nazi ideology which was based on the belief that Nordic blood was the purest of all in Europe. They believed that people from southern Europe were not pure as they had associated themselves with the Moors and many North African peoples, and they wanted to see a pure Aryan race of blond-haired and blue-eyed people superseding all other races. They sought what became known as Nordicism. People had to prove their Aryan ancestry through official records and if it was found they were not of pure German descent they would be labelled *Untermensch*. This included Jews, Poles and many Slavic people. The whole concept derived from Count Joseph de Gobeneau in the 19th century who argued that the darker the skin and the greater the mix of race, the more substandard the peoples. A proponent of this theory was Arthur Schopenhauer, who claimed that white people had evolved as a higher civilisation. The idea of Nordic superiority came to prominence in the 1920s with the publication of Hans F. K. Günther's work *Rassenkunde des deutschen Volkes, Racial Science of German People* in 1922, which cemented the idea of a greater Aryan race, a race superior to all others. When Hitler came to power he saw his chance to change German society into a pure-bred Aryan one. By 1935 the Nuremberg Laws had come into effect forbidding marriage and sex between Aryans and non-Aryans. The punishment for such relationships was death of the non-Aryan and concentration camp for the Aryan.

These courses at Newbury usually went on for days, although some attended longer courses and were reclassified and sent back to Germany earlier than Schran.

Schran's last camp was Camp 25 Lodge Farm at Bayden near Lambourn and he has a camp newspaper from here called *Der Fährman, The Ferryman*. Schran remembered waiting in the morning for the milk lorry and helping unload the heavy milk churns in exchange for a lift into Newbury to the prisoner of war club. He played the guitar in the camp band and he was also the compère, introducing acts and telling jokes, as well as singing. The prisoners used to give concerts in Newbury and Kintbury and these were advertised in the local newspaper. In April 1947 the prisoners gave a concert in St Mary's Hall at Speenhamland near Newbury.

According to the local newspaper the 'spirited performance of light music' was thoroughly enjoyed by the townsfolk who attended and danced the night away. The *Newbury Weekly News* of 4 September 1947 records 300 people in attendance at a POW concert at the Coronation Hall in Kintbury, with about 50 people outside listening to it. 'The musicianship of this band is excellent', it states, noting that at the end of the concert Sir Frank Spikernell 'alluded to the difficulties' the camp orchestra had in acquiring instruments. At least one violin had been handcrafted in the camp itself and 'it was not easy to acquire musical scores'. At the Newbury concert, Schran told the audience some amusing short stories in both English and German – sometimes the jokes were lost on the audience so he began saying 'Now ladies and gentlemen, something to laugh at.' At the concert in Kintbury, prisoner of war Heinz Brandt said in his introduction that the last time the audience had not known what to expect but he supposed going by the numbers that night they had enjoyed it and wanted to come to see them again. Ernst Christoffer was both conductor and solo trumpeter, with Rudi Thering at the piano. The other players were Herbert Schick on the accordion, Herbert Geebel and Artur Schmidt on violin, Rudi Kress on saxophone and clarinet, Schran on guitar and acting as the announcer, Ferdinand Krah on percussion and finally Franz Becker, the solo singer. The last song that night was 'Lily Marlene', which was received with rapturous applause.

––––––––

Schran was repatriated to Bochum on 24 March 1948 but was 'pleased to learn I could come back to England' as on 13 March he had married Agnes Elaine Smith, the baker's daughter, and had been forced to leave her behind. He had met his wife at the prisoner of war club which was held in the Methodist church hall in Northbrook Street in Newbury. She had been involved in the delivery of bread and cakes to Camp 25 Lodge Farm thanks to encouragement from local minister Rev. Bill Meadows, who also happened to marry the couple. After seven months apart, in October 1948, Schran returned to England and his wife. On his registration certificate one of the conditions was that he was only permitted to land if he could 'register at once with the police' which of course he did, on 12 October at Newbury. They were to enjoy many years together before she passed away in February 1982 in his arms. They had no children.

Life after the camp was a daily routine of early rises to bake and make the business the success it was. In the early 1950s the Schrans installed an oil-fired oven to replace the old wood one but kept up the tradition of bread rounds, although this ceased the week before the bakery was sold in 1974. When the business was sold, the flat in which the Schrans lived went with it and they found a new home at The Meadows in Long Lane in which to enjoy their semi-retirement.

In 1964, Newbury and Braunfels in the Hesse region of Germany started a twinning association of which Schran was founder and honorary member. In July 2014 it celebrated its 50th anniversary. It had begun with a visit in 1953 of a delegation of German local government officials visiting Newbury to study British local government. Heinz Hermanns, learning about traffic policy, subsequently made return visits, and in 1958 he became the Bürgermeister of Braunfels. In 1961 Newbury was also approached by St Claude in France regarding a possible twinning but at a meeting of the Town Council the German town won out. The following June, Hermanns and a small delegation visited Newbury once more to finalise the details. At the end of August 1963 Newbury hosted the first part of the twinning ceremony and in November the Newbury–Braunfels committee was formed. In May 1964 a small delegation from the town, including Schran and R. J. Huckle, visited Braunfels to cement the twinning. Huckle later went on to become the chairman of the newly formed Newbury Braunfels Association which superseded the committee that November. Three years later, in 1967, Schran became a member of the local Freemason Lodge and in 1990 he received Grand Lodge Honours from HRH Duke of Kent personally at the Masonic Grand Temple in Great Queen's Street in London. In 1976 Schran and his wife went on a round the world trip, and in 1977 he took a part-time post at Silvers Menswear, selling suits, overcoats and other items of men's clothing.

In 1999 Schran was invited by the BBC to participate in a documentary about life in Hitler's Germany of the 1930s. On Wednesday 18 August he was flown to Berlin, where he spent the following day being filmed and having his recollections recorded. Although hard work he enjoyed the visit and 'felt like a celebrity'.

In October 2004, Schran remarried. He had met German Helma Köhler and they were wed at the Newbury Registry Office. Schran passed away peacefully on 15 July 2015, aged 94 years. He had been a British citizen since 1954 and on numerous occasions had publicly declared his abhorrence of war in any form.

5 | DEATH SENTENCE

Prisoner of war camps were generally pretty mundane places. Routines changed little and life trundled along very slowly for the men while they awaited repatriation. Some kept their heads down and accepted their lot. For others, though, the situation was almost intolerable. They could not believe Germany was losing the war – a war they had given up so much for – and they tried to persuade others that the fight was not over. These were the 'black' Nazis. They believed the Reich would survive and intended to do their bit to ensure that outcome. Those who did not feel this way were seen as weak at best, or traitors at worst. And, as far as the 'black' Nazis were concerned, these traitors had to be dealt with.

Feldwebel Wolfgang Rosterg, prisoner of war number A788778, had been transferred to Comrie by bus along with a group of 30 other prisoners from the Le Marchant prisoner of war camp at Devizes in Wiltshire, Camp 23. The Devizes camp was positioned on a road running out of the town towards the Marlborough Downs and was once a prison, but by 1944 held thousands of German prisoners of war. It was mainly used as a reception centre, where the new contingent of prisoners were deloused and washed, had their hair cut and were medically inspected by captured German army doctors. They were then provisionally politically graded. Special intelligence officers kept back those they believed might have useful information for the Allies. Once they had been fed and watered the prisoners were kitted out in a uniform with the classic patch which segregated them from ordinary civilians. They were then dispatched to other prisoner of war camps, at a rate of approximately 2000 a day when there had been a large influx. Most of the men who went through Devizes were classed as 'white' or 'grey' as they settled into their new routine without fuss. Only the 'black' fanatical Nazis were unrepentant. There were also a few who the British felt were rather an odd choice for sending to war. One, known as Little Hans, was a midget with scoliosis, and was endlessly teased and pointed to as a fine specimen of the Master Race. Another was brought to the camp in the back of a truck, after a call had been placed to the camp from the railway station asking for transport for a prisoner. Captain Spreckley, an interpreter at the camp, asked if the prisoner had wounds, in case an ambulance was required. The prisoner did not – but was 78 years old.

Camp 23 was to go down in British history as being the site of the greatest escape plan ever hatched in a British prisoner of war camp. Walter Maier and his assistant Müller, a one-time professional heavyweight boxer, tried to keep the camp calm and friendly. On arrival, new prisoners were informed by them that the food rations were good, and Red Cross parcels came at regular intervals with their contents evenly distributed among the prisoners by the friendly British guards. An older prisoner often recounted that when the Americans had been guarding them they would barter cigarettes and British money for German watches, German money and old postcards. Prisoners who arrived in the latest contingent in the autumn of 1944 were not overly impressed by what they had been told. One of them was Erich Pallme Koenig. One day near Christmas Koenig asked if that was the radio he could hear playing loudly? Wolfgang Rosterg replied that it was the choir practising for the Christmas concert, to which Koenig replied that they should be planning to escape, not singing 'Silent Night'.

After arrival that autumn Koenig had quickly developed a bond with prisoners Josef Mertens and Kurt Zuehlsdorff, who had begun to turn their thoughts to escape. Mertens somehow managed to smuggle a map of England into the camp, and told them it would be possible to escape the camp, make their way to the south coast and steal a boat to cross the English Channel. He recounted a story about how some Germans had stowed away in an American landing craft moored in the Thames – after overpowering the crew they had made it out into the Channel, although they had all then perished when the German guns stationed on the Normandy coast fired on them, believing them to be Americans. This story is partly true. The Germans did stow away, but none were reported missing and the boat remained under its rightful authority. Rosterg, who was listening to the story, then told the group he had only heard of one escape from the camp, and the prisoner had made it as far as Dover by stealing a car and buying petrol from a British soldier. However, he had been recaptured when he tried to start the motor on a boat. He was returned to camp and put in a cell for 28 days. Rosterg was pressed for more details but had none except how angry the British officers were that this German had managed to get several gallons of petrol when they could not get enough to go home for a weekend. It was also during this time together that Rosterg advised them not to go anywhere near the wire if there was a Polish guard. He said the Poles would shoot to kill, claiming they had a habit of dropping half-smoked cigarettes very near the wire and warning the Germans not to go anywhere near these – he said the last man who did that was riddled with bullets. Zuehlsdorff laughed. Zuehlsdorff had seen the fighting in Russia and France; when he was captured the French partisans forced him to dig his own grave, but he was then rescued by American forces and handed over to the British. He told the assembled group that it was their duty to escape, that they must get back to war, kill British soldiers and take London. He called for a meeting in the camp leader's office but turned to Rosterg and told him he was not invited.

One of the prisoners, Rolf Herzig, was allegedly told to take some men out to scout the immediate countryside and to report back on the situation at the local airfields and at the camp's perimeter fence. Herzig and eight friends managed to cut through the wire with hand-made wire cutters and escape. The following morning Captain Spreckley counted the men at roll call and discovered there were nine missing. He kept calm and suggested they were probably part of a working party but as soon as the prisoners were dismissed he hurriedly ordered the guard to surround the camp and find out where they had escaped from. For two days the nine prisoners remained at large, until a few of them were captured by the local police. The others appeared at the main gate later that evening, hungry, dirty and tired. The camp leader was called to formally identify the men and the prisoners told him they had become lost as all the signposts had been taken down. They were interrogated all night, and the information required was passed round the group of would-be escapees.

A few weeks passed. Then one day the group were holding a meeting when they were interrupted by two Americans, Brandstetter and Hoelzl, who had been attached to the camp to learn more about interrogation techniques. Unbeknown to the prisoners, they were also fluent German speakers and they had heard one of the prisoners say that 'the arms store was key'. The Americans never let on but as they crossed the camp they stopped Captain Craig, the camp's chief interpreter, and mentioned to him that surely the store (which was at the Le Marchant Barracks next door to the camp) was out of bounds to prisoners? Craig stared at them. There could be only one reason why the prisoners were interested in it. It dawned on Craig then why the well-trained group of nine prisoners had returned to camp – they had obviously been on a reconnaissance mission. The escapees were questioned again. One, named Schmitt, unintentionally gave the game away when he boasted about the local airfields being captured by freed German prisoners of war. The camp commandant Lt.-Col. John T. Upton thought that it was feasible he was telling the truth. When the Americans had been in charge of the camp they had installed devices to listen into the conversations of the prisoners but the British had removed them. That night Upton re-instated them and soon it was discovered that Schmitt had indeed been telling the truth. By the end of the first week of December, Upton knew the full details of the escape plan – and waited.

Christmas week had been the time chosen for the escape attempt. It was assumed the British and Americans would be distracted, especially as they believed the war was coming to an end, unlike the Germans who had little time for the festive period. The guards would be thin on the ground – many would be on leave. And it looked like the choir might prove useful after all – the prisoners would strike while they were holding their concert.

The Germans had discovered a weak area in the camp's fencing, and had been watching the movement of the trucks coming and going in the camp, keeping a log of what times the trucks arrived and who was involved in the loading and unloading of them. They had also surreptitiously checked locks as they walked round the perimeter.

The plan was as follows. Led by Joachim Goltz, a group of former SS would jump on the guards and seize their weapons before storming the gate. A number of truck drivers would commandeer trucks, break into the arms store and steal the arms. The telephone cable would also be cut, rendering the camp helpless to contact the outside world. Food would be taken from the stores and loaded onto other trucks. Then the breakout would begin in earnest. They intended to drive north from the camp to pick up more escaped prisoners of war from Camp

17 Lodge Moor near Sheffield. With their numbers increased, they would head towards the east coast where they would radio Germany to be picked up. London would fall and Germany would use British aircraft to beat the country into submission.

Upton had no choice but to inform Lt.-Col. Alexander Scotland at the London District Cage of the impending plot. Officers there had already been hearing of German parachutists dressed as Americans assembling on the French coast. Together these pieces of information were enough to result in an officer from the War Office interrupting a meeting being held by Winston Churchill. Churchill could not quite bring himself to believe what he was hearing –but he ordered the cancellation of leave of all prisoner of war guards over Christmas. The British officers were told to do nothing. On 15 December news reached Camp 23 that a German offensive was to take place the next day, which it did, at dawn. Field Marshal von Rundstedt launched an attack against the Americans along a line 60 miles long. The Ardennes Offensive, as it became known, was underway. Back at Devizes, a prisoner met another at the bath hut. Seen by a couple of British paratroopers, they had no time to hide the piece of paper one of them held in his hand. He tried to swallow it but was prevented by the British. They were frogmarched to the Orderly Room where the paper was unfolded. It was a Hitler Order of the Day which read 'Men of the Freedom Movement. The hour of our liberation is approaching', and continued that it was the duty of every German to fight against 'world Jewry'.

Word about these prisoners being caught spread quickly in the camp, but the success of the Ardennes Offensive, announced on the concealed radio, was met with enthusiasm and the escape plan was definitely still on. Mid-morning, the prisoners were told to prepare for a head count. While this was going on, their huts were searched. Although no guns were found, homemade knives were, along with knuckle dusters and a selection of iron bars. Following the discovery of this homemade weapon cache, the adjutant Captain Hurn crossed the road to warn the American hospital to be prepared for injuries as something was about to happen. Late in the afternoon Hurn spoke to Jim Gaiger and told him to order his men to prepare the fire hoses. Gaiger asked why but was told to just do it then get out. Gaiger then heard the noise of vehicles and turned round to see tanks and armoured cars pulling up into position, their turrets and weaponry focused on the camp. The plot had been foiled. Twenty-eight men were identified as being involved in the Devizes plot and were promptly sent to maximum security cells within the London District Cage. During the journey, the prisoners were overheard vowing to find out who had given their plan away. It was widely held that it was Koenig himself who had let slip about the weapon store – the comment which had been overheard by the Americans Brandstetter and Hoelzl – but this was disproven, so the blame seemed to lie with Schmitt (who had been so boastful at the earlier questioning). He owned up. One of the other prisoners was furious and unleashed his fury on the young German. He hit Schmitt so hard he reeled backwards across the room where he was then set upon by Mertens and Joachim Goltz, both of whom were later implicated in the murder of Rosterg. It was only thanks to the intervention of the British who heard his screams that the young German was saved from serious injury. However, the ringleaders still did not believe Schmitt could have given the game away alone.

They questioned Rosterg and he was adamant he had not spoken to the British officers about the escape – but they did not believe him.

Following their interrogation in London a group of the men were sent north by train to Edinburgh and then transported on to maximum security Camp 21 Comrie, then held to be 'ultra Nazi and horrible', according to Herbert Sulzbach. Amongst them was the liberal Rosterg. Could an administrative error have sent him north? Or was the answer a little more secretive – had he been recruited by the British to spy in the camp? Whatever the reason this liberally thinking former Nazi arrived with the others on a cold December day a few days before Christmas.

––––––––

Rosterg was old for a soldier, having been born on 17 December 1909. As a member of the Rosterg family, who were involved in the potash industry, he was well educated: he could speak seven languages including French and Polish, and spoke English as fluently as his native German. The Rostergs had a holiday home next to Hitler's at Berchtesgaden, and the family were also well known to the senior executives of British chemical manufacturers F. W. Berk. Rosterg had spent time as a trainee with Berk's before the war, living in a bedsit in St Pancras. According to Edger Berk he was a real Nazi in those days. During the war he had been a sergeant in the 5th Grenadiers Infantry Division. At Devizes, he had proved unpopular. He had helped Jim Gaiger, the civilian clerk of works who oversaw the prisoners' work, to maintain the camp buildings, not only in administration but also in meting out punishments to prisoners who were deemed to have lied, stolen something or been involved in creating disturbances. On one occasion he spoke to Gaiger claiming that one of the prisoners was a liar and asked him how he wanted the prisoner punished. He was the sort of man who would withstand little nonsense from fellow Germans and none at all from those from Austria, Hungary and other German regions now under the rule of the Third Reich. This caused many prisoners to mistrust him. It was rumoured, however, that he had deserted in France in 1944 to join the British; if 'blacks' had found this out he would undoubtedly have been a person of interest to them. On arrival at Comrie he was given the post of confidential clerk and almost immediately came to the attention of the fanatics. He asked the camp authorities for a copy of the *Lagerpost*, the camp newspaper, but was promptly told it was full of propaganda and the prisoners were forbidden to read it. Defiantly he turned round and told them he *would* read it, and the English newspapers to boot if they were available.

Shortly after this he proclaimed the Ardennes Offensive was a disaster and whoever thought it would work had been foolish. To the other prisoners in his hut, Hut 4, he exclaimed categorically 'The war is lost'. They looked at him full of contempt. Koenig, who was present, said flatly he, Rosterg, clearly did not believe in National Socialism to which Rosterg replied he did not indeed believe in any of 'that nonsense anymore'. He returned his attention to his newspaper.

Later a conversation was held between prisoners Kurt Zuehlsdorff and Rolf Herzig, both formerly of the Waffen-SS, along with another man. Zuehlsdorff, a one-time grocery assistant, had been a Panzer grenadier, and it is known that he boasted when he was captured about how many men he had killed in battle. They were speaking about the *Lagerpost*, and about what

Rosterg had said to Koenig. Zuehlsdorff proceeded to ask Rosterg outright if he was a Nazi and he told him 'No, I certainly am not'. Zuehlsdorff reported to the others that Rosterg had told him he had seen enough of the world not to believe in Nazism. According to Zuehlsdorff in his later testimony, someone had then said 'Well, we will see about that'.

That night the men in Hut 4 went to bed but sleep was fitful. Sometime after midnight, Rosterg was disturbed by a noise at the side of his bunk. He recognised Koenig kneeling nearby, as the searchlight glowed briefly through the small windows.

'What do you want?' he asked.

Koenig stood up and emptied out Rosterg's kitbag onto the floor. He picked up a diary and some other papers and told Rosterg 'I want these'.

Furiously Rosterg leapt out of bed but he was held back almost immediately by the hands of unseen prisoners. It was to be his final night alive.

————

On the morning of 23 December Oberführer Hans Klein, a Wehrmacht warrant officer who had fought at the Russian front, entered their hut sometime between 6 a.m. and 7 a.m. and ordered Zuehlsdorff and Herzig to go to Hut 4. He had a piece of paper in his hand and had called the names out. The men duly obliged and a witness in the case that was to follow later, Fritz Heubner, followed them to see what was going on. Rumours were already going round that someone was being beaten up. It transpired that the man they were going to see was Wolfgang Rosterg. He had been taken from his hut by a small group of prisoners and questioned about his political beliefs. He stood in front of the stove surrounded by men. Klein said to Zuehlsdorff and Herzig 'Is that the swine who arrived with you yesterday?' and each of them replied yes. Rosterg's face by this time was badly swollen, so much so he was barely recognisable. Blood was coming out of his left eye and his lips were badly swollen. He had a rope round his neck, a noose with the knot at the back and the rest of it wound round his neck, bar four inches or so. Koenig was holding the rope about four inches behind Rosterg's neck and told him 'Every time you scream swine I'll tighten the rope'. Rosterg could only groan for the rope was already too tight around his neck. Another prisoner called Bienek stood in front of Rosterg and read from a piece of paper. He claimed it had been found either on Rosterg or in his kit. Bienek claimed Rosterg had given away bombing targets and had been responsible for the rounding up of German ATS women by the French. During this time a yellow file was being handed round the rest of the prisoners. The name Herbart Wunderlich, a former member of the Luftwaffe, was recorded and there seemed to be lists of other prisoners of war who had been at Devizes. Many in the crowd were saying these were lists of Nazis that were to be given to the British authorities and that they had been made by Rosterg. But Rosterg had been a clerk and interpreter and wore a band with the words 'Compound Sergeant' at Devizes and these lists were of men for such things as delousing squads, nothing more. It was one of the ringleaders who claimed they were lists of Nazis for the British. After Wunderlich saw his name, he marched up to Rosterg and started hitting him in the chest and face repeatedly until he was finally held back by others in the crowd.

After each of the statements was read out, Rosterg was supposed to answer but he could only groan. A crowd of around 100 men watched, among them prisoners Steffan, Recksiek and Goltz. Recksiek picked up the iron poker from the stove and hit Rosterg on the right cheek and temple. He did this each time Rosterg was supposed to answer but could not. Goltz hit him with a square iron bar which was lying in front of the stove and had been used as a poker. Steffan then said he was going to report this to the camp leader Staff Sergeant Pirau. He went off to fetch him and returned within ten minutes. Steffan pushed his way through with Pirau beside him and called for the men to stop hitting Rosterg, then announced they were going to take him to the compound office. Koenig removed the rope from Rosterg's neck and thereafter held it in his hand. Pirau, Steffan and Rosterg left the hut along with Koenig and Goltz.

A crowd of about 20 men who had witnessed the beating followed but waited outside the office. Walter Bretschneider and Rudolf Vollstaedt were clerks in the compound office and had slept in it the night of 22/23 December. In his statement during the later trial Vollstaedt said he rose just before 8 o'clock because he was the room orderly that day but Bretschneider stayed in bed. Rosterg was brought into the office around 8 a.m., accompanied by Pirau and the others. Bretschneider and the interpreter Hellfritsch – who had also slept in the office – left immediately but Vollstaedt continued dressing and making his bed. He never left the office. Rosterg was being questioned. Koenig grabbed him by the shirt and yelled at him to stand to attention but he was barely conscious. Bienek read out some of the documentation he had in his hand; Koenig hit Rosterg in the face with his fist for not standing to attention properly again. The document was to do with the betrayal of the German ATS women, but also alleg-edly included the location of petrol dumps and factories. Koenig said he was a traitor and had many German lives on his conscience to which Rosterg said 'No, I have not done it'. This was followed by several blows to the face. Koenig then said to him 'If you have any honour at all, you will go and hang yourself'. Rosterg replied 'No, I cannot do it'. Five or so minutes later, Koenig came out and announced that Rosterg had signed a confession. He ended by telling the crowd 'You will have him soon'.

Twenty-five minutes later Rosterg appeared, with the rope around his neck once more. Koenig pushed him out and announced 'Well, here you are. Here is the swine. He is going to hang himself and if he doesn't you bloody well know what you have to do'. He looked at Gefreiter Hermann Bultmann and said 'I want to see that this tall fellow here [Bultmann] is a proper national socialist and takes part' in the hanging. Rosterg began to squeal like a pig. Goltz fell onto him and pushed him to the ground. By this time the crowd had started to hit him. Goltz knelt on him and pulled the rope but Rosterg continued squealing. Only after a few minutes did it stop. Zuehlsdorff and Herzig kicked and stamped on Rosterg repeatedly. Josef Mertens of the Kriegsmarine then joined in, kicking him and pushing him with his feet. All this time Goltz held onto the rope. Shouts of 'Hang him, hang him up' rang out from the crowd so Goltz, Herzig and Zuehlsdorff took hold of the rope and dragged him along the ground for 45 yards until they reached the latrines. Hundreds of prisoners now knew what was happening and had formed a crowd through which Rosterg was dragged. Goltz and Zuehlsdorff dragged the body through the narrow entrance to the lavatory, for it was only wide enough for two

Inside a Nissen hut at Camp 21

The Officers' mess at Camp 21

Street view of Camp 21

Rear view of huts at Camp 21

This is the most significant painting done by the soldiers as it lists their deployments to various regions of the world including Aden, Hong Kong, Belize, Northern Ireland, Germany and Bosnia.

Above: The camp could be a dreary, cold place but was brightened by the idea of paradise. The irony was not lost on those who came after this was done.

Left: Soldiers and cadets alike kept a good sense of humour as this depiction shows.

Another painting showing perhaps a rather domineering senior officer bellowing at the young cadet.

Above Although this shows a single cell which could house multiple occupants, there is evidence that originally these were divided to create much smaller individual cells.

Left: Lt. Col. Rupert L.T. Murray served as commandant of Camp 165 Watten where many prisoners from Camp 21 were later sent. (Courtesy of the BlackWatch Museum, Perth)

A neat row of huts with electricity running to them.

Watten – City" 1985
Da hat sich in 40 Jahren
nichts geändert.
Herzl Grüsse von dort
Helmut

Top: A card sent to Weitzel of Watten in Caithness where he spent time as a prisoner of war. The card states the village has not changed much.

Above: Rolf Weitzel, former prisoner of Camp 21 Comrie, went on to work in the WHO library in Geneva following his release.

Left: Schran married Helma Koller, his second wife, at Newbury Registry Office in October 2004.

people at a time. As many prisoners as possible squeezed in to witness the incident. Goltz and Zuehlsdorff took the rope and put it over the pipe in the ceiling, while Mertens pulled on the end. It seemed to be too heavy for Mertens and he said 'Hold him up'. Herzig and Zuehlsdorff did so while Goltz and Zuehlsdorff made a knot round the pipe. As soon as the knot was tight they all ran away. Rosterg hung with his toes about six inches from the ground, unconscious. By this stage it was nearly time for the 8.30 roll call. Many of the men returned to their huts and when Bultmann entered his, Goltz boasted that he would have to go to the wash house 'because I stamped my boot on Rosterg and my boot is full of blood'. Bultmann later testified that the toe cap and the boot up to the laces was indeed filled up with blood.

––––––––––

When he was discovered at 9 a.m. the camp doctor tried to resuscitate him but his efforts were in vain. The post mortem revealed that the most likely cause of death was strangulation. An investigation began immediately. Colonel Wilson stated that as soon as concrete evidence against a suspect was found, he was to be arrested and marched in broad daylight in front of the rest of the prisoners to the detention block. Wilson had help in the investigation in the form of Herbert Sulzbach. Sulzbach arrived at the camp in January 1945 with his wife, sister and niece in tow; they went to live in the village nearby. He got to work straight away and began interpreting the information gathered in the Rosterg case. With him came Staff Sergeant John Wheatley, who had been seconded by the Judge Advocate General's department. The investigation was not straightforward as there was uncertainty over whether it was to be dealt with by the civil authorities or the military ones: initially the civil authorities took it on but only one witness came forward to claim it was murder and not suicide, which was not enough in Scots law for a conviction, so it was passed back to the army. The information was gathered and sent down to London.

In April 1945, Zuehlsdorff, Mertens, Goltz, Wunderlich, Brüling and Steffan were interviewed by a captain in the Intelligence Corps, and written statements were produced for the men to read over and sign.

Eight men eventually stood trial in July 1945 at the London District Cage in Kensington, London. The court was convened by Lieutenant General Sir Henry Charles Loyd with Colonel R. H. A. Kellie presiding over the bench. Also present was Judge Advocate Carl L. Stirling who advised the court on points of law. The prosecution Judge Advocate was Major Richard A. L. Hillard with Major R. Evans representing Herzig, Mertens, Goltz and Brüling. The Barrister at Law representing Zuehlsdorff, Wunderlich, Koenig and Klein was Captain Roger Willis. The charge against them was murder and all eight pleaded not guilty.

Lt.-Col. Scotland of the London District Cage had seen the men and pointed out that no German counsel could possibly defend them properly unless they could speak fluent English and had a good grasp of English law, and it was at this point Willis and Evans were appointed to act together for them. Willis had problems from the start with his clients. They moaned that they should not be facing trial for killing a traitor. Willis explained to Koenig and Zuehlsdorff that murder was seen as a civil crime and as such was a crime against civil law, even though it was a military court. Koenig complained that at a prisoner of war camp at Breslau RAF offic-ers had hanged one of their own who gave away an escape plan and not been punished and questioned why they could get away with it but the Germans could not. Willis mentioned this lynching to the authorities but following an inquiry the Air Ministry could find no evidence to support the allegation.

The prisoners arrived at court clean and well dressed, in new uniforms, and Klein even wore his Iron Cross First Class. They were escorted to and from court by Grenadier Guard sergeants.

During the trial Soldat Charles Lergenmueller came forward to testify that during a visit to Heinz Brüling in Hut 2, Brüling had admitted he had taken part in the death of Rosterg, claiming that Rosterg had betrayed an escape attempt when they had both been at Devizes and 'That's why we killed him'. He then said that he was present and took part in the killing. He already 'knew Rosterg and that Rosterg had come with him from another camp'. Klein was the only one of the accused to ask him any questions, and asked 'Are you a soldier of the German Army or of the Waffen-SS?' to which Lergenmueller replied he was from the Waffen-SS.

Another witness came forward. Gefreiter Wilhelm Schmidt had stayed in Hut 1, the same hut as Zuehlsdorff and Herzig, and had witnessed the two men leaving earlier. In the dining hall at breakfast between 7 a.m. and 7.15 a.m. he was struck by Zuehlsdorff's absence, as he was always there at that time. He heard screaming and went to see what was going on, but then left to go and finish his breakfast on his way back to his hut. He then went towards the camp office, from where he could hear shouts of 'Traitor'. He went to investigate, and on opening the door into the room saw a man standing there who he later realised was Rosterg. He told the court there was blood all over his face. He closed the door quickly and went outside. Later he testified that Mertens had called on him to help in the lavatory with the rope but he refused, a statement backed up by fellow prisoner Klaus Merfeld who witnessed the refusal. He also said he did not go for help as anyone who interfered knew they would suffer the same fate or be clubbed to death by former members of the Afrika Korps in Hut 6. Although there was a mailbox between two huts where a note could have been deposited, it was watched constantly by prisoners so it would have been difficult to safely come forward and tell the authorities.

Other witnesses included Matrose Obergefreiter (Leading Seaman) Fritz Heubner. He testified that during a conversation in Hut 1 the night before Rosterg was killed Zuehlsdorff had said he had asked Rosterg at some point if he was a national socialist, to which he said Rosterg had replied 'No I certainly am not', because he had seen too much of the world to believe in it. Heubner then went on to testify that out of curiosity the following morning he had followed Zuehlsdorff and Herzig to Hut 4 where they had been summoned by Klein when he came over to the hut with a note. When Heubner saw Rosterg his face was badly swollen and Koenig had a rope wrapped around Rosterg's neck. Heubner witnessed the whole incident, in fact, from the use of the poker on Rosterg's head to the beating, kicking and finally the lynching. Zuehlsdorff cross-examined him. He asked 'Can you say definitely that the name Rosterg was mentioned by me or Herzig?' to which Heubner said yes and that he 'knew he was a Feldwebel and slept in Hut 4'. Herzig too cross-examined him, asking what he was wearing that fateful morning. Heubner described his clothing as 'an American pair of fatigue trousers with the letters P. W. on the seat on the hole'. Mertens decided not to cross-examine him but Goltz did, asking 'Could it not be a figment of your imagination that in Hut 4 I hit Rosterg with an iron bar and followed him to the compound office?' Heubner was adamant. 'I am not mistaken', he replied. 'I do not know why I should say something about someone whom I have never seen before unless I saw it happen'. Goltz continued: 'If I bring witnesses that I have not hit him, would you still be certain?' Heubner replied clearly, 'My statement remains, it is the whole truth'. Wunderlich declined to ask him questions, Brüling only asked him if he was sure he was present at the latrine to which he replied 'I am not sure', but Koenig had plenty of questions when he cross-examined him.

Koenig began by asking if he was sure he was in the barracks on the morning of the 23rd to which Heubner replied that he was absolutely certain, 'and', he continued, 'I know you were present when the trial in Hut 4 was interrupted and you took Rosterg to the wash house and he was screaming and the blood was washed off his face and then he was brought back to Hut 4 and the trial continued'. Next Koenig asked 'Can you remember definitely that I held the rope in my hand when Rosterg was taken from the hut to the compound office?' to which Heubner said 'My memory is quite clear'. Next he was cross-examined by Bienek, who asked about the lighting in case Heubner had been mistaken. Again he was adamant. There had been several lights on in the hut and it was light enough outside 'to recognise anybody and anyhow, I knew you because you used to visit my hut'. Bienek then asked 'Why, as you were present during the whole of this affair, did you not fetch any help?' Heubner replied 'Because the whole hut was surrounded by people, some of whom had knives and who were watching for anybody who might go and get help'. Klein was one of the last of the defendants to ask him questions. He asked if Heubner had watched Rosterg 'all the time from the moment you entered the hut till he was hung, except when he was in the compound office?' to which he replied that he had 'only lost sight of him when they took him to the wash room'. The last question came from Jelinsky, also accused of participating in the murder: 'How is it you know me as I only arrived the evening before?' to which Heubner replied 'Because I saw you that morning'.

The next witness called was Gefreiter Hermann Bultmann who had arrived in the same draft as Rosterg so knew him. The last time he had spoken to Rosterg was at 9 p.m. that evening. The following morning a naval prisoner of war called Walproel came into Bultmann's hut, which was Hut 2, and told him and the others who had come up from Devizes 'to get dressed straight away and to come with him…. About seven men left…Wunderlich and Goltz were two of them', and they all went to Hut 4. He stated Rosterg was standing by his bed, his face and lips badly swollen, and with blood coming from his left ear. He saw the rope around Rosterg's neck. It seemed to him that Recksiek was in charge. Bultmann himself was accused of being a traitor so pushed forward and asked Steffan what exactly he was accused of. Steffan had asked if he had been a member of the Hitler Youth to which he said yes but he lied. Bultmann had noted from a yellow file being passed around that Wunderlich's name was on it and 'there were other lists of names of P.W. who had been at Devizes. Lots of the men in the crowd were saying that these lists were lists of Nazis to be given to the British authorities'. But he already knew Rosterg was an interpreter and clerk at Devizes and wore an armband with the words 'Compound Sergeant' on it, which meant these lists were nothing more than lists of men for such things as delousing.

Bultmann, like Heubner, went on to describe the torture inflicted on Rosterg. Zuehlsdorff, Herzig, Mertens, Steffan, Jelinsky and Wunderlich chose not to cross-examine his testament. Goltz was the first to do so, asking if Bultmann had taken part in pulling the rope when Rosterg was hung up in the lavatory – he replied he had been outside at the time. Brüling was next to question him. He asked if he had helped to pull the rope and help Brüling drag Rosterg to the toilet, to which Bultmann replied 'I did not pull the rope. I remember you took me by the collar and pushed me towards the lavatory'. Koenig was next and asked if he could remember someone calling out that Rosterg had had enough and that he should be handed over to the British. He replied 'I don't know who it was'. Bienek was next and asked how Bultmann knew where Rosterg slept and he explained he had been with him the night before, talking to him. He, Bienek, said that he had been calling Rosterg names when he was in the compound office. The last to cross-examine him was Klein, who asked about Bultmann's talk with Rosterg the evening before. Bultmann had received word he was about leave Camp 21 and wanted to spend time with Rosterg before he went. Klein then asked 'Do you remember that in Hut 4 on the morning of the 23rd you and I were standing between two bunks and that I told you that Rosterg had betrayed you and that he was a traitor and that you were a traitor?' Bultmann replied 'I now remember that somebody, and as you are taxing me with it I think it was probably you, accused me of being a traitor and asked Rosterg if I was a member of his clique and he said no'. Klein then asked Bultmann 'Are you sure you have not mixed up me and Steffan?' to which came the reply 'No, I don't think so'.

Throughout the trial, none of the accused called witnesses. All of them gave sworn evidence themselves, cross-examining the witnesses, except for Brüling who had made a sworn statement. Also giving evidence was the medical officer who had examined Rosterg's body at the post mortem. He told the judges that Rosterg was already dead when he was hanged. He reported that his head and face were covered in blood, and grit was embedded in his face and on his nose, consistent with being dragged along rough ground face downwards. In his opinion his death was caused by sudden strangulation but he was alive when he was being dragged along the ground. The trial was reported on worldwide, such was the interest in it; however, the court assured all witnesses that their names would not be made public and the newspapers abided by this.

Two were found not guilty of participating in the murder. These were Obergefreiter Herbart Wunderlich of the Luftwaffe and Oberfeldwebel Klein of the Wehrmacht. The six others were found guilty and sentenced to death, although one, Unteroffizier Rolf Herzig of the Wehrmacht, had his sentence commuted to life imprisonment. The other five were Zuehlsdorff aged 20, formerly of the Waffen-SS, Brüling aged 22, also Waffen-SS, Pallme Koenig aged 21, also Waffen-SS, Goltz aged 20, formerly of the Waffen-SS, and Mertens aged 21, of the Kriegsmarine. Only Mertens showed any remorse for the crime.

In the closing stages of the trial, Hillard refused to accept the Germans' plea that they were right to kill the traitor among them. He said it was immaterial what the motive was and that they had had no right to kill Rosterg simply because he was not a Nazi or if he was indeed a traitor. He said of the accused they had all been complicit in the murder, whether they had been part of the group who had inflicted the violence or had been intending to participate. They were quite simply guilty of murder. During this phase of the trial Koenig, Zuehlsdorff, Mertens, Goltz and Brüling could be seen making little jokes, nudging each other, yawning and doodling as if bored with it.

The condemned men were returned to Pentonville Prison in London. In the few days before their execution, a wing of the prison was temporarily taken over by the military authorities – it is thought the execution chamber was in that wing. All condemned military prisoners were taken there until the end of that year when it returned to its civilian purpose. The men were hanged on 6 October 1945 at Pentonville by Albert Pierrepoint, one in a line of Pierrepoints who carried out executions for the authorities, and buried within its grounds. Three were hanged together, followed within two hours by the double hanging of the next two. Rosterg was initially laid to rest in a grave at Wellshill Cemetery in Perth before being exhumed and re-buried at Cannock Chase, the German military cemetery in Staffordshire, along with another man who had died in mysterious circumstances at Comrie, Oberleutnant Willy Thormann. Thormann had died on 29 November shortly before his 40th birthday and only three weeks before Rosterg was killed. He had fought with the II Battalion 9th Company Fortress Staff Troops, and had last been seen at 10.30 that morning. He was found dead 45 minutes later in the latrines at the camp. According to his death certificate 'Hanging not certified' was written in the 'cause of death' column – although at the time it was thought it was suicide, this could not be fully ascertained. The death was registered by the camp adjutant Croft. Coincidentally Rosterg's death certificate also states as the cause of death 'Hanging not certified' and was again registered by Croft.

The murder of Rosterg was by no means a unique case in the history of war camps. Another incident occurred at Camp 17 Lodge Moor near Sheffield. Once again an escape plan had been hatched, but had been thwarted following the discovery of a tunnel. After the discovery things quietened down for a time but by March a new tunnel was underway. On the morning of 24 March 1945 inspection took place in the hut where the new tunnel started. Thirty-one-year-old Feldwebel Emil Schmittendorf had been relaxing when camp guards entered. Schmittendorf knew by the look on their faces that they knew what was there. They found a false floorboard and asked if he knew anything about it, which of course he denied. At lunchtime he declared that the traitor who had given them away would be found that day, and no one would ever betray them again. Armin Kuehne, an 18-year-old ardent Nazi, told Schmittendorf he knew who it could be and he would deal with it. Most anti-Nazis kept their views to themselves out of fear, but two of the prisoners failed to grasp the danger of speaking out. One of these was Gerhardt Rettig. A few days before a discussion had taken place on when the war would end, and during the conversation he stated he was tired of being held in captivity when the war was lost anyway. Rettig's unnamed friend had stepped in and agreed with Rettig, to which Schmittendorf shouted they would regret saying that.

On the afternoon of the day the tunnel was discovered Retting and his friend were warned by another that meetings had been going on all afternoon to find out who had betrayed the plan and that they were being blamed for revealing the information to the British. Quickly they made their way to the gate and handed over a letter to the guard, requesting they be moved as a matter of urgency as their lives were in danger. The note was handed over to the commandant and later they were ordered to pack their kitbags and wait to be escorted out of the compound. At 5.30 p.m. roll call took place but Rettig and his friend hung back from the rest of the prisoners. Once roll call was over they returned to the hut, but the atmosphere inside was too much for Rettig and he decided to get some air. When he went out he saw the rest of the prisoners standing around in little groups but thought nothing of it as they always gathered like this. From one of these groups Kuehne called 'That's the criminal', and Rettig knew at once that for his safety he would have to get to the gate. But that route was now cut off by other prisoners. He had nowhere to go. He decided his best option was his hut, but just as he reached it Kuehne struck him. He could no longer find safety, as those inside wanted to do him as much damage as those outside. Punches rained down on him, and as blood poured from his face he tried to protect his head with his arm. He sank under the weight of his attackers. Eventually they retreated. Rettig sat cowed in the corner, still covering his face. Schmittendorf pulled at his arm, tugging it away from his bloodied face, and stamped on it. Rettig fell to the floor, semi-conscious, but Schmittendorf was not finished yet. He asked for a bucket of water and threw it over Rettig. Rettig suddenly regained consciousness and like a racing dog out of a trap, instinct took over and he ran for all he was worth. The blood was pouring into his eyes and he could not see where he was going. He ran towards the kitchen but found more prisoners standing in his way, so he tried to get to the wash house. Meanwhile other prisoners were encouraging those participating in the hunt, shouting that they should beat him to death or hang him. He was surrounded again and boots and fists showered blows on him. Eventually he stopped moving and someone called for him to be strung up. Schmittendorf had other ideas though. He called for another prisoner and the two men grabbed Rettig's legs and hauled him over to the bins, where they left him.

By this time the commotion had attracted the attention of the British and they were on their way to see what was going on. As soon as word came they were coming, the camp suddenly became quiet and the thirst for blood disappeared. The British found Rettig after following the trail of blood. The medical orderly was horrified at what he saw, and astonished that he was able to find a pulse. He called for a stretcher and as they made their way through the crowd of prisoners, one of the guards threatened to shoot if any of them got in the way. They could see by his expression he meant business so melted back into their huts. The German doctor who examined Rettig later testified that he was unrecognisable. His head and face were badly swollen and his lip was torn. Two days later Rettig died of his internal injuries. He was 25 years old.

That same day Schmittendorf and another prisoner Unteroffizier Heinz Ditzler escaped from Lodge Moor only to be recaptured soon afterwards. In August Schmittendorf, Kuehne,

Ditzler and Soldat Jurgen Kersting all stood accused of Rettig's murder at the London District Cage. Schmittendorf and Kuehne had bragged in the hours following the beating but now they denied being part of it. One of the men at the trial was Hillard, who had been involved in the Rosterg case, and he knew such brutality was meted out by Germans on fellow prisoners of war but all the prisoners denied they were Nazis. Kuehne wore a Red Cross armband at his trial and vehemently denied having taken part, also claiming he was no Nazi. He stated he had simply been carried along by the crowd. Schmittendorf denied ever hitting Rettig although he did admit to hitting another man. He had also written a letter, which appeared in evidence, that told the recipient to say he had been present in the hut when Rettig was attacked. There was no strong evidence against Ditzler or Kersting so they were both acquitted. Schmittendorf and Kuehne were found guilty of murder and hanged by Albert Pierrepoint at Pentonville Prison on 16 November 1945. In all 14 prisoners of war gave evidence during the trial, their names kept secret from the press.

———

There are cases of note from across the Atlantic as well. The first concerns the death of Werner Drechsler, a former submariner. Drechsler came from Chemnitz in eastern Germany and volunteered for the U-boat service in 1941 where he was assigned to U-118, a brand new submarine which was to be a supply and mine laying vessel, captained by Korvettenkapitän Werner Czygan. On its fourth outing in June 1943 while mine laying near the Azores, the U-boat came under attack from two war planes. Czygan gave the order to dive to try and escape, but less than 40 metres down the U-boat was hit by depth charges. The order was given to resurface. The men opened the hatch ready to man the guns only to realise there were now nine planes honing in on them. None of the submariners made it to the guns. Drechsler had until this point stayed below but as he watched his shipmates burn, he scrambled to the deck where he was hit by a fragment of the U-boat as it split in two following another hit by a depth charge. He was then hit by enemy fire in his right knee. At this point, bleeding from wounds himself, Czygan gave the order to abandon ship. Drechsler jumped into the water. The planes dropped a life raft for the struggling survivors. Of the 58 men, 17 survived and they were picked up around an hour after the U-boat disappeared under the waves by the USS *Osmond Ingram*, where the injured were cared for. The ship took the new prisoners of war back to Norfolk in Virginia where the wounded were taken to the naval hospital. The others were sent on to Fort Meade in Maryland for the first of many interrogations, then on to Stringtown in Oklahoma where most of the U-boat prisoners were being sent at that time.

Yet Drechsler was not to follow the usual pattern. The US navy had informed the army that he seemed to be anti-Nazi, just as Rosterg had been. He had been a very cooperative prisoner and was therefore a valuable commodity as new prisoners arrived at Fort Meade and began to pass through the system. He learned English during this time and spoke freely with the new arrivals, yet it seems he could not manage to gain their trust, regardless of how friendly he was towards them. On 3 February 1944, for reasons unknown, he was transferred to Fort Leonard Wood in Missouri.

Meanwhile, news filtered through to Stringtown about an interrogator at Fort Meade who, although using a different name, soon came to be recognised by other submariners as Drechsler, as everyone else had been accounted for except him and one other from U-118. They concluded he knew too much about U-118 for it to be anyone other than him, and claimed that the interrogations had been bugged. It was unanimously agreed that the traitor at Fort Meade was Drechsler – but they knew they could do nothing about it. In January 1944, this group of men, including Helmut Fischer, Fritz Franke, Guenther Kuelsen, Bernhard Reyak and Rolf Wizuy from U-615 and Heinrich Ludwig from U-199, along with the prisoners from U-118, were transported to Papago Park just outside Phoenix, Arizona.

On Sunday 12 March 1944, 21-year-old Werner Drechsler boarded a train to the one place the US authorities had deliberately stated he should never be sent: a prisoner of war camp holding naval personnel such as submariners. Whether this was an administrative error or a deliberate decision by the US army is unknown but it was to precisely that environment he was sent. This situation has parallels to the Rosterg case and him being sent to Comrie due to a possible administrative error.

The day at Papago began as usual. Then Captain Lelland Hebblewaithe received orders to mass some troops and head to Tempe train station to pick up a new contingent of 350 prisoners from the midday train. He was to classify and identify them at the station, assign them to barracks and settle them in. The train arrived late and as the men disembarked he noted one with a limp and a few others who appeared to have problems. When he asked what was wrong with them it was Drechsler who answered in English that there was nothing serious and that his limp was not an issue. On the way to the camp, taking his place with two others in the back of the ambulance, Drechsler was told he was assigned to Compound 4. On arrival he watched as the other prisoners from the back of the trucks disembarked then the three of them from the ambulance joined them, taking in their new place of residence. He found his bed in the barracks and tried to keep himself to himself, but it was virtually impossible as other prisoners kept asking questions. He soon realised that this compound at least was made up mainly of German naval personnel, including those who had been on his own U-boat 118.

By just after 5 p.m. the news had spread that among the new prisoners was the traitor from Fort Meade. Kuelsen heard the news from a fellow prisoner, who claimed the man had been recognised as the interrogator. Quickly he tried to find his friend Rolf Wizuy, who would recognise him, but he was nowhere to be found as he was still on duty elsewhere. He began to mingle with the new prisoners instead. As fate would have it he began speaking to Drechsler. By the end of the conversation Drechsler had confided that he should not be in the compound but at the hospital.

In just an hour and a half following his arrival 'the traitor' was known to not just Kuelsen but also to Ludwig and to Otto Stengel, a good friend of Wizuy's. Stengel, a self-styled reporter in the compound, sought Drechsler out and began interviewing him. The questions were much the same as Kuelsen's. Stengel knew a prisoner by the name Heinz Richter, who also came from Chemnitz, and asked if Drechsler would like to go and see him – Drechsler said he already knew him and declined politely but Stengel went looking for Richter and told him his friend had arrived. Another prisoner overheard the conversation and stated Drechsler would be dead before the night was out. Richter, perhaps to protect himself, told Stengel he did not wish to see him now and never wanted to.

Meanwhile Kuelsen had found Fischer, along with Fritz Franke and Bernhard Reyak amongst others, and told him the news. Reyak had the advantage over the others that he had met Drechsler briefly, although said he would not be able to identify him. Wizuy could identify him from interrogation but they knew the best man for the job was Heinrich Ludwig.

Ludwig was still busy washing dishes when Obermaat Werner Reinl entered the mess hall of Compound 4. He told Ludwig about Drechsler but Ludwig already knew he was there. Ludwig told Reinl that Wizuy had spent a fair amount of time with him in Washington but that he too would be able to identify him. As Reinl wrote down a list of names of men who may have had contact in Washington, Ludwig stopped and asked if he was planning to do something to Drechsler. Reinl replied that there would be a meeting and nothing was planned, yet.

At around 6.30 p.m. Fischer, Franke, Kuelsen, Wizuy and Reyak made their way to Drechsler in his barracks. Wizuy spoke to him and he and the other men interviewed him. Drechsler denied knowing Wizuy, or anything else for that matter. When they left, Wizuy confirmed this was indeed the man from Washington. They had found the traitor. On their way back to their bunks, they discussed what should happen. There was a phrase used, 'holy ghost', which was the prisoners' code for a severe beating and this would lead to all the other prisoners giving Drechsler a wide berth, but others thought death would be more appropriate. It was the latter that would eventually be carried out.

At 9 p.m. the group met. Fischer had offered to get a rope with which to hang Drechsler in the shower room and he appeared with the noose already tied and ready for the hanging. Wizuy told him it would not be strong enough so the noose was re-tied accordingly. Gloves were distributed but there was a problem. Groups of men were talking. Otto Stengel, still hungry for news, was on the prowl too. He moved from group to group for news about Drechsler until he reached the six men. He asked them outright what they were going to do to him and brazenly they replied 'Kill him'. He probed them further, asking how they would get him out of the barracks – then he offered his services to help them. The group split into two and they entered the barracks from both sides. No other prisoner in that barracks moved from their bed. A confession of sorts spewed from Drechsler. He had been in Washington but had been forced to help the Americans. He pleaded with them to wait until the morning when he would explain everything, but suddenly he was being dragged from the bed by his legs. He desperately fought back, and managed to free himself long enough to make it to the middle of the room, only to be grabbed by the neck from which he found there was no escape. He was kicked in the legs and one kick saw him tumble to the floor where numerous arms, hands and feet began kicking and punching him. With a blow to his nose he fell into unconsciousness and the seven men began to carry him out of the barracks. Drechsler regained consciousness and began flailing about wildly, screaming at the top of his voice. An American army jeep stopped, its spotlight scanning the area, but it did not linger long enough on Drechsler. His assailants scattered with considerable speed into the darkness. Drechsler returned to his hut.

Outside the seven men debated what to do next. Wizuy believed the beating was enough and that it was too dangerous for them to complete their mission. Reyak agreed but Stengel said that Drechsler could well be removed from the camp that night and identify them to the Americans. This changed everyone's mind, except Reyak's. He no longer had the stomach for it. But Stengel persuaded him to see it through. They re-entered the barracks and again Drechsler pleaded for them to wait until tomorrow so he could explain, but they were having none of it. The kicking and punching began again, and again he fought back. Fischer tried to place a handkerchief in Drechsler's mouth to muffle the screaming, but he spat it out. Fischer tried again but this time Drechsler bit down on Fischer's thumb. Fischer yelled in agony but Drechsler kept his teeth firmly clamped until finally Stengel grabbed Drechsler by the neck and forced his fingers into his neck until he released the thumb. Drechsler desperately tried to get up but he was stopped in his tracks by an almighty kick in the groin, which it later transpired had all but crushed one of his testicles. He screamed in pain then lost consciousness. Franke took the opportunity to slip the rope round his neck, using it as a lead and tightening it as he moved Drechsler. Reyak opened the door and the others lifted the limp man and carried him outside. They made their way to the shower room with Franke every so often loosening the rope around his neck to allow Drechsler to suck in air only to tighten it again when he began screaming for help. While Drechsler was in an unconscious state, they lifted him up to the noose that had already been prepared for him in the shower room. Two of them jumped onto the bench while the other four passed him up. Reyak had hung back, speaking to one of the crowd that had gathered. He then heard the bench being knocked over. When he entered he saw Drechsler's limp body swinging gently. His feet were less than 12 inches off the floor.

At 6.30 a.m. the following morning Drechsler's body was found by the Americans. They did not announce the death. Instead they remained silent and the day continued for the prisoners in the normal way. Behind the scenes, though, the investigation was getting underway. The body was cut down and removed to the mortuary in Phoenix but not before photographs had been taken of the murder scene. Captain Hebblewaithe also managed to take three fingerprints from Drechsler's fists, which were by now stiff with rigor mortis, for identification purposes. Captain Parshall was ordered to undertake the investigation and find the perpetrators but no clues were left behind and there was nothing to link the crime to any particular prisoner. That was until there was a breakthrough. Funkobermaat Friedrich Murza cracked under interrogation on 1 June 1944, revealing that the perpetrators had worn gloves when they killed him. It was the information that the inquiry had been waiting for. He repeated his testimony so it could be recorded. Murza admitted he knew who had hanged Drechsler. Hours later Stengel sat and wrote out his own confession and so the story of the German's death unfolded.

A week later eight men had confessed to the murder – Murza as well as Wizuy, Ludwig, Reyak, Kuelsen, Franke, Fischer and Stengel. They were charged then tried for murder. Murza, because he had been involved before Drechsler had been hanged and not involved in the actual hanging, was to be tried as an accessory before the act. The trial took place on 15 August at the Florence prisoner of war camp, but by this time the charges against Murza had been dropped. It lasted two days and on 16 August the verdict was read out. Wizuy, Ludwig, Reyak, Kuelsen,

Franke, Fischer and Stengel were to be hanged by the neck until dead. The sentences were reviewed, especially in light of Stengel's admission that he had participated in the killing on the grounds that Drechsler had killed fellow Germans by betraying them. In November the review was over and the sentences stood. They were to be hanged on 1 May 1945. However, there was a twist. In March the Americans received word that the Germans were prepared to exchange 15 American prisoners of war who had been sentenced to death for 15 German prisoners of war with the same sentence hanging over them. Communications passed between the relevant government departments. By the end of April communications to Berlin had become difficult but there had been assurances that the American prisoners of war would not have their sentences carried out. The hangings were postponed. However, on 13 April President Franklin D. Roosevelt died and with Adolf Hitler's death on 30 April it was still hoped at this point that an exchange of the prisoners could take place. On 8 May Germany surrendered and the war in Europe was over. This changed the position of the Americans. They knew their soldiers were now safe, so no exchange would take place, and the German prisoners should have their sentence carried out. This was confirmed around the end of June/beginning of July.

The new president Harry Truman received the documents so he could personally consider the case against these men.

On the evening of 23 August shortly before lights out, Colonel Ely informed the men that the case against them had been upheld and they were to be hanged at one minute after midnight on 25 August 1945. They had just over 24 hours to live. Each man was led out separately to the noose but they were buried close to one another, just as they had spent their last few hours together. During those last weeks, the camp saw the execution of a total of 14 German prisoners of war and this later became known as the last mass execution in the United States. But the question remains as to why these men were hanged after the war had ended and not repatriated to a German prison. This could also be applied to the prisoners who were hanged following the trial in the Rosterg case. The case itself did not open until 2 July 1945 at the London Cage, almost two months following the end of the war.

———

Another case with similarities to the Rosterg murder is the beating to death of Gefreiter Johannes Kunze at the Tonkawa prisoner of war camp in Oklahoma. Kunze had been captured on 13 May 1943 after the fall of German garrison in Tunisia. During the journey to America, he spoke of his hopes for the future including settling in the United States when the war ended. However, this defeatist attitude did him no favours and those who believed Germany would win the war earmarked him as a traitor as soon as the words were out. He arrived with his fellow prisoners at Tonkawa in August. By November he was dead.

On 4 November, between 10 p.m. and 10.30 p.m., Kunze was beaten and killed after the American guards had left the compound, Compound 1, where he was interred. The body was found near the fourth company's mess hall by fellow prisoner of war Rudolph Scheuer. Kunze's upper body was covered in blood, his trousers twisted around his feet and his face was pressed into the ground. He had compound skull fractures, and blood seeped from his ears and mouth.

There were numerous contusions and abrasions on the face and upper body as well as four deep lacerations running roughly parallel on his head. There was also a star-shaped ragged wound to his head. Inside the mess hall was covered in blood some of which, it seemed, had been scraped with a spade. An empty milk bottle, bloodied, had hair stuck to it. At 10.45 p.m. Kunze was pronounced dead.

All the men in Kunze's company were forced from their beds, and following a search of their clothing and bodies 16 were found to have blood on their uniforms so were segregated immediately. The other three companies from the compound were searched likewise but were returned to barracks when nothing linked them, or the rest of the fourth company, to the killing.

Following a post mortem Kunze was buried with military honours although the prisoners refused to have anything to do with the service. Instead, the prisoners of Compound 1 played football.

After the burial the investigations got properly underway and prisoners were questioned. One of these was Gefreiter Albert Neef, who had been present at the beating but before Kunze had died. The fourth company had been called to the mess hall at around 10 o'clock and there Hauptfeldwebel Walter Beyer had read out two documents which purportedly came from Kunze. The first was a letter from Kunze to his wife and the second an unsigned letter with notes about factories in Germany and military notes about the city of Hamburg. Neef recounted how the beating then started and that as the fists flew at him Kunze protested his innocence. He fell against a table, knocking off some plates, which smashed onto the floor. Neef went on to say that Feldwebel Berthold Seidel announced he was from Hamburg and Kunze was giving away military secrets. Seidel then hit Kunze, he claimed.

The Americans were worried that the death would cause unrest within the confines of the camp. It was difficult to get any straight answers from the prisoners regarding Kunze's demise – the prisoners who had witnessed anything stayed quiet in fear of retribution, much the same as the prisoners at Camp 21 when Rosterg had been found. But the Americans were determined. Their main suspect in the case was the non-commissioned officer Beyer. During his interrogation Beyer denied touching Kunze, although he did admit intercepting the letter from Kunze to his wife, claiming he had a right as company leader to read it. He also claimed an unnamed American officer had asked him to examine all mail written by the prisoners, and that he had specifically targeted this one to compare it to the Hamburg notes which had fallen into the hands of another prisoner, Heisig, and he concluded the handwriting was the same. When Beyer had called the meeting and told his men of his findings, he knew what could happen – but as a parting shot he told his interrogators that if he was guilty of anything it was *thinking* of killing him, not actually doing it. Heisig admitted giving the notes to Beyer but refused to cooperate, stating that he understood how 'the boys felt'. It was quite a coincidence that Heisig disappeared at this point – being replaced with a young American soldier called Kayle Young – and was never heard of at the camp again.

Soon the investigators had another prime suspect in the murder in 30-year-old Seidel, who, like all the others who were questioned, had blood on his uniform. He admitted he had punched Kunze on the nose following the revelations from the Hamburg notes as his family lived in the city, and that blood had emanated from that first blow. He also told them he had dragged Kunze to his feet and had hit him five or six times in the face. The next prisoner to be interrogated was 23-year-old Unteroffizier Hans Demme, who freely admitted beating Kunze and said he had witnessed Seidel beating him too. Obergefreiter Willi Scholz, a 22-year-old, admitted he hit Kunze with three successive blows which caused him to bleed from his mouth and head, and that the blood on his uniform must have splashed onto him as he hit him. He then went to the latrines to try and clean up and was, he said, in bed by 10.30 p.m. The final suspect was 27-year-old Unteroffizier Hans Schomer. He said he never touched Kunze although he was bloodstained too – he did admit that while Kunze was being chased through the dining room, kitchen and finally the store room, if he had been close enough he would have hit him 'as hard as I could'. In all around 15 men took part in the actual beating and killing but only five men were formally accused. The rest kept their silence.

The trial began on Monday 17 January 1944 and heard from numerous witnesses. On the 25th it came to an end. The five men had faced two charges. The first was the commissioning of a riot, for which they were all found guilty. The second was murder. Every one of them was found guilty on that charge too. The court was closed and on a secret ballot, the accused – Beyer, Seidel, Demme, Scholz and Schomer – were all sentenced 'to be hanged by the neck until dead'. It was unanimous. The men returned to Fort Leavenworth's death row. Their final appeal was denied on 2 July 1945 and on 10 July they made their way to the improvised gallows in the disciplinary barracks. Beyer was first, and before the trap opened at 00.06, he told his executioners he could not understand why this was being done to him. Seidel remained silent and was hanged less than 30 minutes later. Demme was next and stated 'A wrong is being done', but could not finish his rehearsed speech. He died at 01.07. At 01.40 Schomer died, followed by the youngest of them all, Scholz, at 02.11.

———

One final case of note is that of the beating to death of Horst Guenther of the Afrika Korps, who like Rosterg, Rettig, Drechsler and Kunze was beaten to death by fellow prisoners of war. Captured in Tunisia in May 1943, he was murdered at Camp Aiken in South Carolina. He had been accused of collaborating with the American authorities and was strangled by Erich Gauss and Rudolf Straub on 6 April 1944. Gauss and Straub stood trial, were found guilty and were hanged on 14 July 1945 at Fort Leavenworth. Straub maintained he had executed Guenther under orders and as a German soldier carried them out. He claimed if he had not he would have been punished on his return to Germany.

This appears to be the stance all of these men took following the killings. They were soldiers and as such had a right to punish those who deserved it, whether under direct orders or not. Traitors had to be dealt with, whether there was compelling evidence or fabricated evidence of something said.

As a final note about the murder of Wolfgang Rosterg: the Crown Office and Procurator Fiscal's Office requested the return of an old ledger which had been passed to the National

Records of Scotland for permanent retention. There is a record that a report was received in the Crown Office from the Procurator Fiscal's Office on 27 December 1944 regarding Rosterg who had been 'murdered by strangulation'. Crown Counsel, senior independent lawyers, sent an instruction back to the Procurator Fiscal's Office on 2 January 1945, intimating there should be no proceedings in this case. All paperwork which had been held has now been destroyed in line with their records retention policy.

6 | PRISONERS OF CAMP 21

Obermaschinenmaat Theo Hunkirchen was taken prisoner of war following his capture in March 1944 in the western Mediterranean Sea. His U-boat was sunk by British destroyers and he was among the 50 or so survivors who went into captivity in both Britain and the United States, remaining there until his release in 1947.

Hunkirchen was born on 27 May 1920 in Cologne. By December 1939, Hunkirchen had been assigned to M-72 as part of the 6th Minensuchflottille, the mine sweepers, but his was a training ship. It had been built during 1917 and was completed just seven months before the Armistice. On 1 July 1940 he was promoted to Maschinengefreiter, the equivalent of corporal, and acted as a Fireman Third Class before being promoted once again a year later to Maschinenobergefreiter, lance corporal, as well as Fireman Second Class. That same month he also attended the naval academy, the Marineschule Wesermünde or MSW, specialising in U-boats to become Mot II, a Mot-Machinist. The academy was established in 1935 for the technical training of machine operators. It was open to crews, officers and sergeants, with specialised courses available. The one downside for Hunkirchen was that these required him to spend time doing maths as well as physics, machine engineering and electrical engineering, followed by an exam at the end of the course. He was no academic, but persevered nonetheless. On 1 December 1941 he was promoted once more to Maschinenmaat, a qualified mechanic, and Fireman First Class while he was at 2. Unterseeboots-Ausbildungsabteilung (UAA), the submarine training department at Neustadt in Germany, and 2. Unterseeboots-Lehrdivision (2ULD), the submarine training division at Gotenhafen (Gdynia) in Poland.

In March 1943 he was on operations with U-622 in Northern Waters off Bergen, Trondheim and Narvik in Norway. This was a brand new submarine under the command of 28-year-old Kapitänleutnant Horst-Thilo Queck, and had been part of the wolf pack Nordwind in January to early February that managed to sink three ships but had now been assigned to Norwegian waters. On the 15th of that month Hunkirchen was awarded the Iron Cross

Second Class by Kapitän zur See and Führer der Unterseeboote Norwegen Hans Rudolf Peters when U-622 arrived intact at Narvik. On 24 July the submarine was hit by US bombers near Trondheim and sank. August that year saw Hunkirchen as part of 9. Flottille at Brest in France. This flotilla had been formed two years previously and ran between Brest and Norway, although its main base was the French town. Hunkirchen was promoted to Obermaschinenmaat, Senior First Class Petty Officer, on 1 December that year.

That month also saw Hunkirchen on U-450 while it was operating in the Mediterranean. This submarine had been commissioned on 12 September 1942 and its commander was Oberleutnant zur See (lieutenant) Kurt Böhme, then a 24-year-old from Elberfeld, Nordrhein-Westfalen, who was decorated in 1943 with the Iron Cross First Class. A Type VIIC, the U-boat was furnished with two supercharged Germaniawerft six-cylinder, four-stroke diesel engines with a total of 2800 and 32,000 brake horse power and could travel at 17.7 knots when surfaced and 7.6 knots when submerged. It carried five torpedo tubes but during its career it never sank a single vessel. It was initially a training vessel with 8. Flottille before seeing active service with 9. Flottille, then 29. Flottille which had bases at La Spazia in Italy, and Toulon in France where Hunkirchen was sent. U-450 had been hit on 6 June 1943 by a British B-17 Flying Fortress as it patrolled some 250 kilometres south of Iceland. One man was killed and seven injured and it was only with help from other U-boats that she made it back to Brest to be repaired. However, she was finally sunk on 10 March 1944 in the western Mediterranean south of Ostia by depth charges from the British destroyers HMS *Blankney*, HMS *Blencathra*, HMS *Brecon* and HMS *Exmoor* along with the US destroyer USS *Madison*. Two of the ships, *Brecon* and *Exmoor*, attacked following 'doubtful' sonar contacts by dropping depth charges. What they had picked up were in fact echoes from U-450. So much damage was caused by the charges that Böhme was forced to surface. As soon as the U-boat did so, *Brecon* and *Exmoor* began firing at her with their guns. Böhme gave the order to abandon the submarine and scuttled it. All the crew survived and were picked up by British destroyers HMS *Brecon*, and HMS *Urchin* which had joined late, and delivered them the same day to Naples in Italy.

And so began Hunkirchen's life as a prisoner of war not only in Britain but in the United States as well. The survivors of the sunken U-boat were held first at Prisoner of War Enclosure 326 at Dugenta near Naples. This was the headquarters of the Mediterranean Theatre of Operations for the United States Army run by the 6619th Prisoner of War Administrative Company at this time, although it had not quite changed its name in time for Hunkirchen. Here each man was assigned a US Internment Serial Number – Hunkirchen's was 81G-237548 (M). A card was sent to his father at his Schwadorf home informing him of his son's capture and stating that he was being held at the North African Theatre of Operations, United States Army PWE 326. He was 23 years old and on his preliminary prisoner of war record was recorded as being roughly 5 feet 7 inches tall (1.67 m), weighing 143 lb (65 kg) and having blond hair and blue eyes. He was missing the first joint on his little finger on his left hand.

On 2 April Hunkirchen was transferred to British custody at Salerno, at a prisoner of war camp at the foot of Mount Vesuvius. Here he was given his British prisoner of war number N 92807. A day later he was transferred aboard the 11,550 ton and aging Belgian steamer

SS *Leopoldville* bound for Glasgow in Scotland. However, by 10 April he was no longer in Scotland: he found himself at Camp 7, Winter Quarters Camp at Ascot near Windsor in Berkshire, which was also the South East Cage for prisoner of war interrogations. But on 9 May he entered through the gates of Camp 21 Comrie following the usual march from the railway station in the village, with his kitbag slung over his shoulder. This contained all his worldly goods, including a hairbrush, toothbrush, comb, two woollen shirts, and trousers as well as cutlery and a canvas groundsheet. He also had a gas mask.

Two days after his arrival Hunkirchen was given a medical and a dental check-up. For the next few weeks he passed his days just like all the inmates, playing games and talking to other internees. But he was not to stay at Comrie very long – after just six weeks he was moved on again, as at this stage Comrie was only a transit camp.

On 18 June Hunkirchen embarked on the *Queen Elizabeth* at Glasgow bound for New York and a new chapter in his prisoner of war life. He arrived at the receiving centre Communipaw in New Jersey four days later. On arrival he was given an internees deposit book into which the prisoners could deposit and withdraw money, although the funds could be withheld by the authorities. Two days later, on 24 June, he arrived at Camp Patrick Henry in Virginia where he spent the next few weeks before being transferred yet again, this time to Camp McCain at Elliot Mississippi on 14 July. At Camp Patrick Henry another prisoner of war card was sent to his father which included the information that he had arrived from Camp 21 Comrie, known also as Lager 21, and the new address of where his son was being held so that he could write to him, and another card was sent when he arrived at Camp McCain. He stayed in Camp McCain for just over nine months. On one of the forms he filled in when here he revealed his religion as Catholic. On another form, an insight is given into his mental state: one of the questions was about his occupation but he refused to answer it, either an act of defiance or simply that he did not know what to put as he did not have one any more. Shortly after his arrival, on 16 July, he was given a receipt for his personal possessions. During September he was immunised against typhoid and given a tetanus injection as well as the smallpox vaccine.

On 27 April 1945 Hunkirchen was assigned to the Greenville Auxiliary Camp, which ran under the McCain camp administration. This camp quartered prisoners formerly from the Afrika Korps. Here he managed to work on the Elkas plantation, owned by William Fox Elkas, who was Jewish. The plantation was located to the north end of Lake Washington near Chatham, south of Greenville in Mississippi.

On 3 March 1946 Hunkirchen was moved briefly to Camp Forrest in Tennessee. Here another inventory of his personal possessions took place. He wore a ring on his finger now but possessed no other jewellery. His possessions also included a cigarette case, two tobacco pouches, a pipe and sunglasses. On 15 March he was sent to Camp Shanks at Orangeburg in Rockland County, New York to await transportation to Europe. Camp Shanks had originally been one of the biggest US staging areas and embarkation points for American troops leaving to go to war during 1942, shortly after America became involved following the Japanese attack on Pearl Harbor in December 1941. More than 1.3 million men and women passed through the camp *en route* to Europe to fight against the Axis nations. The camp was built on 2020 acres and had capacity to house over 46,000 troops but it was its location that was most important, with its access to the Piermont and New York piers. In the death throes of the war it became the staging post for prisoners of war instead.

Shanks had been used to house over 1000 Italian and 800 German prisoners of war between April 1945 and January 1946, although the last German prisoner to leave did so on 22 July 1946. In all some 290,000 prisoners of war had gone through the camp before being transferred back to Europe. Two days after his arrival Hunkirchen was on a Liberty ship sailing from New York to Antwerp in Belgium. He arrived at Camp 2227 at Cedelheim in Belgium on 24 March before being transported once again back to Britain, this time to Camp 185 Springhill Lodge at Blockley in Gloucestershire where he arrived on 14 May. The camp was a base camp made up of a large complex of huts with watchtowers and is still intact today although in some disrepair. He was only there for ten days before he was moved on to Camp 37 Sudeley Castle at Winchcombe, Cheltenham. This was a purpose-built standard camp and operated as a working camp for both Italian and then later German prisoners of war. Finally on 17 December Hunkirchen arrived at Camp 4 Scraptoft, a transit camp at Thumby in Leicestershire (this is opposed to the other Camp 4s of which there are two – Gilling Camp in North Yorkshire and Windlestone Hall Camp in County Durham). On 4 January 1947 he was transferred by ship to Cruxhaven in Germany before entering the Munsterlager or discharge camp on 13 January at Bonn from where he was finally given his freedom. At this time he was given Control Form D2 which stated that he would abide by the instructions for personnel on discharge, and the medical part of the certificate stated he was 'fit'. It was stamped by W. Cahille of the Irish Guards, the discharging officer, and also stamped by the Disbandment Control Unit. He was a free man.

Some months later, on 28 July, Hunkirchen received his Certificate of Clearance. It stated that he was a 'released prisoner of war' and was provisionally classed in accordance with military government regulation number 42. He remained under investigation by the German military authorities regarding the de-Nazification programme even though it was a temporary situation and 'this should be addressed without delay'. When accepting him for employment, any new employer had to see this certificate and have a filled-in questionnaire. This was done through Public Safety (Special Branch) in order to keep an eye on newly released prisoners of war. Hunkirchen had signed up for 12 years of military service and in 1961 he received his Certificate of Service from the German Centre in Berlin-Borsigwalde for notifying the next of kin of martyrs of the former German Wehrmacht.

After the war Hunkirchen returned to Brühl where his parents now lived. He was utterly shocked at the devastation that had been wreaked on Cologne from the Allied bombing raids. The city had been the military command centre or *Militärbereichshauptkommandoquartier* for the military district of Münster. As such it was home to the 211th Infant Regiment and the 26th Artillery Regiment and responsible for the military operations in the likes of Bonn, Aachen and Monschau under the command of Lt.-General Freiherr Roeder von Dierburg. Over the course of the war it suffered 262 Allied air raids, the worst of which occurred on the night of 30/31 May 1942 when 1000 RAF bombers attacked targets during Operation

Millennium. That night 2500 fires broke out, and over 12,000 buildings were either destroyed or damaged to varying degrees including nine hospitals, 16 schools, 14 public buildings, ten buildings of historic interest, six department stores and four hotels, all of which were completely razed to the ground. The loss of civilian life that night was considerable. More than 400 died along with 58 military personnel. Over 45,000 people were bombed out and as a direct result of that bombing around one-fifth of the 700,000 strong population left the city. By the end of the war, over 90% of the population had fled but many returned quickly once it was over. Much of the city had been destroyed, although the famous cathedral, which holds some of the relics of The Three Kings or The Three Wise Men, weathered the storm. Possibly used as a landmark for the bombing raids, it was hit 14 times but its two spires remained standing, giving the people of the city hope. Emergency repairs were carried out in 1944 using bricks and these were left *in situ* until 2005 when they were replaced and it is now restored to its original state. Repairs post-war on the rest of Cologne took until 1956 to complete.

Hunkirchen searched for work and was finally offered a position with the Deutsche Bundesbahn, the German national railway. He later became a signal technician, and following several years of training was appointed to manage the maintenance of train track. He was often working near the Belgian and Netherlands borders so could only return home twice a week. In 1949 Hunkirchen married Josefine who came from a small village near Bonn and whom he had met at a dance. In December 1950 the couple had their first child, a daughter named Marita; sadly, due to complications with the Caesarean birth, Josefine died. Five years later he found happiness again when he met Magdalena, a refugee from Lower Silesia in the small town of Hürth, some 10 kilometres from Cologne. Once again, a dance hall played a part in the romance and the following year they married. In April 1957 they had a son and named him Theo. That year also saw an expansion of living accommodation for the growing family. The Behelfsheim his father had built in 1942 at Brühl as an emergency shelter, just four metres by four metres, was enlarged and made into two stories with two adjacent buildings, meaning they now lived comfortably for the first time. During these early years they had chickens and a pig and along with an abundance of fruit trees, a vegetable patch, berries and potatoes, they had plenty of food. The garden was a favourite place for the children. In 1965 another baby joined the family and she was named Elke. Theo Hunkirchen's private life was a happy one and his country had returned to a democracy. However, one thing truly annoyed him and that was the fact that former Nazis were still holding high positions within the civil sector, mainly in law. He could not fathom out how they managed it considering what had happened during the war years.

On the 30th anniversary of the sinking of U-450, Böhme wrote a letter to his former crewmen, dated 10 March. He began the letter, 'Today it is 30 years since our boat was sunk'. He goes on to say that he initially thought one of their own torpedoes had hit its target but soon realised it was them that had been hit. Despite the adverse circumstances, the boat was still able to be brought to the surface. He continued that it was only thanks to each man's self-discipline that, despite the severe damage to the boat and the additional water pouring into it, everyone emerged unscathed. They were on board one of the few boats, if not the only one, from which in spite of its sinking all had survived. Böhme himself was released from captivity on 5 November 1947 and began a new life. In 1973 he says it was an unforgettable experience to meet with former crew members and their families, thanks to the exemplary organisational efforts of Hans Hörder from Holzappel in Westerwald. Böhme died in July 1984 aged 67.

At the end of March 1979, Theo Hunkirchen died suddenly at home. He was 58 years old. He had gone into Brühl to do some shopping on his bike and it had been a stormy day, and he had a bad heart. He had managed to put his hat on the coat rack before collapsing to the floor. The door closed loudly, causing his wife to stop doing her hand-washing and go downstairs to see what had happened. Magdalena shouted for her son Theo, who was studying in his room for his final exams for an apprenticeship, and he ran down the stairs as soon as he heard her cries. Theo was flat on his back on the tiles, and there was blood on them. They found the pills for his heart scattered over the floor; he must have known to try to take these tablets but it was too late. The cause of death was an embolism.

In September 1993 at Tulln an der Donau at the Romühle Hotel a reunion took place of those still surviving from U-450. Among the topics discussed were the U-boat's functions, where it worked and its history, and a toast to lost comrades, including Hunkirchen. Two years previously there had been a gathering at Kiel.

Incidentally, the Belgian steamer which took Hunkirchen to Scotland, the SS *Leopoldville*, was destroyed by U-486 on Christmas Eve 1944 with the loss of 802 men out of 2235 of the American 66th Infantry Division, many of whom died in the freezing water as she sank.

———

Michael Kickertz was born in 1915, the son of a farmer and one of seven children. They lived in the small village of Üttfeld about 100 kilometres from Cologne. After attending elementary school and working in agriculture, he was called up for the Reich Labour Service, the Reichsarbeitsdienst or RAD. In 1937, Kickertz began his active military service. This lasted for two years and was by then compulsory for every healthy man. Just a few months after he arrived back home from this, the Nazis invaded Poland and the war began. Kickertz was called up and soon afterwards found himself with the fighting troops in Poland. He later spoke of how brave the Poles were in the way they fought for their country, but horses against tanks were a disaster and they were crushingly defeated.

He then got his marching orders to go to Africa. The ship on which he and his 1000 fellow comrades were being transported was sunk close to the African coast. After the hit the ship sank very quickly and only those who dared to jump from a great height into the sea, and then found a plank of wood, had any chance of survival. He made it and swam quickly away from the sinking vessel. Many of the other troops went down with the ship.

In Africa, he was in the 21st Panzer Division under Rommel, a man who he never liked. Rommel told the German troops that the British were inferior but the Germans soon realised this was not the case. Kickertz was wounded before the major battle for Tripoli and also suffered from jaundice, so was taken back to hospital in Germany. After recovering, he was transferred to the Russian front briefly and after a week, he was sent to France. There his unit was stationed at Caen.

By this time he had fallen in love and wanted to marry his sweetheart so on 31 May 1944 the couple tied the knot, during some leave. But his honeymoon was soon over as on 6 June the Allies landed in Normandy. A day later he was sent back to the front.

With three comrades in an advanced observation post he could see the bombardment from the massive shelter they were holed up in and watched the advance of the armoured British personnel and the infantry. A British tank was hit but the advance was well underway and the Germans knew the battle was over. British troops captured Kickertz and his fellow men in that observation post. It was 18 July 1944 and he was now a prisoner of war. As the British assumed it was him and his comrades who had shot and destroyed the tank he was transported to London, where he was interrogated for three weeks under considerable pressure. He was then asked to dig a grave, and thought his life was about to end. However, this was not the case. He was sent to Camp 21 Comrie instead. He often told the story that as the German prisoners made their way along the road to the camp, the local population understandably responded in a very contemptuous way. At the last house in the village they passed an older woman who was standing watching, and she was crying. He was immediately reminded of his mother, who at the time had four sons in the war. He was never to see his mother again as she died before his return home to Germany.

Kickertz remembered the camp was divided into the officers' camp and what he termed the 'team' camp, the one for the ordinary fighters. The prisoners were allowed to keep busy during the day and did not sit around moping, but with only a blanket at night it was often very cold. They helped themselves to keep warm by forming a chain and marching in a circle, almost like a Scottish reel dance.

The food rations when he was there were poor, he remembered. Mostly it was a thin soup and a piece of bread, but not the heavy German-type bread so they often felt hungry after eating it until they were allowed extra. But there were two cigarettes a day, which they quickly smoked one after the other. The German arm of the Red Cross was allowed after a time to send aid packages for the captured men but they went exclusively to the officers. He never forgave the Red Cross for treating the men differently.

After a year he was transferred to Central England to Camp 153 Fulney Park, Spalding in Lincolnshire. There they had the privilege of working with farmers and thus had much better food. He was a further two years in England while he awaited repatriation. He thought of escape, but said to himself 'How do you get off the island since it takes an aircraft or ship?' Thoughts of escape were then abandoned while he waited.

On 10 April 1947 he was released from captivity. After 11 years on military service, war and then captivity he returned back to his home a broken man. For weeks he could barely sit and only walked up and down. His mother had died, their house largely destroyed. He hardly spoke. Later he very rarely talked about anything to do with the war. He had the opportunity of becoming the village policeman but the decision was made: never again would he put on a uniform. So he renounced this very lucrative job and decided to be a joiner instead. He and his wife built everything up themselves, with hard work, and went on to have three sons and one daughter and lived a simple life. He never again wanted to be away from home. He died in 1998.

————————

Another prisoner of war held at the camp was Heinrich Steinmeyer. Only son of Veanhold Steinmeyer and his wife Lena, Steinmeyer died in February 2014, and his story is one of the more extraordinary ones as he asked that his ashes be scattered at or near the camp which once held him prisoner of war. Steinmeyer was born in 1924, the year Adolf Hitler returned to political activity following his incarceration after the attempted coup in Munich. The treaties of the Paris Peace Settlement were impacting on everyday lives and it was this that propelled Hitler into the mainstream on his promises of a better Germany with an improved economy. Many families were poor after World War I reparations took hold, and Steinmeyer's was no different. He recalled a time when he, his three sisters and his parents had one herring between them, which they shared, and how he used to go to school with a single tomato. Shoes too were at a premium and in the summer he went to school barefoot. The local fields were scavenged for anything they could find, from corn to potatoes and even rabbits as they had no meat for most of the time because it was so expensive. In short they had no money – but when Hitler came to power, their lives changed dramatically. His father found work in a brick factory where he worked long shifts seven days a week, but now at least the family could eat properly.

As the Hitler Youth expanded during the 1920s and into the 1930s, it became an escape for many of these impoverished children. Steinmeyer was given a uniform, like other boys from his street, when he joined when he was just eight years old. Meetings were held twice a week and they learned new crafts such as how to use an air rifle and orienteering skills – skills taught with a view to them joining one of the forces when they reached maturity. There were also regular camps which were a world away from the poverty of home life. It was during these years that he decided he would become a soldier. He was exactly the type of youngster Hitler was hoping to recruit. In a speech in 1938 Hitler had told them they were 'our nation's most precious guarantee for a great future', and that they would one day 'rule the world'. Steinmeyer's father never spoke about politics but he knew his mother disliked Hitler, at least to begin with. When she received a widow's pension following the death of her husband she changed her mind.

When Steinmeyer was 17 years old he applied to join the elite Waffen-SS, the 'protection squad'. Being tall and healthy with blond hair and blue eyes, he was the epitome of an Aryan but even so he still had to trace his German ancestry back to the 1800s so the Nazis could be sure he was of true German blood. At that time, he never saw himself as a Nazi but rather as a member of an elite force, which he was fiercely proud to be part of. Before he was accepted he had been apprenticed as a butcher, which was poorly paid, so he decided to better himself and applied to be an officer in the SS, for which no formal qualifications were required, which was unique. He went on to serve with the 12th Panzer Division and trained in Poland to be a squadron leader for the Hitler Youth. He was then sent to Belgium and was to see action at Caen in Normandy in June 1944. He felt it was a great honour to fight for his country, but then on 28 August, aged 19, he was captured by the Allies as he lay hidden in a manhole. The British went from one to the other in their tanks and Steinmeyer knew that if he did not surrender he would be shot. Along with another youngster he raised his arms and they both came out of hiding. They were asked to empty their pockets and when he produced two apples the Scottish soldier told him to keep them as he would need them.

The captured men were transported to the banks of the River Seine where a group of women appeared with butchers' knives in readiness to attack the prisoners, but luckily the Scottish soldier stopped them. Once they were safely on the ferry they began their journey to England. Steinmeyer stood out because of his SS uniform, however. Some of the Poles on board threatened to slit his throat but the British stepped in. Some Scottish guards ushered him and his 18-year-old companion towards them and gave them some hot milky tea. They also gave them big jackets to sleep on during the crossing.

When they docked in Southampton it was raining and they were told to go to the tents, but once again the Scottish guards stepped in. They had seen the Poles threatening the two men again. The Scottish guards told them to go with them, staying close to them for safety. Steinmeyer recalls that some of the English guards would have been happy to let the Poles get on with it however.

As was the norm, he was interviewed but because he was Waffen-SS it was inevitable that Steinmeyer would be classed as a category C prisoner. Until his death he maintained that he was no Nazi. He said that as a youth in Germany in the 1930s you had a choice: join either the Nazi Party or the communists, and he saw himself simply as a soldier fighting for his country. He was assigned to go to Comrie then north to the 'black' camp at Watten in Caithness. Before reaching Comrie he was held at a smaller camp at Crieff but he entered Camp 21 Comrie in September 1944 and was to remain there until June 1945. The Polish guards surrounded the camp and Steinmeyer recalled how they shot and killed the German prisoner Heinrich Schwarz through the fence, as they were not allowed in the camp itself. The Scottish guards did roll call and the days were spent playing skat, chess and Doppelkopf, another card game. They could always hear people outside the camp, but being a category C prisoner he was never allowed out of the compound. He participated in football when it was allowed but on the whole the days passed by slowly.

At some point during his captivity he was shown the photographs of the concentration camps as part of the on-going de-Nazification process. The images were so horrific he thought they were fake and it was all simply propaganda. He recalled that some of the prisoners thought the idea so preposterous that they burst out laughing at the ludicrous photographs. Those who did laugh were punished by being forced to do exercise. Until that point he had believed the camps were being used for political prisoners and even many years later still found it difficult to comprehend.

Steinmeyer was transported north to Watten in the summer of 1945 where later he came under the watchful eye of Lt.-Col. Murray, who he recalled as a 'real gentleman'. Murray was firm but always seen as fair and of course there were no Polish guards at Watten so the Germans felt safer. While at Watten Steinmeyer was able to walk along the perimeter fence. He recalled a time when, once the guards at the camp had been fed, he was asked to hold out a plate in each hand and the plates were filled with food. A YMCA group would also give the Germans tea at no charge, something he never forgot.

After his time at Watten was done, he was sent to Camp 77 at Ladybank in Fife. Here he was allowed to work on Turret and Greenside farms, where they were paid half a crown for their labours. Every night they were given a slice of cake and some meat. It was here that he experienced another act of kindness. One day he asked the family who owned both these farms if he could exchange his coins into a ten shilling note. When the farmer's wife asked what he wanted it for he replied a pair of shoes. She asked what size he was and the next day she went into Leven and bought him not only shoes, but socks and polish as well. She told him she did not want any money from him. She also knew of the food shortages in Germany and sent three food parcels to his mother to help her out.

Steinmeyer was finally released in 1948 but instead of heading back to Germany he decided to stay on and worked on farms in Stranraer, where he settled. He lived in a hostel and worked on the farms for five years along with some 30 other Germans who had decided to stay.

It was not until 1970 that he finally returned to Germany. His mother Lena did not qualify for a pension in the now East Germany so she had asked him to go back and look after her. She died soon after he returned home, but he decided to stay. He found work in the docks at Bremen and built a house in Delmenhorst. He now saw a chance to thank the Scots who had helped him all those years ago. He decided that in his will he would bequeath his house and all his savings to the elderly residents of Comrie as a thank you for the kindness he had been shown throughout his time in the country, as he was divorced and had no issue.

During the early summer of 2003 Radio Scotland invited Steinmeyer back to Cultybraggan to interview him for the broadcast *Return to Freedom*. The BBC flew him back to Scotland from his home and when he entered the camp he met fellow former prisoner of war Werner Busse, who had stayed in Scotland after the war. Busse had been born in December 1925 and lived in Halberstadt near the Hartz Mountains in central Germany. Aged 16 he volunteered for the 10th SS Panzer Division Frundsberg where he became a tank commander. He spent two years on the Russian front before being sent to fight in Normandy. Following the D-Day landings, Busse's tank was hit by a rocket at Caen. Some of the men died but he was thrown clear and only suffered a minor shrapnel wound. He was captured by Scottish soldiers and after his wound was treated at Bayeux, he was sent to Britain as a prisoner of war. He spent time in various camps in the UK including Camp 21. The two men reminisced about their time in the camp. Both claimed to have seen the brutal murder of Wolfgang Rosterg. Steinmeyer always regarded his time at Comrie as a continuation of 'army life in German barracks without the freedom'.

In 2009 Heinrich Steinmeyer returned to Camp 21. It was to be his final visit and a media frenzy ensued as news broke he was leaving his money to the village. His generosity to those who treated him with kindness is his remarkable legacy. His ashes were received from the Bremen undertaker Thomas Cortes by Ken Heiser for scattering on the hills above Comrie. With forward thinking, Steinmeyer had deposited £350 in the Strathearn Ramblers' account.

As for Busse, he also spent time in camps in the United States, picking cotton in Alabama and working on former president Jimmy Carter's peanut farm in Georgia, as well as a cattle ranch in Indiana. He escaped from one of these American camps once but was caught and duly escorted back. He was shipped back to Scotland in 1946 and spent time at Camp 67 Sandyhillock at Craigellachie near Elgin. He worked on a farm at Keith and it was at a barn dance there he met his future wife Molly, the daughter of George Stables, a decorated World War I veteran. They married in Brechin. They both worked at the local Stracathro Hospital before running a hotel in Montrose. From there they moved to Inverness where they ran The Plough for a time then the Imperial Bar, which twice won accolades from Tennants for the best performance in turnover for a pub. But life was not always plain sailing. If anyone came into his pub and he heard them calling him Hermann the German they were duly deposited on the street outside. He had close links with the nearby Fort George Barracks as well as the Cameron Barracks in Inverness, and was an honorary member of the King's Own Scottish Borderers. He and his wife went on to run The Moray for around 20 years before they retired and decided to travel. And it was while travelling in California that he passed away, on 26 June 2008. The couple had two children, Eva and Karin.

––––––––

Helmut Stenger was born on 8 August 1926 at Goldbach, Aschaffenburg am Main in Bavaria in the southwest of Germany some 41 kilometres from Frankfurt am Main. The year after his birth his parents emigrated to Chicago, Illinois in the United States, taking their two children with them, but the marriage failed shortly afterwards. His mother returned to Germany with her son and daughter and left them with her parents while she went back to America, asking them to look after them until she was more settled.

Stenger attended the local school, and during his time there he joined the Hitler Youth. When war broke out he applied for an apprenticeship with the Guldner Motor Company as a draughtsman – they were manufacturers of diesel engines, many of which were now to be used in the building of war ships for the Kriegsmarine. After he had served three years, the young Stenger applied for the U-boat service. He had heard from others that the food rations, as well as the food itself, were the best with them and by this time he had noticed the decline in food in the shops. However, as he was only 16, he was refused and instead did his training with the Reichsarbeitsdienst, the German Labour Service. Once this was completed he returned to Kiel in Schleswig-Holstein on the Baltic coast where he began his basic training with the U-boats, and he graduated as a Fireman Second Class. His first assignment was to the Baltic where he made two trips to the Murmansk area and patrolled the Barents Sea. Most of his time was spent in the engine room, where the work was grimy and hot. When he had time off he would join the other sailors and sing songs or listen to the radio, tuning into Kameradenschaft Dienst.

The U-boat returned to Wilhelmshaven and Stenger was then transferred to France where he met up with the 3rd Flotilla at the depot at Brest. There he saw a notice for U-569 looking for two volunteers which stated they could go on to do officer training after a few trips should they wish. Stenger applied without hesitation. U-569 was an older submarine and had been on eight cruises before he joined *The Old Hare* as she was known. Her captain was Hans Frederick Johannsen and in order to boost morale he had the motto '*Let's Go*' painted on her conning tower. This ninth trip was to be a mid-Atlantic patrol and she was escorted through the minefields by the minesweeper *Sperrbrecher* before reaching her post. She received word there were aircraft close by and after she surfaced for repairs on 22 May 1943, the captain sent a message back to Germany using the Enigma machine he had on board. This was intercepted by the Canadians, however, and passed on to the USS *Bogue* which launched several Avenger aircraft. Up at the conning tower, Stenger was having a smoke with a fellow crewman and saw a plane appear from behind a cloud. No sound came from it as the engines had been cut, but he witnessed a number of missiles being launched directly at the U-boat. As they hit, he and his shipmate were thrown into the ocean but managed to grab hold of a piece of debris from the stricken vessel, and watched as the U-boat dived, hoping to salvage itself. It remained under the sea for around 20 minutes before it resurfaced only to be attacked by another aircraft. The submariners clambered onto the deck and began waving white sheets and towels as a signal they had surrendered.

As U-569 disappeared beneath the waves many of the submariners were rescued by the *Bogue* and HMCS *St Laurent*. Stenger and his friend watched but were not picked up until a few days later when a Canadian destroyer found them clinging to drift wood. Stenger had suffered shrapnel wounds. Once on board the ship he was given a drink then passed out. After landing in Newfoundland most of the crew were sent to Boston, Massachusetts where they were to be interred. But one was not with them: Stenger was hospitalised then shipped over to England where he would see out the rest of the war as a prisoner of war at various camps. He was screened at the London District Cage where he was interrogated about the one-man submarines he had learned about during training. He was classed as a B prisoner and sent north to Comrie. His prisoner of war number was B43666; all prisoners of war remember their number for the rest of their lives.

Stenger was held with other members of the Kriegsmarine but as he was classed as B and not C he was allowed out to work on local farms under the watchful eyes of the guards. On one occasion he remembered a contingent of Irishmen had been on duty and for some reason had left their rifles behind. Stenger and his fellow prisoners simply picked up the weapons and returned them to the camp, minus the bullets which were put safely into Stenger's pocket. For their endeavours they were confined to barracks for 24 hours for being in possession of British weapons then told to march at the double. Being an honest person, Stenger felt he should tell the British that he still had their bullets in his pocket so he tapped the shoulder of a corporal. All hell broke loose. He was suddenly surrounded and pinned to the ground and for touching the corporal he was given another 24 hours in solitary confinement.

So the days passed at Comrie. Stenger received parcels from his mother in America which contained jam but most importantly cigarettes. This changed the attitude of the hard-line Nazis who had until that point treated him rather poorly, and suddenly he had a voice and a reputation. Most of the others in the camp did not receive anything so he was the most popular man in his compound.

Stenger recalled a radio in the camp which the men made themselves and this was their link to the outside world. They soon realised how the war had changed direction, with Germany losing the fight. Although disheartened they continued to listen, hoping for better news which never came. To lift their spirits they played games and organised sporting events such as football. He even recalled a game against Glasgow Rangers. There were also more pressing activities such as stealing a chicken when they managed to slip out of the camp, and even pinching a small Christmas tree, which they decorated with anything they could find.

When in May 1945 the war in Europe was finally declared over, the prisoners found themselves able to go out of the compound more and fraternise with the locals, although some succeeded better than others with this. Stenger recalled a prisoner who had been sent out to work on a local farm only to be returned to the camp by the farmer who found him disagreeable. By now they wore British battle dress but with patches to clearly show they were prisoners of war. When he was transferred to the small camp at Crieff, Stenger was able to work on local farms. He worked on one at Muthill where the Ballantyne family took him in and treated him well. It was the potato harvest and he made friends with the Ballantyne's daughter Vickie. She remembered him as kind and decent. Shirley, Vickie's younger sister, also recalled that he even stayed over in the house on occasion and had to sneak back to camp early so no one would suspect. Their brother Hamish would also loan Stenger clothes so he looked just like the other village boys, and they would take him on picnics and visit local places. He was also sent to Alloa and Tullibody in Clackmannanshire where he became involved in construction work, and was given a basket of fruit by a girl. When they returned to Crieff they would nip into the local chip shop and on Hogmanay 1945 a local police officer invited them to share a wee dram of whisky with him, no doubt not realising they were Germans.

Stenger was then sent to Camp 77 at Ladybank in Fife. He was released from captivity in 1948 and returned to Germany. His home town of Aschaffenburg was in ruins but from the ashes, love blossomed and he married Margot. Shortly afterwards he went to America in search of better prospects and after almost two years of being apart from his wife he returned to Germany to be with her. The next while was spent planning and they arrived in the United States in 1953. But life was not all rosy. In order to stay he had to join the US army as they were now involved in the Korean War. If he had not, he would have been refused entry into the country. He was promoted to sergeant and given army housing, but after two years he was de-mobbed and left the army for good. The now young family moved to Chicago but the weather was not suitable for their baby so the family moved to Phoenix, Arizona where they set up and ran their own business, the Phoenix Music and TV Company. He and Margot had two sons, Ralph and Roy, and a daughter Carol.

In 1955 Stenger joined the German-American Club, and in 1982 he retired. In 2002 he came back to Scotland and visited the Comrie camp. He also met Vickie and Shirley Ballantyne and all three were shown round the camp by Captain Graham as it was then used by the Ministry of Defence. At the prison cells he told them about his time locked up there and told them there were 3000 bricks; he had counted them to pass the time. On 16 April 2005 he passed away at his retreat in the Bradshaw Mountains near Prescott in Arizona, where he had a memorial to his lost comrades of U-569.

7 | REMINISCENCES

This chapter looks back at more local memories of the camp.

————

Grace McLennan recalls a time before the prisoners of war arrived, at the inception of Camp 21, when her father worked for the local Crieff Hydro Hotel (locally known simply as the Hydro) on Ferntower Road. She remembers:

> When war broke out the Crieff Hydro had about a week to clear out residents, staff and all furnishings – carpets, beds, wardrobes, curtains, etc. Any permanent resident had to find accommodation elsewhere, some to Ferntower Road and others to relatives perhaps or friends. We knew the war was on and troops arrived with cars, trucks and buses, ambulances and tanks. The sergeant major drilled the men up at the stables and garage area and we could hear him bawling at the Hydro cottages where we lived. My father who had been head porter for over ten years suddenly found himself along with a few other members of staff on his way to Comrie to help in putting in the electricity at the Cultybraggan camp for prisoners of war. This was before the prisoners arrived at the camp but after the erection of Nissen huts. This became a daily trip and Dad enjoyed the change of scenery and occupation. […] I remember he had to go with the prisoners to Balhaddie and from there to Sheriffmuir where the prisoners had to lift a railway line. There was no trouble as far as I can tell. The Hydro squad came under 'The Garrison Engineer'. Back home my brother Douglas, Harry and Margaret McGregor and I had a great time jogging along on a Hydro lorry to a sand pit where we helped the men, one or two of the staff, with filling sandbags which were now needed for all the ground level windows at the Hydro and the cottages. My father was responsible for the blackout of all the windows – that was quite a task.

Allan Kenny, who now lives in Lancaster, attended Cultybraggan for a week in 1962 as a 14-year-old schoolboy when he was a member of the Dollar Academy Combined Cadet Force (CCF), and again in 1965 and 1966, on summer vacation work in the officers' mess. Of his reminiscences he says 'such recollections, covering a variety of aspects/experiences, would be "light-hearted" and, hopefully, possibly "entertaining" for any readers who had themselves experienced the delights of life at Cultybraggan…or, indeed, hadn't'. The names have been changed by Kenny but all else is as it happened.

Kenny remembers the sergeant major barking 'Right. Get in – double time', in the school grounds:

> [There were about] 30 apprehensive 14-year-old boys, in our khaki CCF uniforms, in late June 1962, ready to clamber aboard the waiting 3-ton Army Bedford trucks, armed only with our kit. Our destination, spoken of by those who had never been and by those who had in soft, reverential and, it seemed, slightly sinister tones, was to be 'Cultybraggan'; our home for the next week of annual CCF camp.

Its reputation, it seems, went before it. He continues:

> For whatever reasons, little was said of their time there by those who had gone before. Questioning of those old hands provoked little other than pause for reflection, a far-away look in the eye and a murmured 'Culty? Aye; you'll see!' Even my brother, who had been three times some years before, was tight-lipped on the subject. This was quite alarming, really, and gave rise to speculation, not all of it good.

And so the cadets clambered into the trucks

> …in double time as ordered, and off we set. Sitting on the low, wooden benches facing one another, kit on the floor between, we swayed from side to side as the truck sped around corners, the wind through the open tail gate causing us to shiver. We felt a little in common with World War II soldiers going to war, or so we thought. Perhaps the only common element was the fact that we didn't really know where we were going, or what we would find when we got there.

Kenny knew the location as it was only 30 miles or so away from his home in Dunblane. But it was only sometime later that he 'discovered it had been a prisoner of war camp, nestling at the entrance to Glen Artney'.

An old saying amongst locals, which his father used to like to mutter with a chuckle every time they were nearby, was 'The hills of Glen Artney are covered in snaw!' Having grown up in Dunblane, he knew the area well, but his recollection of snow-covered hills did not make 'the prospect any more comforting as we approached'.

The cadets disembarked and were ordered by the sergeant major to 'Fall in'. They picked up their kitbags and 'shuffled into three more-or-less straight rows', the sergeant-major inspecting them as he walked up and down the rows. As he did so he said to them 'You're a right shoddy-looking lot', shaking his head, then shouted: 'You'd better buck your ideas up before tomorrow.'

Kenny goes on: 'We came to what we thought passed for attention; he certainly had ours.' The boys were then instructed to move to the right in threes and as the order was given everyone turned right, all except one boy that is, who turned left. 'He was always doing this. Sergeant-major raced towards the miscreant' and told him he was stupid, his face 'three inches' from the boy's now-quivering face. 'We all thought he, or we, were about to be shot.' However, the frightened boy turned 180 degrees. Kenny continues:

> We were reprieved and set off after sergeant-major, who was setting a terrific pace. Our eyes fixed on the square broad-shoulders ahead, we hardly dared to look about us during that short march. Through squinting eyes, all we detected were ranks of low buildings, each with a curved corrugated iron roof, tracking the tarmacadamed roads that fed left and right and around what might pass for playing fields, the largest supporting a pair of bleak rugby posts, standing to attention in welcoming us.

They received the command to halt outside a Nissen hut labelled A4, which would be home for the week. The sergeant-major nodded to one of Dollar school's corporals, 'lounging and smirking in the doorway. "Reveille oh-six hundred hours", barked sergeant-major, turning smartly on his heel and departing, leaving us to the tender care of our nurse-maid.'

The corporal turned out to be an experienced hand of two previous 'Culty' camps and told them to find themselves a bed and drop their kit, after which he was going to show them around the camp before returning and explaining what the rules and regulations were. They were also informed they had the evening free to do as they wished, and to make the most of it. Kenny remembers:

> We stepped inside our hut and gazed around in silence. However humble our own homes may have been, they had not quite prepared us for what we found here. Two rows of double bunk-beds, eight on either side facing each other; uprights of regulation green ironwork, with wire mesh bases which had lost their springiness around 1948, supporting greying mattresses that boasted a depth of no more than an inch. In the middle of the hut, a wood-burning stove, connected to the roof by a narrow metallic chimney. Four narrow windows on either side did not permit the entry of much daylight. The floor was, of course, concrete. Each bed boasted upon it one very firm, very thin pillow, two sheets and pillowcase of similar hue to the mattress and three thin, coarse, grey-black blankets.
>
> 'Come on, hurry up', squawked our corporal from the open door, 'I haven't got all day, you know.'
>
> There was some shuffling about as we each tried to secure what we thought would be the best bunks – they were all identical – to share with best friends, dumping our kit on it, then hastening outside for the 'Grand Tour of Culty'.
>
> We found that the camp comprised about 40 Nissen huts like our own, side by side in serried ranks, surrounding a range of other, larger administrative buildings, including a very lengthy, low-slung one that housed the officers and their Mess. Towards the centre, we found what was to become our haven, our cathedral, there to offer us much-needed succour, the NAAFI canteen.

Busy it certainly was; a stampede of army cadets from many Scottish and indeed English schools, with more senior boys from our own school, who had arrived before us and knew the ropes, well in the vanguard. All these young gentlemen would be our brothers-in-arms for the next week. Together would be trained to become an elite fighting force so that, if the bugle were to sound for the outbreak of World War III, we would be ready to do our duty, for Queen and country.

Meanwhile, there was no time for us to test the delights of the NAAFI.

'Come on', signalled Corporal Anderson, waving his arms about to secure our full attention. 'Mess-tent and latrines next. Follow me, and don't forget to salute any passing officers!'

He needn't have worried. We knew about this. On our way round, in our trepidation, we had been saluting anything that moved, and some things that didn't.

Here were facilities with which we were to become all too familiar in the coming days. The mess-tent was well named – a huge marquee, located on the western fringe of the camp buildings and where us 'other ranks' and NCOs ate all our meals together. A couple of dozen trestle tables and their associated wooden benches were accompanied within by an aroma, almost physical in nature, that appeared each morning and remained all day, the by-product of around 200 fried breakfasts. It was not an aroma to delight the nostrils; in fact many a boy could be found retching, and that was before the meal began.

Suffice to say that the cuisine on offer at mealtimes was perhaps not to everyone's taste, such that the majority seemed quite to lose their appetites as they joined the queue, plate in hand, ready to receive the dollops delivered by the kitchen staff'.

Tea was the staple drink on offer at all mealtimes, with coffee being the preserve of officers only. It was so hot they had to leave it while they ate to make it cool enough to actually drink.

Each cadet had been instructed to bring from home their own mugs, along with knife, fork and spoon,

…often sold in those days as a dinky little set, held together by a crafty clip. After meals, these were washed and rinsed in a communal trough of tepid water, outside the mess-tent. Heaven help your stomach-lining thereafter, if you happened to be numbered from 10 to 200 in the queue to use it!

He remembers the latrines clearly, as the use of them

…formed a none-too-subtle element of a new procedure to which we novices were soon introduced, namely 'ablutions'. This comprised, first thing each morning, a compulsory shower in a draughty building with stone floor but no doors. The water temperature was such as to make the North Sea appear positively inviting. Adjacent, one could relieve oneself courtesy the fairly rudimentary urinal, but it was the facilities available for more substantial relief that will be seared forever in the memory of its customers.

This toilet was communal, consisting of a long tube roughly two feet in diameter, with circular holes which had been cut at regular intervals. Kenny recalls:

117

This remarkable construction was hidden from public view by a series of thin timber cubicles, access to which was gained by pulling aside an almost transparent 'curtain' of sackcloth, nailed to its lintel. One imagined that prisoners of war were its first grateful visitors. When in a seated position, full concentration was required, not so much for the business in hand, but for the sound of the onrushing bore that would cascade along the pipe's length from time to time, to clear whatever detritus had accumulated, and to wash the bottoms of the unsuspecting, who had failed to stand to attention at the appropriate moment. For the duration of our camp, we learned to treat visits to this alarming device with considerable caution.

Reveille for the cadets was at 06.00 each morning:

> …as luck would have it, our Nissen hut was first of four in the queue for our school. Which meant that, at 6 a.m. precisely, our door would burst open to reveal our champion boy bagpiper who, with unconcealed delight, would march around our hut giving 'Highland Laddie', or some such, maximum expression. Its impact was instantaneous. Quiet reverie transformed into bodies falling on the floor in fright. If any further stimulus was necessary, the departing piper, *en route* to the next-door hut, was followed by our duty school corporal…

…shouting at them to get moving as they were to appear on the sports field in their kit in five minutes. The corporal was meticulous on time-keeping and if you were a minute late he informed the culprits they were a disgrace to the school and ordered them to do 20 press-ups. The others who had arrived on time were also ordered to do these; no one escaped the punishment for lateness.

Their days would begin this way throughout their stay, with 'twenty minutes of exercise, which was not easy, as 6 a.m. is not a time with which too many 14-year-old bodies are familiar', declares Kenny. They then had to run back to their hut and change into uniform for breakfast which was served at 6.45 sharp 'and woe betide us if we were late for that too'. Hut inspection was scheduled for 8.00 and 'was a serious business, as it was conducted by one of our school officers, accompanied by sergeant-major, wearing his "I'm not happy" face and a corporal or two, including the one in charge of our hut and whose reputation was about to be put on the line'. The beds had to be stripped,

> …with blankets and sheets folded within a tidy roll – blanket, sheet, blanket, sheet, blanket. The pillowcase was folded on top. Mug, knife, fork, spoon were arranged on top of that. The set was located at the end of the bed, by which stood each cadet, in full uniform and cap – belt and gaiters blancoed, cap badge shining like the sun, boots polished to reflect our anxious faces. Or so we thought.

The officer would inspect the hut, a stick snapping at the side of his leg, and occasionally he would poke a bed roll,

> …usually with some distaste. At times, without comment, a bed roll would be tipped unceremoniously onto the floor, the clatter of tin mug and utensils piercing the silence. Deemed inadequate. The cadet responsible would wince

in mental pain, as would the hut corporal, who would be making a mental note for retribution planning. Occasionally, the officer would stop, in astonishment, by one of his subjects.

'What *is* this, Thompson? Have you just got out of bed?'

'No, sir!'

'No, sir? Look at you, Thompson; you're all over the place. When did that uniform last see an iron? Christmas Day? Your cap's on squint. Look at your boots. Hopeless. Get them polished, Thompson. Today!'

'Yes, sir!'

'Corporal Anderson?'

'Yes, sir!'

'Disappointing, Corporal. I hope I'm going to see an improvement tomorrow?'

'Yes, sir. You will, sir!'

The inspection party left, but not before sergeant-major's face predicted thunder was on its way. The door closed.

'Right, you lot', our corporal would hiss through clenched teeth, and we all knew how we'd be spending the next hour before we were next on parade for marching drills at 9.30.

Kenny remembers that the marching drills took place

…on the fairly extensive parade ground near the centre of the camp but were problematic. Firstly, 14-year-olds don't normally achieve a marching formation that is pleasing on the eye. Secondly, it seemed to our sergeant-major, who took drills, that all other platoons on parade at the same time, not least from other schools, appeared to be a great deal smarter and drill-worthy than us. Thirdly, we had the added complication of each carrying, whilst we drilled, a standard-issue Lee Enfield 303 rifle, ex-World War II stock. Marching, whilst supporting this weapon on the shoulder, in complete synchronicity, was one thing. The procedure for coming to attention with a 303 was quite another. There were a number of carefully-choreographed moves required to achieve this involving body, feet, hands, 303 and head. This proved tricky to master individually, never mind as a cohesive unit, and the sergeant-major let it be known, in no uncertain terms, that he was un-impressed. As rifles slipped unwittingly from grasp to clatter on the ground, on regular occasions, he would become apoplectic.

'McGuire!', he would bellow, 'I hope that weapon's not loaded, or we'll all be dead in a minute.'

The fourth problem was that we would be singled out, in turn, to 'take the squad'. This involved coming out front and, in a commanding and authoritative voice, inviting the 'squad' to 'right-dress', 'come to attention', 'stand easy', 'about turn', 'march', 'salute whilst on the march', 'mark time' and so on.

There were two immediate challenges here to overcome, according to Kenny. The first was to do with the voice. At 14, as puberty was being reached, voices were often breaking. Although orders barked might begin fine in an even manly tone, by the time the order came for 'right turn', the voice 'would suddenly emerge two octaves higher as a squeak to be greeted by smirks and giggles by the rest of the squad. Cue for red-faced embarrassment and loss of esteem'. The second challenge he remembers was using

...the correct word of command at the appropriate moment. Having a squad of 'soldiers' on the move, obeying your every command whatever it was, proved quite unsettling, not to say nerve-shredding. One was exposed and the 'soldiers' knew it, hoping-upon-hope that you would get something wrong, that they would obey anyway and make you look seriously stupid.

This seemed to afflict the poor lad who had turned the wrong way on arrival:

There we would be marching in a straight-ish line, three abreast, arms swinging, doing our 'eyes-right' and saluting a passing officer on Donald's barked instruction then, all of a sudden, we would be advancing at pace towards a 10 foot high brick wall. This called for a 'left wheel', or indeed a 'right wheel'; a 'halt' would suffice. Instead, brain scrambled, mind suddenly a blank, no ideas came to poor Donald. Only an appalled silence as, made rigid by fear, he watched us reach the wall and begin to mark time in front of it, up and down, up and down, up and down, for what seemed like minutes. Until an almighty shriek of 'halt, about turn, quick march' from sergeant-major, 100 yards distant, would send us on our way again.

It took the poor cadet 'months to recover from that one. The rest of us loved it!'

The days were filled with 'map-reading, group tasks and team building, attempting the assault course of obstacles, net-climbing, rope-walking, muddy ditches – all in readiness and preparation for our undertaking of Special Exercises', the first of which took place on their third day at Cultybraggan. They piled into Bedford trucks,

...for a 3 mile sortie into the foothills of Glen Artney, along with most of the camp's residents. Apparently, an 'enemy position' had been located about half-a-mile distant from our drop-off point and it seemed [we discovered later] that the purpose of the exercise was for us, along with around 150 others, to attempt to find it, whilst not giving our position away. War games. We all fanned out, in our case under the direction of our hut corporal, who seemed as clueless as ourselves as to our ultimate objective and strategy for achieving it.

Accordingly, we spent much of the morning and a good bit of the afternoon creeping about the hillside, pushing our way through high bracken forests and between the numerous prickly gorse bushes, searching for what we weren't quite sure. From time to time, we would come across other platoons, equally unenlightened, with whom we would pass the time of day and, on one splendid occasion, share a rather nice picnic spot by a burn, enjoying our packed lunches, an improvement on the usual fare served in the mess-tent.

Around 3 o'clock, word passed about that a visiting Colonel had arrived, to inspect our manoeuvres, so we did our best to manoeuvre about menacingly, gripping our 303 rifles as pugnaciously as we could. We didn't see the Colonel but, shortly thereafter, a red flare was released into the sky, which apparently signalled the end of the exercise, and, hopefully, the Colonel's satisfaction, when we all returned to camp the way we had come.

Two days later the exercise was repeated, but this time at night:

[This] made the negotiation of routes through bracken, gorse bushes, burns, numerous cow dung heaps, night dew and other nocturnal obstacles rather tricky…as [it] did our ability to keep our happy band together, trying not to lose one another, whilst maintaining as much silence as possible in our movements and discourse, so as not to alert the enemy who could be anywhere. If they found us before we found them, the exercise would be over and humiliation would befall the guilty platoon.

For their own pleasure the enemy would, from time to time, release phosphorescent flares that lit up the sky, compelling their hunters spread all over the hillsides to 'hit the deck'. This would be when one discovered exactly where the cow dung heaps were located, judging by the many disgusted squawks that would break the silence of the night.

[At around two in the morning] a red flare was released by the enemy, under instruction, to end our torment. As it turned out, over the preceding 4 hours, our platoon had crept to within 50 yards of their hideout, where they had been relaxing, enjoying copious refreshment, gossiping about girlfriends and playing cards to while away their time. Too late; we'd lost! We hadn't even had a chance to use our trusty 303 rifles, not that we were carrying any ammunition.

But this was about to change, as the cadets climbed aboard the Bedfords and headed for the firing range, located on deserted moorland a few miles northwest of Dunblane:

…and what a day we had! Under very necessary close supervision, we were at last allowed to use ammunition with our Lee Enfields, having been taught previously the filling, loading and unloading of cartridge magazines and also with Bren machine guns, included in our armoury for the day.

We were taught how to lie prone, hold the rifle steady, aim at targets 50, 100 and, with the Bren gun, 200 yards distant, how to breathe and how to squeeze the trigger. Round after round we let off, our patient instructors giving us tips along the way as to how to improve our aim and control. The use and accuracy of the Bren gun was a revelation and, all in all, everyone headed back to camp elated with their accomplishments and the knowledge gained, albeit at the price of a ringing in the ears for 2 days, thanks to the noise of gunfire, and a painful shoulder for 7, thanks to the fierce recoil of the guns.

Given our combined experiences over the previous 6 days, good and bad, we now felt suitably qualified and ready to serve Her Majesty as fully paid-up members of her armed forces.

Such an honour arrived, for some of us, sooner than we might have imagined. For our last night in camp, 6 of us from Hut A4 were selected to man the 'Guard-house' at the entrance to the camp, ostensibly to protect the camp, its residents and armoury from any planned incursions by the IRA. Apparently, the IRA had broken into a barracks somewhere in England a few years before and stolen rifles and ammunition, so Army HQ Scotland was taking no chances of the same happening at Culty.

What it was thought a bunch of wet-behind-the-ears 14-year-olds would do in such an event goodness only knows, but we were briefed in all seriousness on our impending responsibilities and we took these responsibilities very seriously indeed. For about 20 minutes anyway, when dog-tired from all our expeditions, not least the night exercise, we all fell asleep.

Luckily, the IRA did not choose that night to launch an attack and the bonus was that we were not woken at 6 a.m. by the skirling of the pipes, and were excused the subsequent physical jerks on the playing field, but could instead stroll down to the mess-tent for a last, leisurely breakfast. It didn't seem to taste so bad that morning; perhaps it was an acquired taste.

Following breakfast, the cadets assembled with their kit 'ready to say our fond farewell to Cultybraggan Camp, taking away memories that would last a lifetime and to head for home, a long, hot bath and as much food as we could eat'.

In Kenny's case, he was about to change to a school where there was no Combined Cadet Force 'and so, as the Bedford trucks pulled up the hill on our way back, I gazed out of the rear of the vehicle for a final look at the receding camp buildings below, as we rocked and rolled from side to side, thinking that this would be the last I would see of it'. He was wrong. He found himself back at Cultybraggan for a few weeks during the summers of 1965 and 1966, 'this time as a paid employee of Her Majesty's Forces; on the inside, so to speak'.

He worked in the officers' mess,

> ...as one of a staff of 8 to 10 mostly university students, but two of us still at school. In '65, I was there as a general dogsbody: cleaning rooms, making beds, helping in kitchens and the dining room. The following year involved some of this but, more significantly, in the evenings [acting] as a bar steward, serving drinks [at 1s.10d. old money per pint] until whenever the last officer chose to call it a night.
>
> Our accommodation, as before, was in the Nissen huts, but unaccompanied by kit inspections or early morning bagpipers, and we had access to 'latrine' facilities in the officers' mess, which was a relief, in every respect. No saluting was expected. In fact, on many occasions, walking between locations, even whilst wearing civilian clothes and white steward's jacket, our working attire, younger cadets would salute *us*, just in case!
>
> Leisure time would be more relaxed: student parties, numerous trips to the NAAFI café, skinny-dipping during nice weather in the nearby Water of Ruchill and the occasional trip to Comrie for a glass or two of Carlsberg Special, in one of the hotels there, despite the tender years of some of us. It was a most enjoyable experience – and we were being paid for it too!

On one occasion however Kenny decided to volunteer and take on the 'night-shift duties of one student who would sleep overnight by the camp's telephone switchboard, located in the Guard-house, in case of emergencies, for which he was paid a bonus'. It was the student's 21st birthday that day,

> ...and he wanted to share it with the others at a night-time party. Easy money, as there were never any night-time calls. Except that night, around 2 a.m., when I was sound asleep, the switchboard started jangling, alarmingly. Unfortunately, I had not received any training in the use of a cable and jack switchboard, so it took my sleep-addled brain a while to figure out how to take the call – it was internal.
>
> 'Get an ambulance,' came the urgent request, 'and get Stirling Infirmary to ring me'.
>
> The caller rang off. Panic! How to make an outgoing call and how to connect an external caller to an internal one?

Kenny experimented with dials and jacks,

> …and eventually managed to handle these complex transactions and connect the callers to deal with whatever business had brought them together. I collapsed on the camp bed exhausted. Apparently, the head chef, that evening, had fallen out with his boyfriend, had slit his own wrists in the officers' shower room, splattering blood everywhere, and thus required some medical attention. He survived.
>
> Still, I had learned one lesson for life: Be careful for what you volunteer!

––––––

Gordon Burns was in the Cadet corps of Dollar Academy from around 1959 until 1965, and attended the annual retreat to Cultybraggan during that time. He recalls:

> When I was around 15 [around 1962] I went with the Cadet corps to Cultybraggan. The living facilities were primitive, even for someone at boarding school, and we had about 16 to a primitive hut each in a bunk, one on top and one below. I was in a top bunk. One morning, while putting on my socks on my bunk, the window fell in. The primitive window was hinged on the bottom. Thus, when it fell it fell inwards and shattered on my head. Worse, as it continued to fall, the residual glass cut off my nose. Several of my classmates in the room fainted at the sight. Others staunched the blood with sheets. My nose was not entirely severed but was hanging down, held by a few centimetres of tissue.
>
> I too must have passed out for when I came to it was during an argument between Colonel Wilson (aka Mr Wilson, our English teacher) and the army doctor. The doctor stated that 'if it was my boy, I would have him transported to Edinburgh for proper cosmetic surgery'. Mr Wilson (Colonel Wilson) said that he didn't want any fuss and that I should be stitched up at the local hospital. Wilson prevailed and I went to the local hospital. The outcome was that I have a lump at the top of my nose, even now, and a prominent scar down one side of my nose. For the rest of my schooldays I was called 'scar nose'.
>
> My parents sued and were awarded, I believe, £1000. The judge actually said that had I been a girl then the damages would have been much higher for 'cosmetic damages' which in these days did not apply to boys.

Burns also remembers 'the .303 shooting, and the people running up and down the butts at the shooting range waving a flag when someone missed the target entirely'.

––––––

Ian Prentice, who was at Dollar Academy from 1956 to 1962, also gives an insight into his experiences at Cultybraggan:

> [It was] undoubtedly one of the most God-forsaken, dreadful places it has been my misfortune to visit. It was in summer 1960 when I was 16 and just finished 4th year. I had no desire to waste a week or so of my summer holidays playing soldiers but there seemed to be little choice and most of my friends were there also.

He remembers:

> My heart sank as we got out of the trucks in the middle of nowhere to be confronted with squat buildings containing small uncomfortable bunks – I think there were about 20 of us to a building. The first thing many of us did was to light a cigarette. Smoking was banned at school, a ban pretty rigorously enforced, but a blind eye was turned to it at camp so long as it was not blatantly done in front of the officers.

He also vaguely remember a mess hall and describes it as 'an unprepossessing, draughty place with benches and tables. Thank God it was summer!' He continues:

> Perhaps the worst building was the toilet block. It consisted of a passage on either side of which were cubicles through which ran an 18-inch rusty pipe with holes cut in it. Privacy (huh!) was provided by a hessian curtain across the front. One did one's business and every so often a cistern at one end released a torrent of water which swept along the pipe removing all before it, in theory at any rate. I was told that from time to time some wag would station himself in the end cubicle and await the torrent; just as it reached there he would drop a piece of crumpled newspaper, light it and chortle as it scalded the sensitive areas of anyone in the cubicles downstream.

Many former cadets remembered the long sewer pipe that was slightly inclined and ran the whole length of the latrine, with holes cut out of it at regular intervals. The toilet seats were positioned above the holes where the cadets sat to do their business separated by thin wooden walls with a hessian screen to protect their dignity. It gained the nickname 'The Flute' as that is what the whole thing looked like. Every 10 or 15 minutes, as Prentice reports, the toilets would automatically flush from the higher end to the lower, which was rather alarming for those seated. And, as Prentice also reports, mischief could be made with crumpled newspaper. The miscreant would wait at the most uphill stall and as soon as the flow was heard to be on its way, the paper was pushed down, sprayed with lighter fluid then ignited. At that point the perpetrator ran away as fast as their legs could carry them. The ensuing fireball was washed down the pipe and under any bare backsides that happened to be there. Running away was the most important part of the whole operation because if the NCOs caught them, life could be made miserable. Tins of boot polish were also used, set sail fully alight in order to prank junior cadets, who could be heard screaming in agony as they ran out.

As the camp was 'in the middle of nowhere it was ideally suited to playing soldiers across the moors and hills. The nearest town, Comrie, was about 2 miles away and one night a bus was laid on for us to visit'.

One day during his stay a route march was organised for the cadets:

> We were formed into teams of about 5 or 6 cadets, given a map, compass and half a dozen map references. Our role was to find them in our own time, register with those already sent there by vehicle (NCOs played by prefects), answer some questions, and then move on. The only definite time to be at any one of them was lunch at 1 p.m. We saw the first two teams set off and we went the other way, causing some disruption as we were not expected till much later at the map references; I remember crossing almost trackless areas

> of moor seeing not another soul for miles except those manning the target
> map reference locations. We got to the lunch point last, only to be jeered
> by the other teams already there and rested, where we consumed the food
> provided and tea with condensed milk (heaven).

In the afternoon they returned to the camp 'via the remaining target locations, a comparatively short journey as we had broken the back of it in the morning, still seeing little but sheep and not many of them. First back, by some margin' they went for showers while there was plenty of hot water but 'rather less I believe for the later arrivals'.

Prentice and his team won.

All in all he found it 'a most unedifying experience and [I] resolved never to return. Maybe I was just not cut out for the somewhat primitive environment and living conditions'.

––––––––

Bill Oram attended Cultybraggan during the summers of 1960 and 1961. He was a student at the University of St Andrews, and worked for a number of weeks as a civilian at the camp. He remembers:

> We were not a large crowd and for myself and two friends our task was
> drying plates three times a day. The cadets washed them and we dried them.
> Two memories stand out. Firstly, our trio didn't like the idea of sharing
> accommodation in a Nissen hut so we found a ridge tent and erected it
> on a bit of open space. The clever bit was that we laid on our own electric-
> ity supply and ran a wire underground from somewhere. The wire wasn't
> designed for mains electricity never mind being buried in damp ground.
> However, it just lasted out and we lived in a sort of style during our stay. This
> happened one summer only.
>
> Secondly, and perhaps more fun, one of our trio needed a warmer bed and
> being the proud owner of a large but ancient car, came up with a scheme.
> When it was time to turn in, he would get in his car and motor round and
> round the camp. When he thought the time was ripe he parked the car,
> crawled underneath, and drained the now hot water from the radiator into
> his hot water bottle.

Nissen huts were uninsulated: in the early mornings the floor would be running with conden-sation and it was freezing cold – so living in the tent was a better option for the trio.

––––––––

On another occasion a cadet woke up before reveille and whistled cheerily while cleaning his brasses. Unhappy at losing his last few minutes of sleep one of the other cadets threw a boot at him, which hit him behind the ear and knocked him out cold. The boys thought quickly and bundled him back into bed so when the corporal came in to check everyone was up, he was still asleep. The unfortunate cadet had no recollection either of getting out of bed or of being hit with the boot.

––––––––

In May 2007 the *Selkirk Weekend Advertiser* ran a story about Cultybraggan by one of its contributors known as 'The Pilgrim'. He recalled his time at the camp to do military training when he was a youth, having been sent up from Dundonald Camp at Troon. He called it a 'cheerless spot' where the so-called external leadership training, he felt at least, should have been more accurately termed as a 'let the wee beggars suffer for a few days'. It seems Cultybraggan certainly has the reputation of being somewhere no one really wanted to be.

Although he and his fellow boy soldiers were not actually in the camp much – as most of it was spent under canvas in wild and windy locations nearby, occasionally with severe frost – he remembered the training staff clearly and remembers believing back then they had been specially selected for their lack of sympathy for human suffering.

When they did stay in the camp, most of the boys fought over their bed positions in the allocated Nissen hut. The reason was the stove in the centre of the hut – the beds closest to it were warmest. On the dark winter nights as the rain and high winds battered the site, he says, the 16-year-old boy soldier from the 1960s could be forgiven for thinking there were ghosts at the place, knowing about the deaths which had occurred there. Also at that time it was firmly believed Rudolf Hess had spent the night there in 1941 so no one could blame imaginations for running wild.

Many of the boys would pair up and spend as much time as they could in the boiler house, where it was warm and where they would heat up tins of compo stew which they had liberated from the usually unlocked ration store. There they would sit happily eating away in the warmth.

8 | HESS AND CAMP 21

Places which have been left to decay often have stories surrounding them, such as hauntings and supernatural activity, and Cultybraggan is no different – so much so that in 2009 the Glasgow Paranormal Investigators stayed at the camp, recording some ghostly happenings. Footsteps have been heard when there has been no one around, and even singing has been recorded. On one occasion the strange behaviour of cadets was said to have been caused by the appearance of a ghost in one of the derelict Nissen huts, and groaning and other noises have been heard in the latrines. And of course it was built near the site of an ancient Roman fort. It could appear to be a ghost hunter's paradise, were it not for the fact that the buildings are old and creaky and settle as the temperatures drop overnight. But apart from the ghosts and other supernatural concerns there is another mystery which seems to have persisted for decades, and that is the case of Rudolf Hess. The burning question is, did he really stay at the Comrie camp?

Rudolf Walter Richard Hess was born on 26 April 1894 in Alexandria in Egypt, the eldest child of Johann Fritz Hess, known as Fritz, a wealthy merchant, and his wife Klara Münch, also from a wealthy merchant family. Rudolf was joined in 1897 by a brother, Alfred, and later by a sister, Margarete, in 1908. The Hesses were brought up in the German-speaking community in the Egyptian city but learned English, although they did not have much to do with either the locals or the British who were managing the country at that time (it was a British colony). From 1900, Hess studied at the German Protestant School for six years. He was then sent back to Germany to the Otto-Kühne-Schule, the Protestant boarding school, at Bad Godesberg in Bonn, and after this to the École Supérieure de Commerce in Neuchâtel in Switzerland for a year. He was never to return to Egypt.

Hess excelled at mathematics, astronomy and science but his authoritarian father wished him to join the family business Hess & Co., an import firm founded by Rudolf's grandfather which Fritz had taken over in 1888. In 1912 he left school and began an apprenticeship with a business in Hamburg, which his father had forced him to do, but with the outbreak of World War I, he saw an opportunity to defy him. He was not interested in becoming a merchant and so he volunteered and was enlisted in the 7th Bavarian Artillery Regiment before being transferred to the 1st Company of the 1st Infantry Regiment stationed near Arras in France, and in 1916 saw action at Verdun. He was awarded the Iron Cross Second Class and rose to the rank of Corporal Reserve Lieutenant. He was transferred again, this time to the 18th Bavarian Reserve Infantry based in Romania. Although wounded several times before, in 1917 he was shot in the chest and was transferred to a military hospital before recovering enough to return to Meissen in Germany. Once fully recovered he decided on a new venture and applied to be transferred to the Air Service. In January 1918 he went to Munich for a medical and aptitude tests, both of which he passed, and he began flight training in March that year. During that initial training, he crashed a plane but walked away unscathed. In October he joined the Bavarian fighter squadron Jagdstaffel 35b near Mons in Belgium but within weeks the war was over, following Germany's surrender, and the squadron was disbanded. By this time he held the rank of Lieutenant. He wrote to his parents in 1919 after the Treaty of Versailles had been signed, stating that 'The only thing that keeps me high is the hope of the day of vengeance even if it is still so far away'. Like so many other soldiers he felt bewildered and betrayed by the capitulation of the German government and the harsh terms imposed by the settlement.

Hess now found himself penniless. The family's firm had been taken into British hands by the government. In 1919, without any real qualifications, Hess decided to return to education and attended the University of Munich where he studied economics and history. He became friends with his geopolitical professor and flight instructor Karl Haushofer, a friendship that was to last all their lives. Indeed it was Haushofer who first told Hess about *Lebensraum* or living space, which became one of the main policies of Nazi Germany; further it is thought it was Hess himself who spoke to Hitler about it.

While he was staying in digs in 1920 Hess met his future wife Ilse Pröhl. That was also the year he joined NSDAP, the Nationalsozialistische Deutsche Arbeiterpartei, the National Socialist German Workers' Party. Through NSDAP he spent time with the young Adolf Hitler, who had had similar experiences as Hess during the war and who also hated the harsh terms of the Treaty of Versailles imposed on Germany. By this time Hess had also become a member of the Eiserne Faust or Iron Fist, a nationalist organisation, and of the Thule Society, an anti-Semitic group. Hess also formed a nationalist group following a speech made by Hitler at the University of Munich in 1920, founding the 11th Nazi Student-Hundertschaft, the Student Hundred, after he joined the SA, the Sturmabteilung, the paramilitary wing of the Nazi Party.

Meanwhile the Paris Peace Settlement was having a direct effect on the German people. The Deutsche Mark became worthless as the Ruhr was occupied by French and Belgian troops, and families struggled to survive. Both Hess and Hitler believed that the capitulation of Germany was not down to military defeat but down to the Jews and the Bolsheviks who had conspired behind Germany's back. On 4 November 1921, as Hitler gave a speech during a Party meeting, a bomb exploded at the Hofbräuhaus and Hess protected Hitler although he was injured himself. He now worshipped Hitler, hanging on his every word and watching his every movement. He made the ideal replacement for Hess's dominant father.

Hitler meanwhile decided to take matters into his own hands regarding Germany's failing economy and the occupation of the Ruhr. Civil unrest was already occurring all over Germany, and Hitler knew of Benito Mussolini's coup in Italy the previous year. This led to Hitler leading the Munich Putsch of November 1923. Hitler, Hess and a band of SA stormed a meeting of local dignitaries that had been organised by Gustav von Kahr, the region's state commissioner, in the Bürgerbräukeller, a large beer hall, and in front of around 3000 people proclaimed that a revolution had begun. Hess and the SA rounded up some of those they believed were enemies of the state and drove them to a house near Lake Tegern. The following day, Hess left briefly to make a phone call and the hostages managed to persuade the driver to help them escape. Hess was left stranded and had to call Pröhl to come and rescue him.

That same day thousands took to the streets in support of Hitler and Hess but were met by gunfire from the Bavarian state police. In all 16 men were killed, the rest scattered. Hitler was put on trial and on 1 April 1924 was sentenced to five years in prison, although in the end served only eight months. The SA and NSDAP were banned. Hess meanwhile fled to the safety of Austria but eventually gave himself up. He was sentenced to 18 months in prison for his part in the putsch and released on 30 December 1924, just ten days after Hitler. Both men had spent their time at Landsberg Prison, some 40 miles west of Munich. During his time in incarceration, Hitler worked on his memoirs which were later published in one volume under the title *Mein Kampf, My Struggle*. The book was edited by Hess. In February 1925 Hitler announced the re-establishment of the SA and NSDAP and on 27 February Hess was appointed his private secretary. In April Hess dropped out of university. He organised meetings, kept Hitler's work diary and replied to letters on Hitler's behalf. He also managed Hitler's personal affairs, such as his private income. Rumours began to circulate in Munich and Berlin that the pair were having a homosexual affair but Hitler got wind of the rumours and formed a plan. Hess should get married.

———

Hess married Ilse Pröhl on 20 December 1927, with Hitler as their witness, and as time went on Hitler spent more and more time with the Hesses. The following June Hess did a magazine interview in *Der S.A.-Mann* in which he defended the Nazi salute which had become Party policy two years earlier. He explained it was not a copycat of the Italian fascist salute taken from Roman times but had been used in NSDAP since the early 1920s.

During all this time, Hess never lost his love of flying and in April 1929 he gained his private pilot's licence and in July 1930 managed to buy a two-seater monoplane, a Bayerische Flugzeugwerke AG M23b, thanks to the Party's newspaper *Völkischer Beobachter* which was advertised in bold lettering on the side of the aircraft. Hess was delighted and often spent time flying low over opposition rallies, disrupting the meetings.

Hess became Hitler's personal adjutant in July 1929 and accompanied him all over the country. He was always with him during his speeches at political rallies and Party meetings. In December 1932 Hess was appointed as NSDAP's Political Central Commissioner.

By the end of January 1933 Hitler was Chancellor of Germany and on 21 April he appointed Hess as his deputy. He was Minister without Portfolio and was to oversee various governmental departments, from education, health and race affairs to reconstruction, finance and law. He was now based in the Nazi headquarters in Munich although he split his time between here and the Berlin office. In September he was promoted to SS-Obergruppenführer and was to be known as Deputy Führer. However, he was seen as rather ineffectual. Although he had absolute power over the Nazi Party he did not attend charity events, for example, and was either unable or unwilling to take the initiative or implement others' initiatives. He left the day-to-day running to Martin Bormann, who would succeed him in 1941.

Yet as the persecution of the Jews began, Hess implemented the boycotting of Jewish businesses – although being friends with a family who had Jewish blood, he also made it clear that the quarter Jewish children of the marriage were given honorary Aryan status in order to protect them. In April 1933 Hess had submitted proposals to control the position of the Jews in German society, and in 1934 forbade personal interaction between members of the Party and Jews. He introduced the protection of German blood and in 1935 introduced a law for the prevention of genetically diseased offspring, which in essence meant forced sterilisation. In a speech he gave in 1938 he claimed the Spanish Civil War was caused by Jews because the Spanish had recognised them as a people and he predicted the demise of the Jewish race because of it. In 1939 he appointed the Gestapo to check on marriages disallowed because of the Jewish laws to make sure the couples were not co-habiting. As for the church, he made sure that a representative of the Nazi Party was appointed by the church to make sure qualified Nazis filled the municipal offices.

When President Hindenburg died in 1934, the path was cleared for Hitler to become an outright dictator. At a meeting at Nuremberg on 10 September Hess shouted that Hitler was the Party and that the Party was Germany and ended with the now well-recognised slogan 'Heil Hitler! Sieg Heil'. The whole gathering joined in a single voice and shouted 'Sieg Heil' back. Hitler was omnipotent.

––––––––

Although very busy with his work, Hess continued to fly. He took part in competitions and was a competent flyer. But by this time, the Saar, a region lost at Paris, was back in German hands as Hitler slowly destroyed the treaties. Austria had been annexed and the Sudetenland returned to Germany. Czechoslovakia was invaded in March 1939 and Memel in Lithuania was ceded to Germany. Poland would fall when the Nazi troops invaded on 1 September and Britain and France would declare war on the 3rd. However, in August, Britain had received a communiqué from Germany requesting a secret meeting between Herman Göring, the commander-in-chief of the Luftwaffe, and the Prime Minister Neville Chamberlain which the British decided to confirm, although Göring subsequently never appeared. Meanwhile Hess asked permission from Hitler to join the Luftwaffe. At first Hitler refused but eventually a compromise was reached: Hess could fly for a year. Besides, by that time Hitler believed the war would be won.

A year later it was Hess who wanted to make peace with Britain, allegedly with Hitler's knowledge. Many suggestions were made regarding who he could meet but in the end it was decided Air Commodore Douglas Douglas-Hamilton, the Duke of Hamilton, would be the best choice. Before the outbreak of war, in 1936, the Duke had attended the Berlin Olympics and had become friends with Albrecht Haushofer, the man who Hess approached to make initial contact. Haushofer wrote to the Duke in September 1940 asking for a meeting in Lisbon; however, the secret service agency MI5 intercepted the letter and the Duke did not see it until a year later.

During that year Hess visited factories which produced war planes, especially the Messerschmitt factory at Augsburg where the designer Willy Messerschmitt lived. He asked Messerschmitt about flying the twin engine Bf110, which had a long enough range to reach Scotland. Hess began learning to fly it – under the supervision of Willi Stoer, the chief test pilot at the company – and undertook numerous test flights. Unperturbed by the lack of a response from Hamilton, Hess began making plans to fly to his home at Dungavel House close to the historic market town of Strathaven in South Lanarkshire. The house, situated on moorland, had once served as the family's shooting lodge. Only a few people knew of Hess's intention. These included his senior adjutant Karlheinz Pintsch to whom Hess gave two sealed letters, one for Pintsch and one for Hitler should he not return. From 29 March 1941, Hess's personal aircraft was tested out by Helmut Kaden, a test pilot, then Hess himself did a number of test flights and asked Kaden to make some minor changes. Although the aircraft was nearing its perfect state, Hess worried about the weather and knew he would have to choose the right time to make the journey. As he prepared he received daily updates. He would take ten Reichsmarks, and Haushofer's visiting card as well as that of Dr Karl Haushofer, the one which he would personally give the Duke.

––––––

On 1 May 1941 Hess was to be seen in public for the last time in Germany. It was Labour Day and he made a speech at the Augsburg factory on behalf of Hitler. On Saturday 10th he made his ill-fated journey from Germany to Scotland. That morning he spent time with his three-year-old and only child, Wolf, taking him for a walk then to the local zoo. On their return he had lunch with Alfred Rosenberg, who later became Reich Minister for the Eastern Occupied Territories. After Rosenberg had left, Hess dressed in a Luftwaffe captain's uniform, and told his wife he had received orders to go to Berlin, although his actual destination was the Haunstetten airfield. Here Hess put on his flying suit and at 17.45 local time he left his country for good.

The first time his plane was spotted was by the Royal Observer Corps (ROC) post at Embleton, inland from the island of Lindisfarne off the Northumbrian coast. From there on in it was tracked and reported to Fighter Command, the aircraft having been identified at the second ROC post it passed at Chatton, Northumberland. At 22.35, pilot officer William

Cuddie along with Sergeant Hodge of 141 Squadron took off from Ayr to intercept the enemy aircraft. By this time Hess was beginning to get low on fuel. At 22.45 he is recorded as flying close to Dungavel House, but then heading out past Glasgow to empty the fuel tanks before landing. He returned inland and bailed out of the plane at around 23.05; he had tried to land but the Messerschmitt was going too fast. He had endeavoured to land it on its back when he failed to get out using the navigation canopy, but passed out; after regaining consciousness he parachuted out of the rapidly descending aircraft and watched as it smashed into the ground. At just before 23.10 Hess touched Scottish soil and passed out once more.

Hess had landed at Floors Farm near Eaglesham in Renfrewshire. The ploughman who lived in a cottage nearby, David McLean, heard the crash and rushed out and helped Hess to his feet. He soon established that the crashed pilot was German; the pilot gave his name as Alfred Horn and said he had come with a message for the Duke of Hamilton. News of his landing spread quickly, however, and soon he was being transported by car to the Home Guard Headquarters at Busby near Glasgow. While he waited at Giffnock police station to be transferred to Maryhill Barracks, he was searched and his personal possessions taken from him. These included a map, photographs of him with his son, and a vast array of pills and potions, which were examined by the Medical Research Council. Among them were opium alkaloids, aspirin, barbiturates and homeopathic remedies.

Hess was questioned by the Scottish Area Commandant of the ROC Major Graham Donald, during which he continued to claim he was Horn. Donald found him polite and interesting but knew instinctively he was a higher ranking Nazi. The Duke of Hamilton was finally called by Squadron Leader C. Hector MacLean, who had been the duty controller of the Ayr sector that night. The two men knew each other and the Duke agreed to meet this mysterious prisoner. Before the meeting they looked at Hess's belongings then the Duke went into the medical room where Hess was being held alone. Apparently Hess told Hamilton who he really was, and that Germany did not want to fight Britain and how he had tried to organise a meeting with Hamilton in Lisbon. This was the first the Duke had heard of this meeting. He also wanted the Duke to approach the government and have him paroled at the very least as he had come unarmed and of his own free will without coercion of any kind by Berlin. The Duke bluntly told him that no such deal could be done and that he would return with an interpreter to continue their discussion.

Meanwhile McLean had cycled back to the crash site at Bonnyton's field and decided to hide parts of the plane, including a part of the fuselage, in some bushes before it was scooped up by the military. He returned later with his tractor and gave the fuselage to his farmhand friend, 18-year-old Stanley Boyd, as a souvenir. McLean had phoned Boyd to tell him of the German plane crash and how he had handed the prisoner over to the local corporal of the signals unit. The whole wreckage was taken away by the Army Maintenance Unit from Carluke and nothing was left once they had gone, apart from the pieces hidden by McLean. It was much later that the local men discovered who had actually been flying the Messerschmitt and were astonished by the news.

Hamilton met with the Prime Minister Winston Churchill, and the Secretary of State for Air Sir Archibald Sinclair who also happened to be at dinner, at Ditchley Hall near Kidlington. This was the mansion house of the parliamentary private secretary to the Ministry of Information Ronald Tree, and was where Churchill was staying. The following morning, Monday 12 May, the matter was discussed at 10 Downing Street where it was agreed a formal identification should take place. Hess meanwhile had been transferred to Buchanan Castle, a military hospital at Drymen in Stirlingshire, and the following day was woken up and identified by Sir Ivone Kirkpatrick who had met Hess while he was First Secretary to the British Embassy in Berlin before war broke out. It was also confirmed when after his medical examination he was found to have a calcified section which corresponded with other records stating he had at some point suffered from the lung disorder tuberculosis.

It was at this time rumours began circulating. The BBC and other news agencies were allowed to report on Hess's arrival in Scotland and that he was safe but was being held as a prisoner. The broadcasts were heard in Germany of course. On 13 May Hitler and Goebbels began perpetuating the story that Hess was unstable, that he was a mentally disturbed man, and this was the information which was passed on to the British. But both doctors who examined him said he was relatively healthy, and fit to be removed from the hospital. Three days later, on 16 May, Colonel R. A. Lennie sent his final report to the Scottish Command Headquarters stating that Hess was rather neurotic about his health and could talk endlessly about it. That night Hess was taken to Glasgow where he was put on the 7 o'clock train to London. He arrived at the Tower of London the following day and on 21 May he was transferred once more, this time to Mytchett Place in Surrey, otherwise known as Camp Z. This was a secure unit and a more appropriate place for someone of his status, although Hess was by this time furious that he was being held as a prisoner. He repeatedly stated he was on a peace mission and that his treatment was reprehensible. He was held here for the next 13 months, ostensibly for protection because a group of Polish patriots were plotting to kidnap him and beat or kill him for the atrocities carried out in Poland. MI5 files released in 1999 give some credence to this story as they report a gun battle between these Poles and the British guards.

Dr Henry Dicks, an army psychiatrist, visited Hess on 2 June. He was charged with finding out more about the Nazi hierarchy and the mental state of its leaders. When he clapped eyes on Hess for the first time in the flesh, he was utterly astonished. The man before him was not the confident deputy that had been seen so often in the press but rather a man who Dicks wrote was quite simply a 'schizoid psychopath'. He wrote in his journal that his face was more like an animal than a human being. The two men talked and it soon became clear that both Hess and Hitler admired, possibly even adored, the British but also feared them. Dicks wrote that he believed they were trying to 'frighten us but are themselves frightened of us'. Dicks believed that the British were the people the Germans were trying to emulate with their Master Race plans. Throughout the interview Hess showed signs of severe anxiety around the British and Dicks put it down to him feeling inferior. He also noted Hess's absolute devotion to Hitler but believed that through reading British newspapers and journals, this would diminish over time. Hess began talking with the intelligence officer Major Foley and it was clear from these and other meetings just how much he admired the country. These were the first steps towards a de-Nazification programme that was rolled out for all prisoners of war. Dicks later wrote he could not believe Hess could have had so much power in Nazi Germany. He described him as 'pathetic and pitiful' and found him to be a very insecure man who had been damaged by his father's absolute power over him as a youngster. He believed that if he had not been such an important political prisoner, much more could have been done for him to help him recover from the traumas of childhood.

On 16 June Hess tried to commit suicide for the first time by jumping off a balcony, following the refusal of Lord Chancellor John Simon on 10 June to adhere to his demands. He had asked for Dicks in the early hours of the morning and when he saw him, rushed towards him and jumped over the bannisters, breaking his leg. He then came under the care of psychiatrist Captain Munro Johnston of the Royal Army Medical Corps who stated that he was suffering from paranoia and suggested he would try and kill himself again. Hess also began having bouts of false amnesia, and in June 1942 he was sent to Maindiff Court Hospital near Abergavenny in South Wales. In February 1945 Hess tried to kill himself once more, by stabbing himself in the chest with a bread knife.

With the ending of hostilities in Europe on 8 May 1945, some 22 leading Nazis appeared before an International Military Tribunal at Nuremberg, including Hess on 20 November. The case against him began on 7 February the following year. The court had ascertained Hess was sane enough to stand trial, though during it onlookers could see his mental deterioration. He had developed a tick and bodily contortions and he seemed not to take in any of the proceedings whatsoever. In September Hess was found guilty on charges relating to 'Common Plan or Conspiracy' and 'Crimes against Peace'. He was sentenced to life imprisonment. On 18 July 1947 the seven prisoners sentenced to life were taken to RAF Gatow near Berlin and transferred to the Allied military prison in Spandau.

During his incarceration, Hess stayed away from Sunday services in the prison chapel and he refused to work, seeing it as beneath his station. This irritated some of the other prisoners. He was also a hypochondriac, claiming to be in pain all the time, but after he was given a placebo the pain miraculously dissipated. Erich Raeder, Karl Donitz and Baldur von Schirach complained about his screaming and moaning day and night and argued he was simply attention-seeking. Hess would also be wary of the food he was given, believing it to be poisoned. He was allowed not to do some work but not all. He was visited by Albert Speer, the one-time minister for armaments, and Walther Funk, both prisoners. Speer defended Hess's behaviour to Funk, which the latter found irritating, and he also defended him to the prison guards. Raeder was released in 1955 and Funk in 1957, both due to ill health. Both died in 1960. Donitz was released in 1956 and died on Christmas Eve 1980. Speer and Schirach were released in 1966, leaving Hess alone in the prison to serve out his life sentence. In 1959, Hess had tried to commit suicide once more by breaking his glasses and cutting his wrists.

Due to his mental health issues, the prison authorities decided to relax their rules for him. He was allowed to move into a larger prison cell which was equipped with a kettle so he could make his own tea or coffee. His cell was kept unlocked and he was free to visit the prison library, and he had unrestricted access to the washing facilities. On Christmas Eve 1969 while he was in the British Military Hospital being treated for a duodenal ulcer he saw his wife and son for the first time since he had landed in Scotland.

––––––––

On numerous occasions Hess appealed for an early release but the Soviet Union vetoed it every time. Even hard-line anti-Nazis began to question his incarceration and the British Chief Prosecutor at the Nuremburg Trials Sir Hartley Shawcross stated publicly in 1977 that it was a scandal he was still in prison. Eight years previously the renowned British history professor A. J. P. Taylor had released a statement citing the injustices regarding Hess's incarceration. He said that Hess had come as a peace ambassador in order to restore peace between Germany and Britain and had acted in good faith. As such, he was 'unjustly treated as a prisoner of war', and after the war 'we could have released him'. He went on to say that no evidence of a crime was ever proven against Hess and there were no records showing he was ever present at any secret discussions Hitler had regarding war plans. The statement went on to say that Hess was the only one at the Nuremberg Trials to have sought peace and had risked his life for it, but having been 'found guilty of "crimes against peace" was certainly the Tribunal's most ironic perversion of justice'. Even Churchill wrote in his book *The Grand Alliance* in 1950 that he was 'glad not to be responsible for the way in which Hess has been and is being treated'. He went on, 'He came to us of his own free will, and, though without authority, had some of the quality of an envoy'. He said that Hess was a medical case and not a criminal one and should have been treated as such. During the 1970s and 1980s numerous politicians from all sides tried to have him released on humanitarian grounds. German President Gustav Heinemann tried writing to the Allied governments but it was all to no avail. Even his son Wolf Rüdiger Hess tried to secure his release. In 1967 he set up Community Freedom for Rudolf Hess, which in 1989 became the Rudolf Hess Company whose main objectives were to clarify the history of Hess and to delve into the circumstances surrounding his death.

In February 1977 Hess tried once more to kill himself. On 17 August 1987 he succeeded by hanging himself, having spent over 45 years in captivity. (Ironically, according to *Der Spiegel* on 13 April that year, Russian President Mikhail Gorbachev planned to secure his release.) An autopsy was carried out by James Cameron and the cause of death was hanging from an extension cord tied to a window. He had spent time outside every day doing a daily walk in the secure garden and was last seen sitting enjoying a rest. He was buried at a secret location before being exhumed and reinterred at the family plot at Wunsiedel in March 1988. In 2011, when the lease for the plot came up for renewal, the church refused. Neo-Nazi marches were diminishing in the town and it was hoped this would further encourage this trend. He was disinterred on 20 July 2011, cremated and his ashes scattered at sea.

These annual neo-Nazi marches were called the Rudolf Hess Memorial Marches. From 1988 to 1990 the marches had the blessing of the local courts but between 1991 and 2000 they were banned – but went ahead anyway, not only in Germany but also in Belgium and

Denmark. In 2001 the town of Wunsiedel allowed a march. Around 2500 people attended. In 2004 nearly 4000 people turned up, with the approval of the Federal Constitutional Court. The people of the town decided to set up a counter-march and promote tolerance. In 2007 all marches were banned as it was the 20th anniversary of Hess's death.

Following his death, Hess's family ordered a second autopsy as they were dissatisfied with the British one. After all, the man was 93 years old and in poor health. He could hardly walk, could not tie his shoelaces or raise his arms above his head, they suggested. The second autopsy was carried out at the Institut für Rechtsmedizin, the Institute of Legal Medicine at the University of Munich, by Wolfgang Spann and Wolfgang Eisenmenger. Asked to determine whether it was strangulation or hanging, the doctors were not in a position to say as the trachea, thyroid artery and larynx had all been removed in Britain therefore no evidence of murder could be ascertained. However, in 2013 it came to light under the Freedom of Information Act that two British agents were allegedly involved in his death. Ex-military surgeon Hugh Thomas gave Detective Chief Superintendent Howard Jones the names of two men he claimed killed Hess on the orders of the British government as he had secret information pertaining to World War II, especially regarding a plot to overthrow Winston Churchill. It is not known if the suspects were ever interviewed but in May 1989 the Director of Public Prosecutions Sir Allan Green QC declared the investigation closed with no further action. In November that year Parliament was told by Sir Nicholas Lyell, the then Solicitor General, there was no 'cogent' evidence to suggest Hess was murdered. Whatever happened, Rudolf Hess left yet another controversy in his wake.

————

There have been many conspiracy theories regarding Hess over the years, such as it was a doppelgänger that landed in Scotland and not the real Hess, or that the RAF allowed Hess to fly over Britain unhindered, or even that Hitler sanctioned him coming to Britain to broker a peace deal, but none has perpetuated so much or caused so much controversy in Perthshire as Hess being held at Cultybraggan Camp. He was not, at any point, held at the Comrie camp, because at that time it was not in a position to hold him as it did not have the facilities to treat him; rather he remained at Drymen where he was receiving the appropriate treatment and where the interviews with Kirkpatrick, and to a lesser extent Hamilton, were taking place. After all, these interviews took place on 13th, 14th and 15th May and on the 16th it is known Kirkpatrick was still at the hospital as he played golf with the hospital commander, the same day Hess was later transported to London. The following day Kirkpatrick returned to the capital. However, it has done the camp no harm being associated with Hitler's deputy over the years.

In 2013 historian Peter Padfield claimed he had evidence that when Hess crashed in 1941 he had brought with him a detailed peace treaty in which the Nazis would agree to withdraw troops from Western Europe if Britain agreed to remain neutral when Germany attacked Russia in the east. Britain would keep her independence and Empire while Germany redirected its war effort to the Eastern Front to stop the advance of Communism. He also claimed an informant came forward who said that German speakers were asked to translate the treaty for MI6 at the BBC headquarters at Portland Place in London. The treaty, he believed, was found near a burn at the crash site and given to the police, who knew of its existence and whisked it away; it was at this point two inventories of Hess's belongings were made which remain sealed to the public. If such a treaty did exist, it would have had major repercussions for the Churchill government, for there was a large peace party in the country and if the public had got wind of him refusing a peace deal, he would have probably lost his seat in government. But Padfield believed Churchill could not bring himself to trust Hitler and it would have been too damaging for relations between Britain and the European governments and the United States.

Stanley Boyd sold the fuselage from Hess's plane in the 1960s to the former assistant secretary of the Battle of Britain Association which then handed it over to a private collection in the United States called The War Museum. It went up for auction in May 2014 and sold on 5 June for just over $8000 (about £5000). The Imperial War Museum has another piece of the fuselage and one of the engines, while another engine is on display at the RAF museum in London.

All British documents pertaining to Hess will be released in the UK in 2017.

9 | ROC POST AND THE BUNKER

In the northeast corner of Cultybraggan Camp lie the Royal Observer Corps (ROC) post and Cold War bunker. In this chapter we look at the fascinating history of these two structures, both of them a response to the threat of nuclear war following the dawning of the Cold War between the Communist Bloc countries and the West.

––––––––

In 1945, following the end of World War II, a conference was held at Potsdam in Germany. British Prime Minister Winston Churchill, and later Clement Atlee, United States President Harry Truman and the Soviet leader Josef Stalin met to thrash out an agreement among the victors. They all agreed Germany had to be punished following her unconditional surrender on 8 May, and drew up a plan of how this would be done. First, Germany would be occupied by the Allies as they implemented their programmes of demilitarisation, de-Nazification and the reintroduction of democracy to the country. Both Germany and Austria were to be divided into four occupation zones – British, French, American and Soviet – with their respective capitals Berlin and Vienna also being divided along the same lines. In addition the annexation of areas such as the Sudetenland and Alsace-Lorraine were to be reconsidered. Germany automatically lost almost 25% of her 1937 size as borders in the east were changed – these now ran along the Oder–Neisse line, losing East and West Prussia, Silesia and two-thirds of Pomerania. Poland was to regain these areas but she had already lost land in the east in 1939 and the Soviet Union was not in the mood to give it back. Poland, Czechoslovakia and Hungary were to return all German nationals back to Germany in a peaceful but organised way. All civilian shipyards and aircraft factories were to be dismantled. Germany's hugely successful chemical and metals industries were to be reduced to minimum output and the country was encouraged to concentrate on peaceful domestic industries such as agriculture, textiles and beer. Nazi war criminals were to stand trial.

Meanwhile, however, war still raged on the other side of the world. Japan was still at war and the Allies wanted its surrender. Towards the end of the Potsdam Conference the country was given an ultimatum by America, Britain and China. It was to surrender or face prompt and utter destruction. Japan's Prime Minister Kantaro Suzuki remained silent following the threat and this was construed as him ignoring it, so on 6 August the United States unleashed its most secret and terrifying weapon – an atom bomb. It dropped its payload on the city of Hiroshima, followed three days later by another bomb on the city Nagasaki. These cities were seen as military targets and Truman believed these actions would bring the war swiftly to an end, saving countless American lives. Truman had hinted to Stalin that America had something up its sleeve but did not furnish him with details. Following Japan's surrender, Stalin wanted this ultimate killing machine for his own country.

Suddenly Europe had a new issue. With peace now in place, Truman saw no need for American troops in the region and had told those at the Yalta Conference of February 1945 that as soon as peace had returned, they would be withdrawn over the following two years. This made Britain and Western Europe twitchy. Without the Americans, the exhausted Europeans would be no match for a threat from the Soviet Union. After all, it still controlled Latvia, Lithuania and Estonia, and had annexed eastern Finland, eastern Poland and northern Romania. The Soviet Union's sphere of influence included its satellite states of the German Democratic Republic, Bulgaria, Poland, Hungary, Czechoslovakia, Romania and Albania. The Soviet Union had created the Eastern Bloc and Communism had spread much further than the West had ever anticipated. Thousands of people in these areas migrated but restrictions were implemented, and during the Cold War period very few people managed to cross the border into Western Europe.

On 5 March 1946, Churchill gave a speech at Westminster College at Fulton, Missouri in which he famously first talked about the so-called 'Iron Curtain' which had fallen across Europe. The speech called for an Anglo-American Alliance, which the Soviet leadership interpreted as a possible first step in war against them.

By 1947 the Marshall Plan had been put forward by the Americans. It hoped to reactivate the German economy, and the restrictions on German industrial production were to be eased considerably. However, the Soviets were unconvinced, fearing a stronger Germany, and refused to take any further part in the discussions. In June George Marshall announced American assistance to any country in Europe that wished to take them up on the offer. Stalin wholly opposed the plan, however, fearing Americanism would start to take over Europe, and forbade any of the countries under Moscow's influence to accept aid. Following its implementation, Germany formed a new currency, the Deutsche Mark, and during elections, the communists were heavily defeated. This led to the Berlin blockade in June 1948 when the Soviets cut off road access to the city and cut all supplies of non-Soviet food, water and other products to the areas of the city controlled by the Allies. Berlin, it must be remembered, was a city inside the Democratic Republic of Germany, so the only way to get food in for the western-controlled areas was by air. A massive aerial supply chain was formed and in May 1949 the Soviets lifted their blockade. By this time Stalin was furious with Truman, who now decided not to pay the

Soviet Union reparations as the German economy had begun to improve and he believed it would hinder such progress. As tensions grew between the two major powers, so the world descended into the Cold War era.

––––––––

In 1953, the United States had a new president, Dwight D. Eisenhower. This was also the year Soviet stalwart Stalin died, and Nikita Khrushchev became leader. Eisenhower was keen to show the Soviets America's military might and at the top of his list was the retention and expansion of the atom bomb technology. Between 1953 and 1961, America increased its number of nuclear warheads from 1000 to around 18,000; and in 1955 the B-52, a bomber capable of carrying the nuclear arsenal, was hailed as a huge success. The States also turned its attention to Europe, and in 1961 its Turkish allies allowed it to house 15 intermediate-range ballistic missiles on their soil, with each one pointed at the Soviet Union.

Meanwhile Khrushchev was amassing his own nuclear arsenal, although this was very small as the military were against the use of the weapons. Most of his time was spent dealing with the numerous uprisings in the satellite states following Stalin's death, such as the East German Uprising in 1953 and the Hungarian Uprising of 1956. The next major crisis was the Berlin Crisis of 1961. Previously, in 1958, Khrushchev had given the Allies who still occupied the city an ultimatum to leave it within six months so it could become a free city; if they refused, he would give East Germany complete control of communications. In 1959, however, Khrushchev met with the foreign secretaries of Britain, France and the United States and the outcome was that peaceful negotiations would take place. In 1961, the Soviet leader once again threatened Berlin. On 25 July American President John F. Kennedy sent more American troops to the city. More chillingly he asked for money to build fall-out shelters in the event of a nuclear attack. Many began fleeing to the west of the city but this was halted when the border between East Berlin and West Berlin was closed on Sunday 13 August 1961.

With these events taking place Britain saw the need to install increased numbers of ROC posts. The Royal Observer Corps was a civil defence organisation made up mainly of civilian volunteers. Although the Corps had been established in the 1920s, and had played a major role during the Battle of Britain in 1941, its main aim was to supplement early radar warning stations which had been built along Britain's coastline in the event of enemy aircraft approaching. The ROC posts were the inland cousins of these stations and tracked and identified aircraft. But with the advent of the Cold War the situation changed and in 1955 ROC posts were given the task of detecting nuclear explosions and the associated fall-out. This data would then be sent to the United Kingdom Warning and Monitoring Organisation which would provide the authorities with the essential information gathered in the event of a nuclear attack.

The Comrie post was opened in August 1960. By 1968 it was one of 1563 throughout the UK, with each post approximately eight miles apart and each one costing in the region of £5000. All of them were built to a depth of approximately 25 feet, made of reinforced concrete and had a waterproof course of bitumen. Inside there was room only for a small number of personnel, usually three members of staff who worked an eight-hour shift so it was working 24 hours a day. They kept records and at the Comrie post there were two ROC cupboards. The ceiling at Comrie was covered in polystyrene tiles and there was evidence of a telephone line, a logbook and a fire blanket. The remains of the post lie to the eastern side of the bunker, in the northeast corner of the camp, where the hatch to enter can be seen as well as the ventilation shaft. Access into it was by means of a ladder. It closed in September 1991. The last Chief ROC Observer at Comrie was Graham Taylor. On 23 March 1992, Observers Taylor and MacGregor checked the post for the last time, but it remained the responsibility of those members of the ROC who were not being stood down and any observations were to be reported to Taylor, or Observer Williamson at RAF Pitreavie.

———

The purpose-built Regional Government Headquarters at Cultybraggan was begun in the late 1980s and completed in 1990 but was never utilised, thus making it basically a folly. It was built with a view to housing the Scottish Office in the event of a nuclear attack, following the planned closure of 'Scotland's Secret Bunker' at Troywood near St Andrews in Fife in 1992. By then, however, the Cold War was over thanks in the main to the Soviet leader Mikhail Gorbachev who pursued his policies of 'glasnost' or openness within Soviet institutions and the government, and 'perestroika', meaning reconstruction, in particular referring to the Soviet political and economic systems. These were widely seen as the major factors in the dissolution of the Soviet Union and in the revolutions in Eastern Europe during the later 1980s.

The bunker, all 26,000 square feet of it, sits within its own fenced and locked ground, with an aerial mast on its northern side and a brick ventilation tower on its roof. It has two levels, the uppermost one being covered with soil to act as camouflage. On the west side is a blast door which is also its main entrance, that leads into the lobby area. Here is a door to the decontamination room and another blast door leads the way directly into the bowels of the bunker. At the guard room, where anyone entering would have had to show their identification card and papers, there is a bulletproof panel in case the enemy, or indeed some crazed activist, wanted to shoot those in the bunker. The control room houses the fire and the intruder alarms and controls for the filters and ventilation plant. There is a preparation room, and in the decontamination room there are three shower blocks. The main room in the bunker is a huge open plan office which takes up approximately two-thirds of the length and breadth of the bunker; before it was sold it had been stripped bare. A partition at the back would have provided private space for meetings. On the north side of this room were housed tele-printers, and next to that was a small tearoom. There was also a plant room where the ventilation plant would have been located, and as well as control panels there were two air compressors for pumping out the sewage. Every time the toilet had been flushed the compressor would have come on. There was a ladder here which led down to the lower plant room. Near the entrance of the bunker stairs down led to dormitories, as well as another plant room containing a water tank. At the far end was a generator room with two large generators.

The bunker also housed a BBC studio measuring around eight feet by eight feet which was entered via a larger soundproofed room. A red light on the door would have alerted people that a broadcast was taking place. The studio had a chair, a mixing desk, a cassette player, a reel-to-reel tape recorder and a microphone. Nearby was the BT room with its emergency communications network unit, and there was a room where two operators would have worked. Next to this was a radio room which contained radio equipment with its receiver and transmitter in a neighbouring room.

There was also a medical room within the bunker, where there were two beds for casualties, a moveable screen and a private WC. There were also washing and drying facilities for the bedding and of course clothing, and a canteen with sinks, cooking facilities and preparation area. In all there were 50 rooms at the facility. Although the bunker was not built for its luxury, it was comfortable enough as it had carpets, good lighting and air conditioning.

The bunker was built for 130 personnel and would have sustained them for 30 days following a nuclear attack thanks to its one and a half metre thick concrete walls. It was the last one to be built in Scotland and it is estimated it cost around £30 million to construct. It was handed over to the army and was used as classrooms until it was finally closed in 2004.

Some of the historic items were passed on to the museum at Troywood and the BBC office and studio equipment were taken to Hack Green Museum in Cheshire. The Troywood bunker, although closed in 1992, re-opened two years later as a visitor attraction although some of the rooms remained locked at that time.

Following the community buyout of Cultybraggan Camp, the bunker went on sale in early 2011 with a price tag of £350,000. It attracted global attention, with a South African couple interested in living there and an American who wanted to use it so he could survive Doomsday. The Lincoln-based communications firm GCI Comm Group Ltd was the eventual successful bidder, but the sale fell through and the property went on the market once more. On 16 May 2014 the bunker was sold for £150,000 to Bogons Ltd, a technology firm, to be converted to a data centre and media archive site. Bogons is co-owned by the BBC's chief scientist Brandon Butterworth.

In the meantime, in June 2013 the bunker hit the news for all the wrong reasons. Around £30,000 worth of copper was stolen and up to £100,000 worth of damage done internally. It was thought the raider or raiders had entered the camp via a local farm so they would remain undetected by security cameras.

SCOTLAND'S PRISONER OF WAR CAMPS

Camp 21 Comrie was just one in a long chain of prisoner of war camps in Scotland, born out of a need to house thousands of prisoners of war. Politics of course played an important role but it is the men who worked there, who were imprisoned there or who constructed them who tell the greatest histories of the camps and life within them. Without their testimonies much of this history would be lost. The camp at Comrie, however, is unique. It began life as a training camp, changed to become a prisoner of war camp – first as a transit camp then a base camp – and then became a military training base once more until the early 2000s. Its history did not stop like so many other camps, which had closed by the spring of 1948, but continues to this day with innovative ideas and community involvement. It remains the best-preserved camp in Scotland.

Below is a list of all Scotland's prisoner of war camps, to the best of my knowledge. Many of them have been lost over time but perhaps original streets exist, like those at Watten in Caithness, or maybe the odd building still remains, or possibly little artefacts turn up in gardens. Whatever does or does not remain, they existed, and housed many thousands of foreign prisoners of war before the gates closed.

2	Woodhouselee Camp, Milton Bridge, Midlothian
3	Balhary Camp, Alyth, Perthshire
6	Glenbranter Camp, Argyll
12	Donaldson's School, Edinburgh
14	Doonfoot Camp, Ayrshire
15	Donaldson's School Camp, Edinburgh
16	Gosford Camp, Longniddry, East Lothian
19	Happenden Camp, Douglas, South Lanarkshire
19	Douglas Castle, Douglas, South Lanarkshire
21	Comrie Camp, Comrie, Perthshire
22	Pennylands Camp, Cumnock, Ayrshire
24	Knapdale, Lochgilphead, Argyll
34	Warebank Camp, Orkney
60	Lamb Holm Camp, Orkney
62	The Moor Camp, Biggar, Lanarkshire
63	Balhary Estate Camp, Alyth, Perthshire
64	Castle Rankine Camp, Denny, Stirlingshire
66	Calvine Camp, Blair Atholl, Perthshire

66	Dundee Camp, Dundee
67	Sandyhillock Camp, Craigellachie, Banffshire
68	Hallmuir Camp, Lockerbie, Dumfriesshire
75/76	North Hill Camp, Laurencekirk, Kincardineshire
77	Annsmuir Camp, Ladybank, Fife
105	Inchdrewer House, Colinton, Edinburgh
109	Brahan Castle, Dingwall, Ross-shire
110	Stuartfield Camp, Mintlaw Station, Aberdeenshire
111	Deerpark Camp, Monymusk, Aberdeenshire
112	Kingencleuch Camp, Mauchline, Ayrshire
113	Holm Camp, Newton Stewart, Wigtownshire
120	Sunlaws Camp, Kelso, Roxburghshire
123	Dalmahoy Camp, Kirknewton, Midlothian
165	Watten Camp, Watten, Caithness
182	Barony Camp, Dumfries Base Camp
188	Johnstone Castle Camp, Johnstone, Renfrewshire
230	Stuckendoff Camp, Shandon, Helensburgh, Dunbartonshire
236	Ninewells Camp, Chirnside, Duns, Berwickshire
242	Cowden Camp, Comrie, Perthshire
243	Amisfield Camp, Haddington, East Lothian
274	Errol Airfield Camp, Errol, Perthshire
275/275a	Kinnell Camp, Friockheim, Angus
293	Carronbridge Camp, Carronbridge, Dumfries
298	Barony Camp, Dumfries
559	Abbeycraig Park Camp, Causewayhead, Stirling
571	ST2 Camp, Stranraer, Wigtownshire
582	Blairvadoch Camp, Rhu, Helensburgh, Dunbartonshire
593	Rob Roy Camp, Aberfoyle
612	Honduras Camp, Kirkpatrick, Fleming, Dumfriesshire
617	Dryffeholme Camp, Lockerbie, Dumfriesshire
625	Patterton Camp, Newton Mearns, Glasgow
640	Manse Croft, Twynholm, Kirkcudbright, Kirkcudbrightshire
641	Earls Cross House Camp, Dornoch, Sutherland
660	Patterton Camp, Thornliebank, Glasgow
661	Leffnoll Camp, Cairnryan, Stranraer, Wigtownshire
1013	Deer Park Camp, Dalkeith, Midlothian
1024	Deer Park Camp, Dalkeith, Midlothian
	Bonnytown, St Andrews, Fife
	Bruckley Castle, Bruckley, Aberdeenshire
	Culreoch Camp, Stranraer
	Duff House, Banff

Kirkton Farm, Balblair, Dingwall
Lathocker Camp, Lathocker, Fife
Maidens Camp, Maidens, Ayrshire
Methven Airfield, Methven, Perthshire
Peterculter Camp, Peterculter, Aberdeenshire
Rickarton Camp, Stonehaven, Kincardineshire
Tealing Airfield, Tealing, Angus
Tullos Hill, Aberdeen

SELECTED BIBLIOGRAPHY

Allen, M. (2004) *The Hitler–Hess Deception*, Harper Collins, new edition.

Bishop, C. (2004) *The Rise of Hitler's Third Reich*, Spellmount Publishers Ltd.

Cultybraggan Local History Group (2010) *Camp 21 Cultybraggan: A History*, Cultybraggan Local History Group.

De Normann, R. (2009/1996) *For Führer and Fatherland*, The History Press.

Gaddis, J. L. (2007) *The Cold War*, Penguin.

Harris, J. and Trow, M. J. (2011) *Hess: The British Conspiracy*, Andrew Deutsch Ltd.

Hess, I. (1954) *Prisoner of Peace: The Flight to Britain and its Aftermath*, Bloomfield Books.

Jackson, R. (1966) *A Taste of Freedom*, Four Square.

Jackson, S. (2010) *Churchill's Unexpected Guests: Prisoners of War in Britain in World War II*, The History Press.

Jordan, D. (2004) *The Fall of Hitler's Third Reich*, Spellmount Publishers Ltd.

Kershaw, I. (2001) *The Hitler Myth: Image and Reality in the Third Reich*, Oxford Paperbacks.

Marwick, A. (2001) *Total War and Historical Change: Europe 1914–1955*, Oxford University Press.

McCauley, M. (2008) *Origins of the Cold War*, Routledge, 3rd edition.

McGinty, S. (2012) *Camp Z*, Quercus.

McGonagall, W. T. (1934) *Library Omnibus*, David Winter & Son Ltd.

Nesbit, R. C. and Van Acker, G. (2007/1999) *The Flight of Rudolf Hess*, Sutton Publishing.

Overy, P. (2005) *The Dictators: Hitler's Germany and Stalin's Russia*, Penguin.

Padfield, P. (1991) *Flight for the Führer*, Weidenfeld and Nicholson.

Padfield, P. (2013) *Hess, Hitler and Churchill: The Real Turning Point in the Second World War – A Secret History*, Icon Books.

Parnell, W. and Taber, R. (1981) *The Killing of Corporal Kunze*, Lyall Stuart.

Picknett, L. *et al.* (2005) *Double Standards: The Rudolf Hess Cover-up*, Sphere, new edition.

Rees, J. R. (1947) *The Case of Rudolf Hess: A Problem in Diagnosis and Forensic Psychiatry*, William Heinemann.

Roberts, J. M. (2003) *Europe 1880–1945*, Routledge, 3rd edition.

Scotland, A. P. (1957) *The London Cage*, Evan Bros.

Sewell, M. (2002) *The Cold War*, Cambridge University Press.

Snyder, L. L. (1998) *Encyclopaedia of the Third Reich*, Wordsworth.

Speer, A. (1971) *Inside the Third Reich*, Weidenfeld and Nicholson.

Stafford, D. (2014) *Flight from Reality*, Thistle Publishing.

Sullivan, M. B. (1979) *Thresholds of Peace*, Hamish Hamilton.

Sutherland, J. and Sutherland, D. (2012) *Prisoner of War Camps in Britain During the Second World War*, Golden Guides Press Ltd.

Thomas, H. (1979) *The Murder of Rudolf Hess*, Hodder & Stoughton.

Various Authors (1976) *Total War to Total Trust*, Oswald Wolff.

Whittingham, R. (1997/1971) *Martial Justice*, Bluejacket Books.

SELECTED WEBSITES

In order of interest:

www.comrie.org.uk
www.comriedevelopmenttrust.org
www.secretscotland.org.uk
www.facebook.com/cultybraggancamp
www.bbc.co.uk
www.thecourier.co.uk
www.buildingsatrisk.org.uk
www.alternative-perth.co.uk
www.urbanglasgow.co.uk
www.breadalbane.org
www.archaeologyscotland.org.uk
www.ads.org.uk
www.highlandstrathearn.com
www.canmore.org.uk
www.historicenvironment.scot
www.28dayslater.co.uk
www.theguardian.com
www.devizesheritage.com
www.islandfarm.fsnet.co.uk
www.feldgrau.net
www.uboatarchive.net
www.wartimememories.co.uk
www.theindependent.co.uk
www.thescotsman.com
www.thetelegraph.co.uk
www.ihr.org
www.pprune.org
www.selkirkweekendadvertiser.co.uk
www.iwm.org.uk
www.thegpi.co.uk
www.royalpioneercorps.co.uk
www.ajr.org.uk
www.heraldscotland.com
www.invernesscourier.co.uk
www.legacy.com

www.basehorinfo.com
www.trauer.hna.de
www.newburytwintown.org.uk
www.pkc.gov.uk

ISBN 978-184995-005-3   £16.99

After 60 years the full story of the camp that held high-ranking Hitler aides is revealed. A new book lifts the lid on the PoW camp at Watten ... where leaders of the Hitler regime were 're-educated' before being sent back home to Germany. *The Scotsman*

...[the] camp had an extraordinary secret role as a place where some of the most notorious figures in Hitler's Third Reich were locked up, interrogated and, where possible, subjected to 'de-Nazification. *Scotland on Sunday*

www.whittlespublishing.com

ISBN 978-184995-039-8 £16.99

…it is remarkable how many people from Caithness have gone on to leave their mark on the world, and in some cases on ours as well. …the fascinating collection of men (and one woman) assembled here fall into two main groups: those who made significant contributions to science, engineering or in others ways in the UK, and those who made their mark in far flung lands. ***Undiscovered Scotland***

…a cross-section of Caithness 'chiels' who have left their indelible mark on the world. … There is a wealth and breadth of talent and absorbing information in this detailed and thoroughly-researched book. That it helps put Caithness and her gifted sons and daughters on the map, so much the better. ***The Scots Magazine***

www.whittlespublishing.com